Preface

The physiotherapy and medical professions involved in pain diagnosis and management are facing major challenges. These are exciting times that should reap the rewards of the mature and well controlled research that is now available. Our professional profile can only benefit if we start to show that we are acting on the knowledge and messages coming from this high quality work.

In a very timely editorial to the journal *Pain* Steven Linton (1998) persuasively argues the case for the instigation of early preventive programmes in the management of acute low back pain:

> '...we found that a secondary prevention program in primary care, for first time sufferers, significantly reduced disability and reduced the risk of becoming chronic by 8-fold as compared to "treatment as usual". The program included a thorough examination by a doctor and physical therapist, information designed to reduce fear, uncertainty and anxiety, self-care recommendations, and the recommendation to remain active and continue everyday routines' (Linton 1998).

He also makes a plea for the early instigation of adequate pain control since it is well established that intense pain in the acute phase of a disorder is a significant risk factor for chronicity. He bluntly points out that if 'medical' risk factors such as 'pain intensity' are being missed by clinicians, then 'what kind of job is being done with "yellow flag" risk factors?'. 'Yellow flag' is the term used to represent the psychosocial factors which have been shown to be powerful and very useful predictors of chronicity and poor outcome for treatment (see Kendall et al 1997). They have been shown to have far greater predictive power for a poor outcome than many biologic/structural/anatomic/biomechanical/pathology based findings. These psychosocial yellow flags need our understanding and attention.

Linton (1998) highlights the work of Indahl and colleagues (1995) whose recent paper title is in itself great food for thought: 'Good prognosis for low back pain when left untampered. A randomized clinical trial'. What they did was provide a straight-forward and low cost intervention for people off work more than 8 weeks because of back pain. First they provided a 'classic clinical examination by a physician', tested physical capacity, and took X-rays. The patients were informed about the findings and advice was provided. Patients were told that 'light activity would not injure the disc, but instead would speed recovery. This message was given even where discs had verified herniations where surgery was not recommended. They placed great emphasis on removing fear about the back pain and specific recommendations about movements and lifting were provided. In their randomised clinical trial this 'minimal' treatment was shown to significantly reduce sick leave as compared to the control group and the return-to-work rate was more than twice as high in the intervention group.

Linton (1998) notes seven common features of the highly successful programmes for acute or subacute low back pain he reviewed for the editorial:

1   They all appear to take a multidimensional view of the problem. A major emphasis is placed on the psychosocial aspects of the problem e.g. fear and worry involved.
2   A thorough, but 'low tech' examination is provided.
3   After the examination, time is taken to communicate the results to the patient. i.e. why it hurts, and provision of advice as to how to best manage the problem.
4   There is an emphasis on self-care i.e. 'that the patients behaviour is an integral part in the recovery process'. But also, the use of effective drug therapy and/or non-drug therapy to help control the pain is seen as vital. Linton notes that reducing pain appears to lessen fear and other psychological factors that may 'fuel long term problems'.
5   There is an attempt to reduce any unfounded fear or anxiety concerning the pain.
6   The programmes provide crystal clear recommendations concerning activities and in some cases help patients regain function by providing graded exercises.
7   The programmes do not *medicalise* the pain. By this he means, for example: the indiscriminant use of high tech exams, referrals as a starting point, sick certificates of more than a few days, providing extensive prescriptions, or advising the patient to 'take it easy' or bed rest.

This Yearbook is about starting to understand pain and its management using whiplash associated disorders rather than low back pain as a vehicle for discussion. Even so, the practical messages that Steven Linton brings to us are largely the same. This yearbook is about starting to understand some of the neglected but very powerful factors that enhance and maintain physical disability—the patient's beliefs, their fears and their anxieties about movement, about structure and about pain—and how we may begin to challenge these beliefs and help patients to restore their physical confidence. It is also about how we must be aware that our interactions can just as easily help as hinder

Topical Issues in Pain

Whiplash—science and management
Fear-avoidance beliefs and behaviour

Editor

Louis Gifford MCSP BSc MAppSc

Foreword

Heather Muncey BA MCSP RMN

NOI Press - Falmouth, Adelaide

NOI Press, Kestrel, Swanpool, Falmouth, Cornwall TR11 5BD, UK
Email: louisgifford@compuserve.com

ISBN 0 9533423 0 1

British Library Cataloguing in Publication Data
Physiotherapy Pain Association Yearbook 1998-1999: Topical issues in Pain. Whiplash science and management. Fear avoidance beliefs and behaviour.
Edited by Louis Gifford
Includes bibliographical references and index.
616.047.2 dc21

Editing: JJ Editorial Services
Indexing: Master Indexing
Typesetting: Sangar Services Pty Ltd
Printed and bound in Britain

Foreword

This is the first Yearbook of the Physiotherapy Pain Association for Chartered Physiotherapists. It represents issues considered in study days during the first years of the Association and provides a flavour of its philosophy and approach to pain.

The PPA was formed in September 1994 by physiotherapists interested in the relief and management of pain, as well as in the prevention of prolonged pain and the resulting disability. The consideration of the multifactorial nature of pain, its progress and management underpins the Association's philosophy and provides its clear identity, defining the difference between it and other Clinical Interest Groups for physiotherapists. In the current climate of evidence-based practice and the need to demonstrate clinical effectiveness, the Association is at the cutting edge of leading the profession into a changing role for the future. There are many areas of physiotherapy where scientific evidence to support practice is sadly lacking but there are also areas where evidence is available against traditionally accepted practices. The profession must mature and grow in order to shed these and move forward into new practices supported by more robust science. This is a challenging process both for individuals within the profession and for the profession itself, but it must take place if we are to survive as key and valued contributors to health care in the 21st century.

Part I considers whiplash injury. This problem, commonly seen in physiotherapy departments through its various stages from acute to chronic, is discussed in terms of tissue damage and the vexed question of where the lesion may lie, and puts this in the context of a biological model. It then builds on this by looking at the biopsychosocial model to make sense of progression from the acute phase into prolonged pain and developing incapacity. A description of the cognitive behavioural approach and how it may enhance physical therapy is given in the chapters on assessment and prevention and management of chronicity and on understanding people with chronic pain. The evidence for physiotherapy management is reviewed.

Part II sets out an important concept in the physiotherapy assessment and management of any patient suffering pain, that is, fear-avoidance beliefs and behaviour. The model is described along with other related health psychology models as a background to the relationship between anxiety and fear and activity and exercise behaviour. The vital role this plays in what we say to patients and the prevention of chronic pain and incapacity is evident in the approach to back pain rehabilitation described in this part as well as in the final chapter. The penultimate chapter scrutinises the therapist and the patient/therapist relationship with a question for us all to ponder—are we being patientist?

This book summarises one year's study days and is evidence of the fruitful relationship between physiotherapists and clinical psychologists in the clinical and educational setting, and of the relevance of broader models of care to physiotherapy practice. I would like to thank all the contributors for their interest, enthusiasm and hard work for the PPA and this text!

Let us hope that the challenge encompassed here is met by our profession as a whole and that our interventions may, as in one definition of clinical effectiveness, do more good than harm!

Heather Muncey, PPA Chairperson 1994–1998

the patient's progress and that we need to fully aware of the delicate nature of the therapeutic relationship.

I believe that pain, in particular chronic pain, is one of the most difficult challenges in medicine. I also believe that physiotherapy has lacked the respect it deserves for its efforts in trying to tackle this vast and complicated area. I hope that this Yearbook is a beginning that reflects the hard work and unique clinical awareness of the many physiotherapists who are dedicated to seeing that things change for the better.

Thank you to all the current contributors, I hope your high standard of work serves as a challenging benchmark for the contributors to our future Yearbooks.

Louis Gifford, April 1998

REFERENCES

Indahl A, Velund L, Reikeraas O 1995 Good prognosis for low back pain when left untampered. A randomized clinical trial. Spine 20(4):473–477

Kendall N A S, Linton S J, Main C J 1997 Guide to assessing psychosocial yellow flags in acute low back pain: Risk factors for long-term disability and work loss. Accident Rehabilitation & Compensation Insurance Corporation of New Zealand and the National Health Committee, Wellington, NZ

Linton S J 1998 The socioeconomic impact of chronic back pain: is anyone benefiting? Pain 75:163–168

Contributors

David Butler M App Sc
Physiotherapist
31 Angus St, Goodwood 5034 AUSTRALIA

Louis Gifford M App Sc, BSc MCSP
Physiotherapist
Kestrel, Swanpool, Falmouth. Cornwall TR11 5BD

Vicki Harding MCSP
Research and Superintendent Physiotherapist
INPUT Pain Management Unit, St Thomas' Hospital,
London SE1 7EH

Patrick Hill BA, MSc C.Psychol
Health Psychologist
Department of Staff Development, Bath and Wessex House,
Royal United Hospital, Bath BA1 3NG

Michael J Rose PhD MCSP
Back Pain Rehabilitation Programme
Willow House, Clatterbridge Hospital
Bebington, Wirral
Merseyside L63 4JY

Suzanne Shorland MCSP
Superintendent Physiotherapist
Pain Management Dept.
National Hospital for Neurology and Neurosugery
Queen Square, London WC1A 3BG
also at:
COPE, The Middlesex Hospital, London W1P 9PG

Michael A Thacker MSc MCSP
Senior Lecturer
Faculty of Health Care Science
St Georges Hospital Medical School
Cranmer Terrace
London SW17 0RE

Katharine F Treves MSc C.Psychol
Chartered Clinical Psychologist
INPUT Pain Management Unit,
St. Thomas' Hospital,
London SE1 7EH

Max Zusman Dip Physio, B App Sc, Grad Dip Hth Sc, M App Sc
Lecturer
School of Physiotherapy,
Curtin University of Technology
Selby Street, Shenton Park 6018
Australia

Contents

Integrating pain awareness into physiotherapy—wise action for the future

DAVID BUTLER

Introduction

We have a problem with pain. 'Gate control' theory has been taught to physiotherapy students for decades. Postgraduate and undergraduate Physiotherapy courses nearly always include lectures on pain. A chapter on pain now seems to be obligatory in manual therapy textbooks. This is all praiseworthy, considering that pain is the phenomenon that almost always brings patients to clinicians. However I believe that pain and all its related issues has hardly been integrated into current physiotherapy practice. This is unfortunate because the pain phenomenon provides a superb paradigm for reviewing current physiotherapy practice to facilitate the utilisation of new knowledge and skills. It is all about integration. To integrate pain, clinicians must have a clinical reasoning framework in operation, preferably one that is adaptable and open to change. This reasoning is no easy thing—there is a science in it which I believe physiotherapy needs to evaluate closely. With this essay I aim to encourage the integration of pain awareness into current clinical and research practice and present the notion that clinical reasoning can provide a framework to allow physiotherapists to take on the phenomenon of pain.

The clinicians are becoming disturbed

Professionally, we are surrounded by scientific advances in areas such as neurobiology, pain and disability, epidemiology, and pain management. The 1990s have been dominated by what Epstein (1990) termed the 'outcomes movement' where evidence-based medicine and practice have come to the fore with willing government support, particularly in the United States and the United Kingdom. The outcomes movement emerged in the United States in response to the obvious need for health cost containment and the competition between Health Maintenance Organisations for the industrial buyer's dollar, with price the basis for competition. It also occurred due to the exposure of great geographical differences in the use of medical procedures (Epstein 1990). By evidence-based medicine, I refer to all the scientific evidence at hand including biological findings and clinical trials of techniques.

Clinicians who have followed the content of mainstream journals such as *Spine* and *Pain* will have noted a powerful message emerging from recent scientific interest in pain and disability related to spinal conditions. There is increasing support for the contention that chronic pain development and responses to treatment have more to do with psychosocial factors, such as pain beliefs, job satisfaction and childhood experiences, than with physical factors such as the injury and ranges of limb movement. Editorials comment frequently on the increasing costs of disability after injury. Some physiotherapists in practice may well begin to wonder their worth. I think we may all go through this, but on the positive side, the outcomes movement is providing the most powerful stimulus for change ever.

Clinician/scientist relationships

I wish to discuss the relationship in this essay since I believe that integrating science is a stumbling block for clinicians. Clinicians are scientists in their own right, and mutual respect is surely required for the best outcomes. Clinician/scientist relationships have always been a little edgy, sometimes testy; and often clinicians completely reject scientific evidence that doesn't support their management framework. Some instinctively rebel against science, and most clinicians would wonder what a statistician knows about pain and suffering.

It's not that clinicians distrust science, it is more that the structure of science may concern them, in particular the advancement of academic careers linked to publication. It is obvious that research workers want results which validate their choice of subject, their world concept and, indeed, validate their choice of career. 'Research is like motherhood—there is no such thing as an ugly baby' was an interviewee's comment in Greer (1987). From the clinician's viewpoint, scientists may be seen as professional subscribers to journals— they have a common language and it seems that much is dialogue between researchers. 'What does it contribute to the literature?' is the question of the researcher, while the clinician thinks 'What does it do for my patients?'. Literature is often seen more as a meandering discourse rather than as a guide to action. Research conclusions will always be tentative at least initially, yet the practitioner often demands guidelines for conclusive action. There is a need for clinicians to be able to translate/extrapolate and extract the scientific information into useful clinical material. Many of us may not have these skills.

Few clinicians will reject the overall legitimacy of the outcomes movement, particularly after the exposure of the huge geographical variations in clinical practice (e.g. Wennenberg et al 1987). However the outcomes movement presents some philosophical difficulties. According to Tanenbaum (1993) the danger is that it may present statistical analysis as superior rather than complementary to other forms of knowledge. The statisticians and those who pay them understandably want neat figures. However uncertainty and subjectivity are at the heart of any clinical encounter. As any clinician knows, good evidence can lead to bad practice if applied in an uncaring way or in an unappealing atmosphere. The clinician wants to know where empathy and the experience of accumulated cases fits in the equation. Crossed professional purposes exist. Clinicians are there to assist healing, alter pain and help restore function. This goal may be at odds with research where the goal is the advancement of knowledge. Clinicians recognise instinctively that it is a leap of faith to expand the results of a trial to a broad therapeutic principle (Kenny 1997) and many clinicians take quiet umbrage at the randomised clinical trial as it holds all clinicians equal suggesting that the specific clinician does not matter. There are suspicions of trials that test a technique—the clinician realises all the time that a single technique is only a part of the total management package that they provide. The other aspects of the treatment, such as associated techniques, explanations with models, empathy, the phone call after the treatment, and the friendly healing clinical environment that the clinician carefully constructed, seem unnoticed. And, as any good clinician knows from hard earned cumulative experience, there are subgroups of pain patterns and physical features within the diagnosis of neuromusculoskeletal pain for which a certain approach or technique works better than in others. These need to be documented better.

There is also suspicion that the outcomes movement is coming on with too much speed and that it could stop development in certain areas (Epstein 1990). I would be concerned if meta-analyses have the final say rather than their being tools which expose errors in practice which may be correctable. And after all, isn't science about proving things wrong? For example, exercise may offer little help for acute spinal pain according to Waddell et al (1996). However, refine the exercise, change the environment in which the exercises are performed, realise that exercise is not just for muscle strength, provide more knowledge and motivation, and specify the group for whom the exercises are given—and more efficacy would probably be demonstrated. As Scott and Black (1991) point out, great care should be taken that meta-analyses are not pooling ignorance as much as distilling medicine.

Despite these differences, which I have presented from my one sided clinical viewpoint, clinicians and researchers in physiotherapy need to review our relationship with science urgently. Traditional physiotherapeutic approaches must engage a broader science therefore, a shift from traditional experiential based approaches to approaches that adopt evidence critically. At the risk of sounding like most editorials in physiotherapy journals, I believe that physiotherapy and, indeed, all medically related professions are facing challenges to change which have never been so powerful. The outcomes movement is one, but closely linked, and unnoticed by some, is the neurobiological revolution. Both forces of change can be met by reviewing practice and taking on the paradigm of pain and all the issues it brings with it. Uncorrupted reasoning science is necessary for this, particularly if the 'grey zones' in which physiotherapists work are contemplated.

The grey zones of physiotherapy practice

Most physiotherapists work in what has been termed 'grey zones of practice (Naylor 1995) where all is obviously not black and white. Here the pathoanatomy of the underlying pain states is not fully known and neither are the risk/benefit ratios of treatment known. Spinal and head pain come into this grey zone. Indeed, any symptoms which last for longer than the expected healing times of tissues under the painful area could be considered. Compare non-specific low back pain, which sits right in the middle of the grey zone, with rheumatoid arthritis for example, where the pathophysiology is reasonably well understood.

The grey zone is massive. This is an era of new, chronic and stress related disorders where there is neither vaccine nor cure. And with the grey zone comes an unprecedented growth in new treatments, machines, and professions proclaiming an answer. There will be huge grey areas until the generation of new research (Naylor 1995). Considering that a properly carried out randomised clinical trial may cost £200 000, this will require a massive financial and social investment.

At this stage, clinical reasoning must be applied to traverse the grey zones (Naylor 1995); reasoning which includes and integrates relevant evidence-based work as it comes about.

Clinical reasoning

Many researchers, particularly in physiotherapy, medicine and occupational therapy, have studied this science of clinical reasoning. In physiotherapy, clinical reasoning has been referred to as '... the thinking and decision making processes which are integral to clinical practice' (Higgs & Jones 1995). That is, the approach is dynamic, integrating a broad view of science and the individuality of each patient. Clinical reasoning should actually be evidence-based medicine. The opposite of clinical reasoning is 'recipe management' where clinicians apply similar techniques and principles to all patients. All physiotherapists have routine aspects of their management, particularly when patients have familiar problems, however the more complex a problem becomes, the more decision making skills will be required. This definition of clinical reasoning should be considered not only on a per patient bsis but also for total professional development. The outcomes movement can appear to devalue the reasoning science we use. Greer (1987) suggests the notion that clinicians are slow scientists or scientific dabblers should be rejected immediately. Science is a system of facts and principles concerning any subject (Hayward & Sparkes 1982). Reasoning is a science.

Clinical reasoning has been termed many things, such as clinical judgement and clinical decision making. A useful term is 'wise action' (Jones 1997). It's more catchy in the clinic and I find more teaching utility in asking a student 'Is that a wise action?' rather than 'Are you reasoning clinically?'. I hope that the broader use of available science can be seen as a 'wise action'.

Reasoning and Gurus

Manual therapists usually, and sometimes fervently, follow a school of thought. As Grant (1995) noted, there are paradigms of practice where practitioners use expert's names such as Cyriax, McKenzie or Maitland, or geographical attachments such as the Norwegian or the Australian approach. There are anatomically based approaches, such as the craniosacral or myofascial approach. The development of paradigms in this way has meant that each has its focal points which are often mutually exclusive. A more overlapping scenario is now required. I believe that the ideal approach in the clinic should be one that encompasses three things: the best skills from current therapies, the best information from science, and the best therapeutic relationship with a particular patient (Fig. 1).

Fig. 1 Clinical reasoning—the wise action approach. (From Butler DS, Gifford LS 1999 The dynamic nervous system. NOI Press, Adelaide, in press. With permission)

The best of current therapies acknowledges that there are good techniques, exercises, management strategies and conceptual approaches that are either self taught or have been learnt from others which are very useful, particularly if the right patient for the approach can be selected. For example I would consider that the self management concept of McKenzie, the inherent reasoning strategies of Maitland, the skill in joint management of Kaltenborn/ Evjenth and Paris are superb aspects of physiotherapy management that we must never lose, but adapt. There are approaches outside traditional physiotherapy which have skills to offer, such as counselling. There is much work yet to be done on the efficacy of current therapies.

The best of science means the most current and relevant science related to pathological movement. For physiotherapists this surely includes pain sciences, tissue pathophysiology, movement science, and rehabilitation science. The skill is to 'search' the brain for the science to fit the clinical pattern. However, if we are to take on the paradigm of pain in reasoning, our knowledge deficits are exposed instantly. For example, this may be, depending where and how you were taught, knowledge of synaptic activity, neurotransmitters, exercise prescription, or knowledge of results of randomised clinical trials.

The best of the patient implies that a skilled, analytical and defensible physical and subjective examination appropriate to the patient will be undertaken. This also implies that a relationship based on an appropriate amount of empathy is engendered and that the patient is involved in collaborative decision making.

These three aspects of reasoning rely on basic knowledge common to a profession and referred to as declarative knowledge.

Declarative knowledge

'Declarative knowledge' is a term that means to have 'knowledge about a topic so that one may declare that knowledge to be theirs' (Biggs & Telfer 1987). This could be considered in a personal sense but also in a professional sense. In the professional sense it should relate to the knowledge which is specific to that profession and it should relate to skills that only that profession has or uses in a particular way. Good clinical reasoning should allow a focus on the uniqueness of a profession—it should make the boundaries clearer.

In some professions the declarative knowledge is quite obvious, for example, dentistry has a near monopoly on the mouth, and neonatal cardiologists have few challengers. In the manual therapies it is much more open—there are many professions vying for management rights of painful states. There are many professions with a great interest in the brain.

'Pathokinesiology' (Hislop 1975) has been suggested as the distinguishing central concept in physiotherapy. This is certainly the primary paradigm in physiotherapy, though perhaps 'pathological movement' or 'movement dysfunction' are more modern terms. Hislop's (1975) concept was also strongly grounded in social and cultural needs and she considered that movement dysfunction could not be considered outside a sociocultural and a scientific framework (Purtilo 1986, Grant 1995).

The mission statements of most national physiotherapy associations are similar. For example, the American Physical Therapy Association (1998) says its mission is '...to further the profession's role in the prevention, diagnosis and treatment of movement dysfunctions and the enhancement of the physical health and functional abilities of members of the public.'

I doubt that these goals have changed in the lifetime of physiotherapy and other professions involved in manual medicine. What has changed rapidly as part of the outcomes and pain sciences movements is the knowledge of the mechanisms behind the faulty movement and dysfunction, and the best methods to assess and manage it.

As stated above, the general outcome of the mass of epidemiological data looking at factors related to the development of chronicity of spinal pain points to psychosocial factors, including patient beliefs, job satisfaction and educational level (e.g. Burton et al 1995, Kendall et al 1997), as being more important than the physical health of tissues, although certainly not denying the role of tissue health and fitness. Physiotherapists must become increasingly aware that sensitivity to movement is related not only to tissues but also to changes in central circuitry (see Chs 2-5). If a patient's pathological movement is a result of lack of knowledge, or inappropriate knowledge provided by a health professional, particularly unnecessary fear of movement or belief that reinjury is imminent, then physiotherapists must do something about it. We should be well placed to contribute here, due to our numbers, time with patients, existing movement improvement strategies, and biological and kinaesiological knowledge. Indeed we now see repeatedly in the physiotherapy literature the call for change; that modern physical rehabilitation cannot limit itself to physical methods only (e.g. Lieberman et al 1994, Feuerstein & Beattie 1995, Harding & Williams 1995, Watson 1996, Ford & Gordon 1997, Gifford & Butler 1997, Martinez et al 1997) . However, the critical question arises— is our current declarative knowledge adequate to handle this?

A critical look at current declarative knowledge

In physiotherapy and medicine, a very dominant tissue or structure based approach undoubtedly still exists. I am not aware of any major physiotherapy spinal treatment teaching programme in the world which is **not** dominated by the structural approach, or what could be called a 'bottom up' approach, where it is all bottom and little up; that is, the approach is dominated by tissues especially joints and muscles. This is the approach I was taught, and then taught myself for many years. It is a relevant and necessary approach when disease and injury are in tissues, particularly in acute cases. In Figure 2, this approach is illustrated. The arrows reveal the deeper and deeper search into the tissues for an answer to a patient's pain. In this model the joint is used as an example, but it could equally be fascia, muscle or any tissue. It shows that for adequate management of tissue problems we need anatomical and pathoanatomical knowledge of all tissues including knowledge at a gross anatomical level and down to the molecular level. This approach holds that pain is a passive process beginning at end terminals, and relates to impulses going in a straight line to the brain. It appears to neglect current concepts of pain as an endogenous active process, the role of fear and anxiety, beliefs, and the fact that the brain is 'on all the time' (McCrone 1997) and thus may not be dependent on peripheral input for activation and output. We can say that the phenomenon of pain, particularly when ongoing or recurrent, challenges this approach.

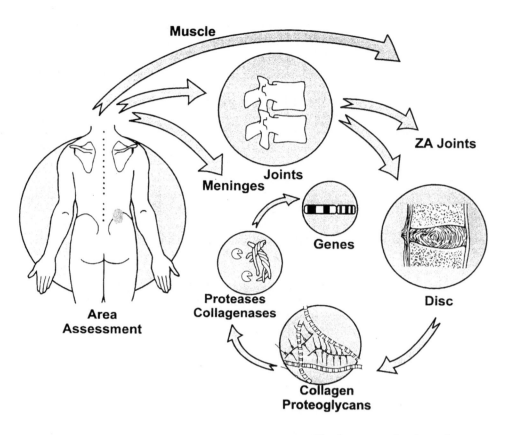

Fig. 2 The tissue based approach. (From Butler DS, Gifford LS 1999 The dynamic nervous system. NOI Press, Adelaide, in press. With permission)

In Figure 3, which I adapted from Shepherd's classic textbook (Shepherd 1994), a neurobiological approach is presented. Louis Gifford and I (Butler & Gifford 1999, in press) are urging the careful and diplomatic integration of this material into current physiotherapy practice, i.e. expanding out declarative knowledge. Again looking down to the less visible levels, our lack of knowledge is exposed. We believe physiotherapists need more knowledge about health related behaviour in general. This includes pain behaviour, illness behaviour, and the reasons for it. We need knowledge about neurological centres and pathways. Traditional education has provided us with knowledge about sensory and motor pathways; the more mysterious hypothalamus-pituitary-adrenal axis was left out. We didn't discuss limbic and reticular systems, and the autonomic nervous system was never for serious study. We must have knowledge of these centres if we are to understand pathological movement and provide a scientific rationale for management. No one is calling for a great depth of knowledge; keeping up with lay science journals, e.g. *New*

Scientist or *Science and Medicine,* and review articles in physiotherapy and mainstream science journals should be adequate for clinicians.

In the model (Fig. 3) some knowledge about the function of neurones, synapses, neurone connectivity, receptors and ion channels is also required. Soon we must take more knowledge of genetics into our declarative knowledge. The proteins which constitute ion channels and receptors in the axolemma of nerve fibres and which ultimately dictate sensitivity are produced by genetic instruction in response to environmental forces. Perhaps a good example of the need for knowledge down to a genetic/molecular level is recent knowledge (e.g. Devor 1994) that in post peripheral nerve injury, the genetic machinery can alter the expression of receptors at the injury site to make them more responsive to circulating adrenaline. This means that stress may drive a neuropathic pain in a direct way. Physiotherapists must be professional conduits of this knowledge to patients. I believe that most physiotherapists would like to take on this new material, we just require some assistance with the process.

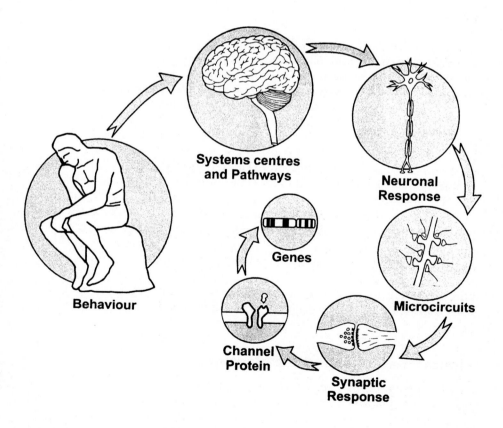

Fig. 3 The neurobiological model. (From Butler DS, Gifford LS 1999 The dynamic nervous system. NOI Press, Adelaide, in press. With permission)

Utilising a wider declarative knowledge in a clinical reasoning model may assist physiotherapists to get more involved with chronic pain professionally. It is well known that most physiotherapists prefer not to work with patients with chronic pain—all but 4% in a US study (Wolff et al 1991). It seems that acute injuries and sports injuries are the preferred options, although it is very likely that physiotherapists conceptualise recurrent back pain as acute rather than the chronic pains they should be framed as. The acute care model predominates in physiotherapy and I believe it is often forgotten that the expression of acute pain depends on peripherally activated central pathways. Not enough is taught about the physiological and cognitive mechanisms in undergraduate training (Wolff et al 1991). The same problem exists in medicine according to Cherkin (1988). The neurobiological model is as appropriate for acute pain management as it is for chronic pain management.

Role of the clinician's experience

Where does experience fit in? Management models that propose new information and the integration of evidence-based medicine downplay or can appear to downplay the importance of experience. Experience was always the dominant feature of traditional management paradigms (e.g. Goldner & Bilsker 1995). This is particularly so in physiotherapy, especially in the area of manipulative physiotherapy where gurus are powerful and many clinicians try to merge the best aspects of all that the gurus offer. In this traditional paradigm, when faced with a patient clinicians will reflect on experiences with similar presentations, reflect on underlying theory and consult an expert (Higgs & Jones 1995, Gilroy 1996). This is clinical reasoning; we all do it, and most of us reason subconsciously. However, the current underlying theory base needs an injection of pain science and I believe we must be diplomatically critical of who we consider an expert. Clearly, given the grey areas of spinal pain management, experience still dominates and is a key part of reasoning. However there are clinicians who have had 20 years of experience in 20 years of clinical practice, there are others who have 20 years of experience in one year of clinical practice. The latter have reasoned, learnt, experimented with management techniques, remained open, aware of the outcomes movement, read widely, and are likely to be amongst the growing number who are becoming disillusioned with what is taught in many schools and continuing education programmes.

Clinical reasoning and the placebo

Any discussion on pain and clinician/patient relationships must include the placebo. The placebo is rarely discussed in clinical practice and in the clinical reasoning literature, and as Wall (1992) comments it is 'an uncomfortable topic'. Yet we must discuss it urgently because it is at the heart of the clinical reasoning encounter.

The placebo can also be used as a framework to discuss the biology and power of the clinician-patient relationship, in itself (if healthy) a positive outcome predictor (e.g. Western Ontario 1986, Henbest & Stewart 1990). To talk about pain is to talk about the placebo. To begin to understand pain is to begin to understand the placebo.

Placebos are commonly thought to be an inert prescription of treatment, but the term should also relate to a method or any type of therapy as was in original definitions. The placebo response or effect is the nonspecific psychophysiological therapeutic effect produced by the therapy (Shapiro & Shapiro 1997). Placebo issues often carry much disparagement and misunderstanding. Spiro (1997) suggests a name change to 'seal'. At first it sounds a bit offputting, but it is worth some thought. Spiro describes it as 'the icon of loyalty between patient and clinicians, the contract, the sign of the physicians willingness to help'. In essence it is the positive aspects in the entire relationship between clinicians and patients. It includes the welcome and the goodbye, the laying on of hands, the ritual in the delivery of a treatment, or handing over a prescription or list of exercises. It may be unfair to call these non-specific effects. In the skilful enquiry demanded by quality reasoning with 'grey zone' patients, the respect for the client is communicated and enhanced. Support for patient's rights to seek their own management and the ability to talk to the patient on a comfortable equal level all engender a placebo response. Just the art of listening and providing enough non-verbals for the patient to be aware that you are with them, can be placebo. As Jensen (1996) points out, this is not necessarily agreeing with the patient; it is acceptance of the story without any blame or judgement. An 'accepted' person then can spend more time considering what they want and need to do, rather than defending what they have done. This is no light topic because placebos relieve pain better than anything else.

Consideration of the placebo also highlights the dissonance between science and modern medical practice (Spiro 1997), an issue raised earlier in this essay. Science wants cures and outcomes; patients want that too, but they also want care. It will be inevitable that the outcomes movement will turn more to the placebo discussion. For example the clinician will justifiably ask, '…if electrotherapy is not worthwhile (Klaber Moffett et al 1996) and manipulation and exercise don't help many, what it is that gets my patients better?', Or they will think, 'Did I get them better?'. It is timely for physiotherapists to consider the seal between us and the patients, how we can harness it, how measurable it is, and for scientists to consider how blind is double blind.

The placebo is a healing thing; it may even be an adaptive human survival mechanism to seek it out. There is an opposite—the nocebo, perhaps more realised in the relationship process than the delivery of a drug or technique. Sometimes clinicians just don't see eye to eye with patients for a multitude of reasons. While some clinicians are natural walking placebos, others may have to work hard at patient/relationship issues. There is a placebo/nocebo component or percentage in all we do as clinicians. Any clinician/patient relationship engenders it, skilled clinical reasoning with its respectful questioning and appropriate empathy content surely enhances the placebo aspects. Good clinicians are subconsciously aware of it, but it is a subject for study. Patients who feel comfortable in the physiotherapy environment and who know they must undress and be touched by knowing hands over their sore areas may be primed for it. There can be a healthy ritual in management that may not involve the physiotherapists/receptionists performing their jobs— the powerful image of the electric up and down bed, the air of positivity, the certificates on the wall, and happy healthy looking patients waiting in the waiting room reading the latest magazines. These are all factors related to the paradigm of pain. Understanding their power is to begin to understand pain.

Great care is needed here. While conveying the words 'I will take care of you' and 'I think I can explain your problem and map out an approach' is a powerful placebo and appropriate in acute illness and acute pain, it may not be entirely appropriate in chronic pain. 'I will help you to look after yourself' may be a better placebo with a longer lasting effect. We all see patients with great hope at first, but then this slowly diminishes as placebo power diminishes. Such is the power of this word *placebo,* that it is worth repeating that I am using it in a non-derogatory way.

It may be that different professions have different needs in relation to evidence-based medicine. This may relate to the amount of placebo involvement in the profession. Physiotherapists do not deliver drugs, injections or surgery, but while there are techniques and some electrical machinery, there is a powerful human physical and verbal interaction. We usually have more time with patients than doctors, thus providing great potential for the power of the placebo. I would suggest that the best clinicians in the field worked out long before Bass et al (1986) showed it, that physician-patient agreement about the nature of a problem was a major variable related to outcome. If we can consider that much of what we do is related to a process of change and adaptation rather than 'fix-it', then the power of the placebo or seal is more easily realised.

The real art in physiotherapy is to harness the placebo to assist in the delivery of a management programme which targets apparent or reasoned pathophysiological and pathomechanical processes which are relevant to the patient's troubles.

The placebo responses alter the neural representation of the injury, disability and the injury circumstances. Neurobiology can provide an understanding of the placebo responses. The effects occur due to modifications in the pain modulating central nervous system circuitry, autonomic, and neuroendocrine and neuroimmune systems. A good summary of these effects is in Fields and Price (1997) and in this yearbook (Chapters 2-5).

A clinical reasoning model to include pain

Reasoning models for physiotherapy are in widespread current use. There are aspects of decision making in all manual therapy concepts, best articulated by Mark Jones (1992, 1995; Higgs & Jones 1995). This model can be expanded to include the paradigm of pain and all that it brings with it (Butler 1994, Gifford & Butler 1997, Gifford 1997, Butler & Gifford in press). It will require going back to basics and considering what the pain paradigm is; for example, the tricky secondary hyperalgesia which can be an assault on one's existing rationality. I suggest that physiotherapists seek a broad answer and read widely in pathophysiological areas (e.g. Melzack & Wall 1996) but also in sociocultural areas (e.g. Morris 1991, Delvecchio-Good et al 1992). Meanwhile, the IASP definition (Merskey & Bogduk 1994) that 'pain is an unpleasant sensory and emotional experience associated with actual or potential tissue damage or described in terms of such damage', is the best starting point and one which acknowledges the key word 'experience'.

Hypotheses categories

Reasoning requires that the practitioner makes educated hypotheses about all kinds of information and processes related to the patient's management. These can be categorised. A reasoning category is a category or 'box' of information collected, with the ultimate goal being successful management of the patient (Higgs & Jones 1995). For example, a clinician collects information from a range of sources (e.g. patient interview, imaging tests, the literature, 'gut feeling', previous experiences with similar problems) which allows identification of a troublesome tissue, hints of a disease process, and prognosis. Although in the following discussion, categories are placed in a certain order, the relative importance of each to a particular patient will vary. These categories are now in use in the post-graduate manipulative physiotherapy programme at the University of South Australia.

The whole reasoning process may collapse if the clinician cannot provide reasoned information in all categories (Fig. 4). Reflecting on cases of failed management, it should be easy to see which category was not reasoned adequately. These categories are briefly discussed below.

Fig. 4 Clinical reasoning categories. Clinicians must be able to provide information in all categories to ensure a balanced approach. (From Butler DS, Gifford LS 1999 The dynamic nervous system. NOI Press, Adelaide, in press. With permission)

Pathobiological mechanisms

Pathobiology is the physiology of suffering, disease and injury and is obviously a central concept in modern medicine. It is clear that it has not been included adequately in current models of manual therapy.

Pathobiology includes mechanisms related to all involved biological systems (e.g. motor, endocrine, nervous) as well as pathological events that are involved in response to injury and other stressful input. It is in this category that pain can be engaged and our shortcomings in declarative knowledge made evident.

This category can be divided up into mechanisms related to tissues and mechanisms related to pain. Pathobiological mechanisms are discussed in greater detail elsewhere in this yearbook (Chs 2–5).

Pathobiological mechanisms related to tissue injury/disease

We ought to be good at this because this is where the majority of our training focussed. This includes making hypotheses about the actual tissue(s) injured, the nature of the injury, the stage of healing, the amount of inflammation, and the amount of scarring.

Pathobiological mechanisms related to pain

This category may be new to many physiotherapists. This is essentially making a decision on the class of pain a patient has. The stimulus came from Patrick Wall as I was reading through a superb paper that I unfortunately have misplaced. It doesn't matter. In the paper was a comment that went something like 'When a patient is in front of you, management decisions will relate not only to tissues at fault but also to the class of pain the patient has'. There are classes of pain all based on pathophysiological processes unearthed by pain sciences in the last two decades and which relate in particular to peripheral and central pain mechanisms. Note that the relative importance of peripheral or central mechanisms cannot yet be judged scientifically. Clinical reasoning is needed to transcend the gap. It appears that there has been a gross error in reasoning in the past with the insistence that all pain should have a tissue source.

Pain mechanisms can be conveniently divided into those related to input (e.g. nerve injury, muscle injury), those related to processing (e.g. central nervous system plasticity changes, cognitive influences) and those related to output systems (e.g. sympathetic nervous system, immune and endocrine systems). Gifford's model (1998) in Chapter 2 of this yearbook, has great clinical utility here. Recent useful reviews on pain mechanisms include Sidall (1997), Devor (1996) and Markenson (1996).

Symptoms related to input

There are two categories here: nociceptive pain and peripheral neurogenic pain. Nociceptive pain is pain arising from the tissues, pain which emerges at the ends of neurones, for example from changes in joint, muscles, dura mater, urethra and skin. The main pain evoking mechanisms will be mechanical and inflammatory. For recent reviews see Chapter 3, Gifford, (1997), and Gifford and Butler (1997). Note that it also include the connective tissues of the nervous system such as epineurium and dura mater. The reader may wonder what the difference is between the category of tissue injury and nociceptive pain. The point is that tissue injury does not necessarily have to hurt. To understand pain mechanisms is to understand why an injury may hurt one person but not another.

Peripheral neurogenic pain includes pain generated from peripheral nerves and the cell bodies of peripheral nerve fibres. This includes nerve root injury and nerve entrapment. It also includes injury to cranial nerves and roots. Any injury or disease outside the dorsal horn of the spinal cord, or the medullary horn in the case of the cranial nerves, could be considered as peripheral neurogenic. In peripheral neurogenic pain the split between the tissue approach and the neurobiological approach can be seen. Two very well known scientists Devor (1994) and Lundborg (Lundborg &1996, Lundborg & Dahlin 1997) have written widely about peripheral nerve injury but, as far as I can see, never mention each other. Devor is more interested in the neurobiology of pain, Lundborg, more interested in tissue health issues such as circulation and axoplasmic flow. These references are highly recommended readings for physiotherapists.

Related to processing

Pain related to input mechanisms is quite understandable. This is how we were taught. A quick review of what pain is helps here. If it was all related to input, it would be easy. It would make pain a passive process, a registering of impulse trains in the central nervous system following alterations of input. It is more accurate to consider it as something a person creates or processes actively, and which is highly reliant on endogenous processes. (Chapman et al 1997). The input mechanisms relating to pain are not in use all the time, however the brain is 'on' all the time. This involves complex processing involving multiple inputs such as feelings and moods, links to existing neural circuitry (memory) which may have been established years previously, and biological events including alterations in responsiveness of neurones, receptive fields increases, and new neuronal connections. Chapters of this Yearbook provide more detail.

Related to output

The human as a control system will have an output in response to input and processing. Sometimes these output mechanisms can be considered as pain evoking mechanisms in their own right. Clinicians will be familiar with the sympathetic nervous system, but considerations here should also include the parasympathetic system, the endocrine system, and the motor system (see Chs 2-5).

It is critical that readers realise that all these process will be occurring at one time in both acute and chronic pain, however there may be a clinical dominance of one mechanism rather than the other. By pattern generation, a reasoned decision about the dominant mechanism(s) in operation may be made. These patterns are discussed elsewhere (Butler 1994, Gifford & Butler 1997, Gifford 1997, Butler & Gifford in press).

Dysfunction

A pathobiological mechanism may result in variable disturbances of function (dysfunction) which hopefully recede as the injury gets better. Sometimes members of the public bring these dysfunctions in varying states of recovery to clinicians and then the person becomes a patient. Dysfunctions are what we observe and find in the clinic.

There are various categories of dysfunction which must be understood by clinicians if they are going to integrate pain (Gifford & Butler 1997, Gifford 1997). All categories should be considered by the clinician.

First is **general physical dysfunction**. This may be an inability to walk properly; it could be a limp, poor use of crutches, an inability to perform a particular sporting manoeuvre, lack of fitness etc. This needs closer attention from physiotherapists. Arguably, the rush to find a tissue at fault means that these general physical dysfunctions and the fact that they may not need to be associated with unhealthy tissues may be overlooked.

Second is **specific physical dysfunction**. This is what clinicians find on examination. It could be a tight or weak muscle, a loss of reflex, an adherent tight piece of scar, a limited Upper Limb Tension Test, or pain on pressure over a certain body part. Physiotherapists are usually well skilled at this aspect of examination. By themselves, specific physical dysfunctions are only clinical findings. Their relevance must be reasoned.

Third is **mental or psychological dysfunction**. This is what patients think and feel, as a result of their injury, about their injury, about you, and about the treatment and society's approach to their injury.

Obviously all are related. A patient would have to have general physical dysfunction before a therapist went looking for relevant specific physical dysfunction. General physical dysfunction may be more determined by beliefs, attitudes and motivation than by actual tissue pathology; it thus has a great relationship to mental/psychological dysfunction.

To make more sense in a reasoning approach, dysfunctions have to be seen as adaptive or maladaptive (Gifford 1997). This can be difficult. Who are we to say that a certain behaviour or way of thinking is adaptive or maladaptive if the complete picture of what pain is, is not explored. For example it may be quite adaptive and assist healing in certain cultures to exclaim and wail loudly, perhaps seeking as much placebo from society as possible. But in practice we can usually make decisions about when a limp or movement pattern or posture is serving a healing purpose (adaptive), or if there is no such benefit in the action (maladaptive). Pathobiological knowledge helps.

We all have dysfunctions. When manual therapists examine people who are in no distress, even top level athletes, they will usually find some dysfunction—stiff joints here, a tight nerve there, altered cranial rhythms, etc; sometimes it depends on the particular bent of the therapist. Here is where we need to be careful—they may not be relevant, just like the findings on a X-ray or MRI may not be relevant (Jensen et al 1994). We accumulate dysfunction as we get older, the 'kisses of time' in antique dealer language. Taking on the paradigm of pain helps us determine the relevance of what we find. In the past we have surely found and treated dysfunctions that have no relevance to the patient. We may well have provided a healthy dose of placebo by the ritual of treatment and alleviated a problem which was elsewhere. We should have no trouble admitting this. It has surely happened in all fields of medicine (Shapiro & Shapiro 1997).

Sources

Sources means the actual anatomical location of the pathobiological mechanisms. Sources may be explained as 'If you had a magic bullet to fix the patient, where would you fire it?'. In the case of acute injury and nociceptive pain, you may need only one bullet aimed at tissues and nociceptors supplying the tissues. In the case of a more complex pain presentation, then perhaps one bullet may not be enough and a machine gun approach may be more necessary—perhaps aim for the tissues, the central nervous system, and one in the pituitary!

Clinicians can consider two aspects to sources—**source(s) of the dysfunction** and **sources(s) of the mechanisms**. Patients also have hypotheses about the anatomical location of their problem and this requires respect. Patients may not care much about sources of mechanisms. For a musician who is having difficulty playing an instrument the source of the mechanisms may be in the peripheral and central nervous system, but the source of the dysfunction could be the hand.

Contributing factors

This category includes any factor related to the predisposition, development and maintenance of a problem. This includes psychosocial, genetic, anthropometric, and ergonomic factors. In understanding this hypothesis category and being aware of the various issues and states which drive a pain state, there should be repercussions for overall management.

Psychosocial means the interaction between a person and their environment and the resultant influences on behaviour. In the last five years the outcomes movement has provided a mass of research in this area. For example, psychosocial factors which have been shown to have a link to the development of pain chronicity include beliefs that all pain is harmful and disabling (Kendall et al 1997), provision of rational explanations of the problem (Indahl et al 1995), fear of pain (Klenerman et al 1995), level of work satisfaction (Bigos et al 1992), and significant childhood psychological trauma (Goldberg 1994). A full summary of these data appears in Butler and Gifford (1999, in press). This reasoning category will provide powerful direction for physiotherapy in the future. Knowledge of it, thus creating an awareness of the multiple influences and effects of pain, should emphasise how important it is to include contributing factors into our declarative knowledge.

Prognosis

This is perhaps one of the most difficult hypothesis categories to make a decision on. It can be a humbling learning process to make a note on a patient chart detailing how many treatments a patient will require and for what result, on the patient's first attendance. This category like others will draw information from all the other reasoning categories. In terms of chronic ongoing pain, the prognosis for pain relief may be poor, while that for restoration of functional movement and quality of movement can be excellent.

Precautions

'Do no harm' should be foremost. Or if manual therapy is performed then the least force for the maximum safe gain should be the ideal. In recent years the terms 'red flags' and 'yellow flags' have been used. (Kendall et al 1997) Red flags are physical risk factors and often require urgent referral for specialist attention. An example would be a sudden visual deficit after a neck injury, or a rapid loss of weight when there is no obvious reason. Yellow flags refer to psychosocial factors. Given the phenomenon of pain and the influences upon it, there should not only be precautions in what we do, but in what we say and how we act as well.

Management

Management has to be a reasoning category also, as what we actually do can only be a hypothesis. It has been said that the management of spinal pain is up for grabs (Spitzer 1993) with no professional group showing any great lead over others at this stage. A technique is only a part of overall management. Management also links into the other reasoning categories and it includes knowing when to stop, and when to use other professionals. Given that pain, particularly chronic pain, is something that we may never cure, management becomes a critical word. There will always be a place for passively delivered techniques. They are often useful and society demands it. However the addition of the paradigm of pain to reasoning makes it obvious that skills including interprofessional work, provision of knowledge, goal setting, activity pacing and rehabilitation of fitness are also critical (see Chs 8 & 9).

The process of reasoning

Reasoning is about falsifiable hypotheses. The key thought is that a hypothesis is not wrong or even fraudulent as the name suggests, but something which is subject to being disproven. It can be disproven by response to treatment and various aspects of science. It could be said that hypotheses must be null hypotheses

Clinical reasoning must be an evolving model. This is perhaps the most critical issue in reasoning (Jones et al 1995). Knowledge evolves, patients and their injury context evolve, politics evolve, and the cultural dimensions of health and illness evolve. For clinicians to keep pace with these evolutions, they must look continually for new patterns and challenge existing beliefs constantly. Figure 5 illustrates the process of reasoning.

The key points are:

* Reasoning is an evolving process.
* All hypothesis categories will be broad at first and then refined, rejected, or new hypotheses added.
* Information to formulate hypotheses is gained from two main sources— assessment of the patient and the therapist's knowledge, understanding and previous experiences.
* Patients must be a part of the reasoning process. They have hypotheses (beliefs) in all the reasoning categories which will alter as the process of management proceeds.
* Placebo effects could occur anywhere in the process.

Errors are easily made in reasoning. Two of the most common are adding pragmatic influences and jumping to favourite hypotheses (Jones 1992), but also read Sagan (1996) and Sutherland (1994).

If a patient says they have a 'pain in the hip', it is an easy often pragmatic thing for a therapist to believe them. However this 'hip pain' could be arising from a number of structures and be related to various mechanisms. Patients' concepts of where their hips are surely vary. There are often difficulties in convincing a patient that their hip pain is perhaps referred from the spinal tissue or is related to maladaptive central processing. Placebo power is required.

Because 'favourite hypotheses' exist in manual therapy there are those who will see every problem as a joint, or a nerve, or something myofascial, or a maladaptive central pain state. It may relate to the last course they were on or to the most recent successful intervention they may have had. Sometimes it may be the first tissue examined. This also relates to sampling too few hypotheses. We can all be guilty here. Ask yourself why you like the hypothesis and compare it fairly with others. A larger declarative knowledge, particularly one that embraces pain sciences, will often be required to make the mistakes obvious.

Conclusion

This essay is directed at clinicians and their future. There are powerful forces for change in operation and I hope readers can see that taking on the paradigm of pain is one way of addressing these forces. I also hope that readers can see that there is a developing clinical reasoning process in physiotherapy which is

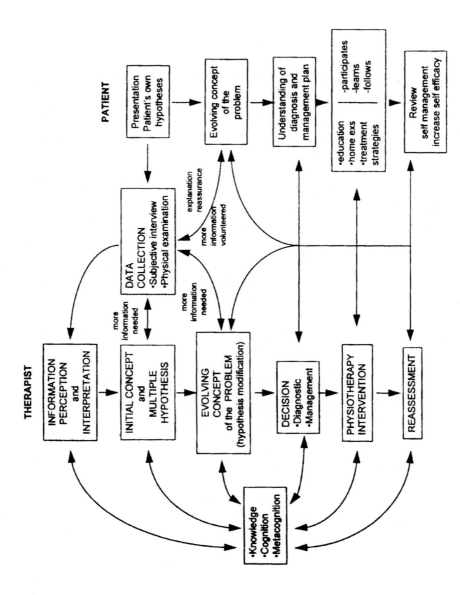

Fig. 5 The clinical reasoning process emphasising co-operative decision making between patient and therapist. (Jones 1995)

open to change and which facilitates the integration of pain into the clinical and research processes, and in itself can engender useful placebo responses. It is as if pain is there for the taking.

REFERENCES

American Physical Therapy Association 1998 APTA Mission Statement.

Bass M J, Buck C, Turner L et al 1986 The physician's actions in the outcome of illness in family practice. Journal of Family Practice 23:43–49

Biggs J B, Telfer R 1987 The process of learning. Prentice-Hall, Sydney

Bigos S J, Battie M C, Spengler D M et al 1992 A longitudinal, prospective study of industrial back injury reporting. Clinical Orthopaedics and Related Research 279:21–34

Burton K A, Tillotson K M, Main C J et al 1995 Psychological predictors of outcome in acute and subchronic low back trouble. Spine 20:722–28

Butler D S 1994 The upper limb tension test revisited. In: Grant R (ed) Physical therapy of the cervical and thoracic spines. 2nd edn. Churchill Livingstone, New York

Butler D S, Gifford L S 1999 in press The dynamic nervous system. NOI Press, Adelaide

Chapman R C, Oka S, Jacobson R C 1997 Phasic pupil dilation response to noxious stimulation in humans. In: Jensen T S, Turner J A, Wiesenfeld Z (eds) Proceedings of the 8th World Congress on Pain. IASP Press, Seattle

Cherkin D C 1988 Commentary. Journal of Family Practice 27:488

Delvecchio-Good M, Brodwin P E, Good B J et al (ed) 1992 Pain as human experience. Oxford, University of California Press

Devor M 1994 The pathophysiology of damaged peripheral nerves. In: Wall P D, Melzack R (eds) Textbook of pain. 3rd edn. Churchill Livingstone, Edinburgh

Devor M 1996 Pain mechanisms and pain syndromes. In: Campbell J N (ed) Pain 1996: An updated review. IASP Press, Seattle

Epstein A M 1990 The outcomes movement. Will it get us where we want? New England Journal of Medicine 323:266–270

Feuerstein M, Beattie P 1995 Biobehavioural factors affecting pain and disability in low back pain: mechanisms and assessment. Physical Therapy 75:267–280

Fields H L, Price D D 1997 Towards a neurobiology of placebo analgesia. In: Harrington A (ed) The placebo effect. Harvard University Press, Cambridge, Mass.

Ford I W, Gordon S 1997 Perspectives of sports physiotherapists on the freequence and significance of psychological factors in professional practice: Implications for curriculum design in professional training. The Australian Journal of Science and Medicine in Sport 29:34–40

Gifford L, Butler D 1997 The integration of pain sciences into clinical practice. The Journal of Hand Therapy 10:86–95

Gifford L S 1997 Pain. In: Pitt-Brooke J, Reid H, Lockwood J et al (eds) Rehabilitation of movement. W.B. Saunders, London

Gifford L S 1998 Pain, the tissues and the nervous system. A conceptual model. Physiotherapy 84:27–36

Gilroy A 1996 'Our own kind of medicine'. Inscape 1:52–60

Goldberg R T 1994 Childhood abuse, depression, and chronic pain. The Clinical Journal of Pain 10: 277–281

Goldner E M, Bilsker D 1995 Evidence-based practice in Psychiatry. Canadian Journal of Psychiatry 40:97–101

Grant R, 1995 1995 The pursuit of excellence in the face of constant change. Physiotherapy 81:338–344

Greer A L 1987 The two cultures of biomedicine: Can there be consensus. The Journal of the American Medical Association 258: 2739–2740

Harding V, Williams A de C 1995 Extending physiotherapy skills using a psychological approach: cognitive behavioural management of chronic pain. Physiotherapy 81:681–688

Hayward A L, Sparkes J J 1982 The Concise English Dictionary. Omega Books, London

Henbest R J, Stewart M 1990 Patient-centredness in consultation. 2. Does it make a difference ? Family Practice 7:28

Higgs J, Jones M A 1995 Clinical reasoning in the health professions. Butterworth-Heinnemann, London

Hislop H J 1975 The not-so-impossible dream. Physical Therapy 55:1069–1080

Indahl A, Velund L, Reikeraas O 1995 Good prognosis for low back pain when left untampered: a randomized clinical trial. Spine 20:473–477

Jensen M C, Brant-Zawadzki M N, Obuchowski N et al 1994 Magnetic resonance imaging of the lumbar spine in people without back pain. The New England Journal of Medicine 331:69–73

Jensen M P 1996 Enhancing motivation to change in pain treatment. In: Gatchel R J, Turk D C (eds) Psychological approaches to pain. Guildford Press, New York

Jones M, Jensen G, Rothstein J 1995 Clinical reasoning in physiotherapy. In: Higgs J M, Jones M A (eds) Clinical reasoning in the health professions. Butterworth-Heinemann, Oxford

Jones M A 1992 Clinical reasoning in manual therapy. Physical Therapy 72:875–883

Jones MA 1995 Clinical reasoning and pain. Manual Therapy 1:17–24

Jones M A 1997 Clinical reasoning: the foundation of clinical practice. Part 1. Australian Journal of Physiotherapy 43:167–170

Kendall N A S, Linton S J, Main C J 1997 Guide to assessing psychosocial yellow flags in acute low back pain: risk factors for long term disability and work loss. Accident Rehabilitation & Compensation Insurance Corporation of New Zealand and the National Health Committee, Wellington

Kenny N P 1997 Does good science make good medicine? Canadian Medical Association Journal 157:33–36

Klaber Moffett J A, Richardson P H, Frost H et al 1996 A placebo controlled double blind trial to evaluatethe effectiveness of pulsed short wave therapy for osteoarthritic hip and knee pain. Pain 67:121–127

Klenerman L, Slade P D, Stanley I M et al 1995 The prediction of chronicity in patients with an acute attack of low back pain in a general practice setting. Spine 20:478–484

Lieberman A, Lieberman M B, Lieberman B R 1994 Psychosocial aspects of physical rehabilitation. In: O'Sullivan S B, Schmitz T J (eds) Physical rehabilitation. 3rd edn. F.A. Davis Company, Philadelphia

Lundborg G, Dahlin L 1997 Pathophysiology of peripheral nerve trauma. In: Omer G E, Spinner M, Van Beek A L (eds) Management of peripheral nerve problems. 2nd edn. W.B. Saunders Company, Philadelphia

Lundborg G, Dahlin L B 1996 Anatomy, function and pathophysiology of peripheral nerves and nerve compression. Hand Clinics 12:185–193

Markenson J A 1996 Mechanisms of chronic pain. American Journal of Medicine. 101 (suppl 1A): 6S–18S

Martinez A, Simmonds M J, Novy D M 1997 Physiotherapy for patients with chronic pain: An operant-behavioural approach. Physiotherapy Pactice and Theory 13:97–108

McCrone J 1997 Wild minds. New Scientist 156:26–30

Melzack R, Wall P D 1996 The challenge of pain. London, Penguin.

Merskey H, Bogduk N 1994 Classification of chronic pain. IASP Press, Seattle

Morris D 1991 The culture of pain. University of California Press, Berkeley

Naylor C D 1995 Grey zones of clinical practice: some limits to evidence-based medicine. The Lancet 345:840–842

Predictors of outcome in headache patients presenting to family physicians—a one year prospective study. The Headache Study Group of the University of Western Ontario 1986. Headache 26:285

Purtilo R B 1986 Definitionl issues in pathokinesiology—A retrospective and a look ahead. Physical Therapy 66:372–374

Sagan C 1996 The demon haunted world. Headline, London

Scott E, Black N 1991 When does consensus exist in expert panels? Journal of Public Health Medicine 13: 344

Shapiro A K, Shapiro E 1997 The powerful placebo. John Hopkins University Press, Baltimore

Shepherd G M 1994 Neurobiology. Oxford University Press, Oxford

Sidall P J, Cousins M J 1997 Spinal update: Spinal pain mechanisms. Spine 22:98–101

Spiro H 1997 Clinical reflections on the placebo phenomenon. In: Harrington A (ed) The placebo effect. Harvard University Press, Cambridge, Mass.

Spitzer W O 1993 Low back pain in the workplace: attainable benefits not attained. British Journal of Industrial Medicine 50:385–388

Sutherland S 1994 Irrationality. Penguin, London

Tanenbaum S J 1993 What physicians know. The New England Journal of Medicine 329:1268–1270

Waddell G, Feder G, McIntosh A et al 1996 Low back pain evidence review. Royal College of General Practitioners, London

Wall P D 1992 The placebo effect: an unpopular topic. Pain 51:1–3

Watson G 1996 Neuromusculoskeletal physiotherapy: encouraging self-management. Physiotherapy 82:352–357

Wennenberg J E, Freeman J L, Culp W J 1987 Are hospital services rationed in New Haven or over-utilised in Boston. Lancet 1:1185–1189

Wolff M S, Hoskins-Michel T, Krebs D E et al 1991 Chronic pain—assessment of orthopedic physical therapists' knowledge and attitudes. Physical Therapy 71:207–214

1

Whiplash—science and management

1

Whiplash—is there a lesion?

MICHAEL A THACKER

Introduction

This chapter is based on a review of the current literature but also includes some critical appraisal relevant to clinical practice. A major aim is to present the accumulating and convincing evidence for a wide range of tissue injuries following a whiplash incident. The first four sections introduce the topic by giving an outline of the terminology, epidemiology, aetiology and pathomechanics of 'whiplash'.

Definition

It was Crowe in 1928 who first used the term whiplash to describe 'the manner in which the head was moved to produce a sprain in the neck.' Since then many other definitions have been used to describe the condition. For example, Bogduk (1986) defines whiplash using a somewhat mechanistic/causal perspective:

> an injury to one or more elements of the cervical spine that arises from inertial forces being applied to the head in the course of a Motor Vehicle accident that results in the perception of neck pain.

The publication of the Quebec Task Force (QTF) report into whiplash injury in 1995 (Spitzer et al 1995) was a major development which amassed and assessed much of the available data and literature on the topic. The report proposes that the term whiplash be replaced as it: 'indicates mechanism, the injury itself, various clinical manifestations consequent to injury and constellations of signs and symptoms'. This is a view shared by several authors including Robinson and Cassar-Pullicino(1993) who believe the term whiplash to be 'emotive'. The problems with definition are further enhanced by the use of many synonymous terms in the literature (see Box 1). This led the QTF (Spitzer et al 1995) to redefine whiplash in the following manner:

> whiplash is an acceleration/deceleration mechanism of transfer to the neck. It may result from rear-end or side impact motor vehicle collisions , but can occur during diving or other mishaps. The impact may result in bony or soft tissue injuries (whiplash injury), which in turn may lead to a variety of clinical manifestations (whiplash associated disorders).

The author feels that this is an encouraging progression in the understanding of this condition and will use this terminology throughout this account.

Box 1

Synonymous terms used in the literature

Whiplash like neck distortions (Jonsson et al 1994)
Whiplash syndrome (Twomey and Taylor 1993)
Neck sprain (Galasko et al 1993)
Acute neck sprain—whiplash emotive (Robinson & Cassar-Pullicino 1993)
Whiplash associated disorder (Spitzer et al 1995)

Epidemiology

This is a confused topic as figures are given differently for the incidence of whiplash events versus the reporting of those events which result in the production of clinical features, i.e. whiplash associated disorders (WAD). This review deals only with the incidence of whiplash associated disorders.

Barnsley et al (1994) reported an incidence of 3.8/1000 in the USA, but pointed out that this was not a population based figure. They quoted figures for several other countries ranging from as low as 0.1/1000 (New Zealand) to 2/1000 (Norway). The QTF (Spitzer et al 1995) found an incidence of 70/100 000 in their study. They quoted the remarkable figure of 700/100 000 for the Canadian province of Saskatchewan and interestingly commented that this huge figure may reflect differences in insurance cover. Twomey and Taylor (1993) estimate that 20% of all MVA result in a whiplash injury in Australia.

Because of the paucity of figures for some countries it is difficult to give an accurate overall average incidence. In spite of this Barnsley et al (1994) have suggested that in western societies there is an approximate incidence of 1/1000.

An interesting point is that the incidence seems to have increased in those countries that have a compulsory seat belt wearing law (Spitzer et al 1995).

Aetiology

It is well established that a rear end collision is the greatest cause of whiplash injuries.

The mechanism of injury was long held to be due to forced flexion (see Barnsley et al 1994). However, this is no longer thought to be the case. It is now hypothesised that the injury is due to a relative extension caused by the force of collision, moving the vehicle and body of the subject forwards whilst the head remains stationary. Thus, as the shoulders move forwards, the head and neck are placed in a relative position of extension. The head and neck then move into flexion once the initial inertia is overcome (Bogduk 1986). The forces involved may be considerable. Severy et al 1955 (cited in Barnsley et al 1994) found that at an impact at 20 mph there is a peak acceleration of 12G into extension. Barnsley et al (1994) speculate that these forces will be magnified if the head is in a non-neutral position.

The work of McConnell et al (1993) on this subject is recommended reading. They researched the effects of low velocity impacts (speeds of 6–8 km/h) on human subjects and found that the forces generated reached up to 4.5G. They concluded that this force was the threshold for mild cervical sprains. Surprisingly, they found no hyperextension or flexion occurred, but instead observed a compression-tension cycle directed axially through the cervical spine.

An interesting aside is the finding that the use of headrests, specifically intended to diminish the effects of these incidents, have been shown to have no real effect (Spitzer et al 1995, Bogduk 1986, Barnsley et al. 1994). This may due to poor headrest design or to incorrect adjustment and positioning. The QTF (Spitzer et al 1995) suggest that problems may arise if the headrest and seat are made of different materials. They point out that headrests are often composed of slow rebound foam whereas seats have fast recoil springs. This results in the torso rebounding rapidly, compared with the head/neck (differential recoil), thus accentuating the problem. Also, if the headrest is too far back (or the seat to which it is attached inclined backwards) or too low, it will not prevent any extension occurring and may actually increase it (Bogduk 1986, Spitzer et al 1995). The QTF (Spitzer et al 1995) recommend that the headrest should be as close to the back of the head as is comfortable and that it should extend 70mm above the eye level of the user. They further recommend that the rest and seat be of a one piece construction. Lastly, if the findings of McConnell et al (1993) are correct, then headrests will not serve any great purpose, as the damaging forces are vertically acting.

As mentioned , there is evidence that the wearing of seat-belts may increase the effects of a whiplash incident (Spitzer et al 1995, Galasko et al 1993). On the other hand, 'cervical problems from the use of seat-belts are minor compared with the morbidity and mortality avoided by their use' (Galasko et al 1993).

Pathomechanics

Taking account of the nature of a whiplash, and the 'agreed' direction of forces and movements, the anatomical focus of injury has been inferred or assumed. This perspective has given rise to lists of structures damaged in the extension and flexion phases of the whiplash (see Box 2).

Box 2   Summary of the major tissues injured in the different phases of the whiplash injury.

Extension phase

Prevertebral muscles strained
Anterior longitudinal ligament strained
Intervertebral disc strain /Annulus fibrosus tear
Cartilage end plate fractures
Oesophagus and pharynx damaged and bleeding—haematoma.
    Anterior swelling due to blood and oedema
Posteriorly—zygapophysial joint compression and fracture. Capsule
    tears and bleeds
Cranio-cervical junction—the odontoid may fracture
Tempero mandibular joint may strain due to violent opening
    of the mouth
Brain may be contused—intra-cranial vessels may be torn

Flexion phase

Vertebral body compression and possible fracture
Interspinous ligament tear
Spinous process tip fracture
Tears of posterior muscles at occipital insertion.

Criticising this perspective, Jonnson et al (1994) state: ' the trajectory of forces, moments, acceleration/deceleration events and other biomechanical events are not only unknown, (but cannot be appraised by non engineering laymen [physicians, lawyers, insurance providers]).'

It seems that the list and approach given above is too simplified and that specific lesions are difficult to predict, a view which led Barnsley et al (1994) to state:

Notwithstanding theoretical considerations as to which structures are mechanically at risk, the actual likelihood of a lesion occurring cannot be extrapolated from such analysis alone. The exact distribution of force and the specific tolerances of the different tissues, as well as any interactions, would need to be considered. Consequently, in the absence of such precise and comprehensive data, pathological lesions predicted from the biomechanical observations need to be ratified by experimental or observational studies.

Those workers who have attempted to satisfy the last sentence of this quote have relied heavily on questionably appropriate experimental models. These have included animals, cadavers and crash dummies as subjects (MacNab 1971, Deng 1989). Clearly it is wise to view the results from these investigations with some scepticism. For example, correct responses cannot be obtained due to discrepancies in anthropometrics, body mass and tissue compliance. In contrast, the work carried out by McConnell et al (1993) is the only study found which was based on live human subjects. It reveals uniquely that the mechanisms of injury may not be in line with the findings of studies using inauthentic models.

Pathology—is there a lesion?

The controversy over whether whiplash associated injuries exist as organic entities is now beginning to resolve. It has been a long held belief that many cases of symptomatic presentation following a whiplash could be assigned to either neurosis or the desire for compensation and that patients in this group were more likely to develop chronicity of their symptoms. Many authors have shown in controlled studies that there is not a direct causal link between chronicity and litigation/compensation claims (e.g. Mendelson 1995, Swartzman et al 1996, Parmar & Raymakers 1993, Mayou & Bryant 1996) but readers are also directed to the discussion in Chapter 15. While there is evidence to suggest that those patients involved in legal action do report more pain, this is felt to be secondary to the stress of the legal process itself, and/or that those patients seeking recompense are at the more severe end of the injury scale and are therefore in greater discomfort!

Interestingly there appears to be a direct link between the report of early onset of pain post injury and the likelihood of ongoing symptoms (Parmar & Raymakers 1993, Wallis et al 1996).

Wallis et al (1996) were able to show that the psychological profiles of patients suffering WAD were almost identical to patients suffering chronic low back pain and rheumatoid arthritis. They concluded that there was a common psychological profile in patients suffering specific types of chronic pain. This may reflect the tendency for ongoing pain to result in secondary psychological dysfunctions (Mendelson 1995). This stance is supported by the work of Mayou and Bryant (1996) who demonstrated a strong link between psychological factors and social impairment despite the absence of a relationship between baseline psychological measures and symptoms. They suggested that the patients were exhibiting a degree of post traumatic stress disorder (see Ch. 10). This opinion is also shared by Maimaris et al (1988) who found in a retrospective study that those patients still complaining of symptoms at 2 months were likely to report long term disability (30% of their study population reported ongoing symptoms and functional impairments at 2 years post injury).

It is evident from the above that there are long term psychological sequelae as a result of whiplash injuries. It is clear however that these arise as a direct result of tissue injury to specific tissues of the cervical spine. The evidence for the occurrence of these injuries forms the topic for the following section.

Tissue pathology

The classical clinical features of whiplash would appear to indicate that there are multiple pathologies occurring at many levels. A list of reported tissue lesions (Box 3) reveals several points that must be considered.

Box 3   A summary from the literature of reported tissue injuries following whiplash—including a key to their presence in humans, repair rate and clinical detection.

Reported injuries following whiplash injuries

Facet joints—sprain and fractures*$
Synovial/ capsular tears*
Long term spondylosis

Disc prolapse*
Annular tear*/ Blood in annulus*
End plate fracture/detachment from the disc$
Clefts in cartilage end plates—rim lesions affects at the insertion of the
    annulus fibrosus*$

Tempero mandibular joint injury—strains*^

Sternocleidomastoid, longus colli—strains* ^
Trigger points—most do not satisfy the criteria to be diagnosed as a
    trigger point

Ligaments—sprains—anterior longitudinal ligament, ligamentum
    nuchae, interspinous ligament, posterior longitudinal ligament,
    ligamentum flavum*

Spinal cord and nerve roots—traction injuries*^
Blood tracking down the sub arachnoid space
Hind/fore brain—bleeds*
Sympathetic ganglia?
Brachial plexus trauma*

Stapes subluxation, perilymph fistulas*^
Odontoid fracture*^

*   denotes proven lesion in human patients
$ denotes slow repairing lesion
^   Detectable via clinical tests

The following questions are pertinent to the review and discussion which follows:

- Is the lesion seen in humans?
- In those studies carried out at postmortem on cadavers are the forces involved excessive compared to those that have occurred in patients?
- Is the lesion observed attributable to the whiplash incident?
- Is the diagnostic tool reliable and definitive?

Facet joints

Facet joint damage has been repeatedly linked to whiplash injuries. Barnsley et al (1994) argue that facet joint damage could be a plausible explanation for the chronic pain encountered in the management of the WAD patient.

This is supported by the earlier work of Bogduk (1986) which presented strong evidence that the zygapophysial joints were damaged following whiplash injuries. His studies included both cadavaric and animal models. Bogduk (1986) made the important point that lesions associated with whiplash injuries were difficult to diagnose *in vivo* as radiographs, CT scans and MRI images are inconclusive. Further study led him and his co-workers (Barnsley et al 1994, Lord et al 1996a,b.) to propose that the only satisfactory way of diagnosing the facet joints as a potential source of symptoms was to use a diagnostic local anaesthetic 'facet blocking' protocol. Using a blinded and controlled blocking procedure they found that 54% of a series of 38 patients who had suffered a whiplash injury could be confirmed as having one or several zygapophysial joints responsible for their ongoing pain (see Lord 1996a). In further work, 60% of a series of 52 patients were diagnosed as having a zygapophysial lesion. The patients in this group had suffered post whiplash associated pain of greater than 3 months (Lord 1996b). The work is very compelling and offers a logical and easily assimilated arthrogenic model for a remarkably large percentage of patients suffering ongoing symptoms of WAD. However, some very important criticisms of this work and its conclusions have been made in the literature (see discussion section).

In their cadavaric study Twomey and Taylor (1993) documented the findings of 32 postmortem cervical spines, 16 of which had died following an MVA. The remaining 16 'control' spines had no history of trauma. Amongst their extensive findings Twomey and Taylor (1993) described 21 soft tissue injuries affecting the zygapophysial joints in the accident victims. The lesions observed were predominantly haemarthrosis and capsular/synovial tears. A point of note is that the forces involved in accidents were enough to kill the patients. This may mean that the observed lesions are only likely to occur when particularly high forces are involved.

Jonsson et al (1994) surgically revealed extensive rupture of the facet joints in 2 of 11 patients who had suffered a whiplash. Cervical radiographs in both the patients revealed marked facet gapping in flexion. Davis et al (1991) have demonstrated subluxation of the facet joint on MRI scanning of whiplash patients.

Disc injuries

Jonsson et al (1994) have revealed different grades of disc prolapse associated with whiplash injury in 13 out of 24 patients who reported the persistence of pain 6 weeks post whiplash injury. They suggested that the discs were the likely source of the ongoing symptoms in the subjects studied. Significantly, they reported that the injuries observed were in fact disc bulges and that frank protrusions were a very rare occurrence. In all those subjects with large lateral bulges the dorsal root ganglion was found to be severely compromised. This may have clinical significance since the dorsal root ganglion is known to have a high mechanical sensitivity and is commonly thought to be responsible for the classic symptoms associated with nerve root compression.

Using MRI scanning, Davis et al (1991) studied nine patients following whiplash injury and showed that four of the subjects had acute postero-lateral disc herniation large enough to indent or displace the cord. All developed neurological deficits after several weeks and three showed a positive Spurling's test to the side of the herniation. (Spurling's test for root compression sensitivity involves cervical extension, rotation towards the side of pain and finally the addition of compression.). In these patients symptoms started immediately after the incident. This provides an interesting contrast with delayed symptom onset associated with ligamentous damage (see below). Davis et al (1991) suggested that injury to the disc was worse adjacent to an area of previous degeneration.

The reporting of disc bulges seen on imaging following whiplash injury should take into account the work of Boden et al (1990). These researchers demonstrated that 19% of their group of asymptomatic subjects showed significant disc bulges, i.e. that entered the lateral recess. They concluded that any symptoms occurring in injured subjects even in the presence of a positive scan, could not be attributed with accuracy to the bulge. They suggested that some patients may well have had pre-existing disc bulges that were either extended due to the injury or that could act as a mechanical irritant to newly acquired damage in adjacent tissue. For example, the nerve roots and dorsal root ganglion could increase their sensitivity making any pre-existing bulge become a cause of irritation. The subtle point is that the cause of the pain, the nerve root, is different from the tissue that mechanically irritates it (the bulge) and which so often gets the blame.

Hamar et al (1993) showed that the incidence of a previous whiplash injury in the history of a group of 215 patients who had undergone anterior discectomies and fusions, was twice that in a group of 800 general orthopaedic patients. They felt that these patients were probably at the more extreme end of the injury spectrum.

In their extensive review Barnsley et al (1994) concluded that the most common injury to a disc is an avulsion of the annulus from the vertebral end plate (the end plate itself is often found to have fractured.) This is supported by the work of Davis et al (1991) and Jonsson et al (1994). The cadaver study of Twomey and Taylor (1993) found evidence of linear clefts in the cartilage end plate that were most commonly situated parallel to the plate and close to the rim of the vertebra. They also found a large proportion of the discs contained signs of bleeding within the annulus.

Muscles

Muscle injuries ranging from acute strains to complete rupture have been described in the literature (see Barnsley et al 1994). However, there is a general paucity of reporting of these injuries.

Some interesting findings relevant to physiotherapy diagnosis come from a recent study by Maxwell (1996). Maxwell (1996) investigated physiotherapists' knowledge of the structures assessed to be injured in whiplash patients. Anterior neck muscle injuries were the fourth most commonly reported injury (as assessed by 60% of physiotherapists) and posterior muscle injuries were the most common (reported by 80%). This highlights a critical discrepancy between clinical observation/perception and the reporting of these injuries in the literature. Is it possible that muscle injuries lack the glamour and appeal of the other 'surgically correctable' or 'blockable' injuries previously discussed? Or does it highlight the inaccuracies of clinical assessments that so often rely on the patient's report of tissue sensitivity? It would seem reasonable to expect that if facet joints and discs can be injured, the muscles are very likely to be as well.

Barnsley et al (1994) discuss and dismiss the notion that muscle injuries could be a source of ongoing pain in WAD patients. Their reasoning is that these injuries routinely heal within a few weeks and cannot therefore be a residual cause of ongoing pain. Hancock (1995) argues with this assumption stating that: 'muscles, presumably, still need to be included for it is known that they are structurally changed in whiplash patients'. This could be said to be true of all muscle injuries beyond a mild strain since muscles heal by repair (scar tissue formation) and not by regeneration (Noonan & Garrett 1992). It would seem prudent to avoid categorically dismissing the potential role of any structure in maintaining an ongoing pain complaint. Even a repaired muscle may provide a significantly altered central barrage of sensory impulses to have some influence on the maintenance of pain and sensitivity (see Chs 2-5). From a surgical or interventionist stand-point a repaired muscle is understandably uninteresting since there is not a lot that can be done. Contrast the situation for those involved in physical rehabilitation who know that muscles are particularly responsive to dynamic activity and training. Perhaps this is a good reason for biasing our interest towards them.

Bogduk (1986) speculated that severe bleeding from muscular injuries could lead to soft tissue swelling which in turn may lead to compression of the oesophagus and pharynx. Further evidence for this comes from the work of Davis et al (1991) who demonstrated injury to the longus colli and longus capitus muscles with associated pre-vertebral fluid collection. They also described injuries to the sternocleidomastoid and the scalenes.

Some authors have promoted a role for trigger points in symptom production following whiplash injury (e.g. Fricton 1993). Trigger points are themselves an area of contention (e.g. see Barnsley et al 1994, Hancock 1995). Friction (1993) states that trigger points remain the greatest cause of ongoing pain following whiplash injuries. This perspective may need re-examination since there is growing evidence that trigger points are in fact an epiphenomenon. Rather than being the originator of the pain, they are more a consequence of it, i.e. an area of secondary hyperalgesia which may not have any significant biological changes (see Chs 2-5). The work of Cohen (1996) and Wall (1993) are worth consulting on this topic.

Neurological tissue

Injury to the brain, spinal cord and nerve roots have all been reported. There is also evidence to indicate damage to the meninges (see Barnsley et al 1994, Yeung et al 1997). As well as direct trauma, damage to tissues adjacent to the nervous system could cause haemorrhaging that may surround the neural tissues and hence result in irritation and possible later development of scar tissue and neural tethering.

Evidence suggests that damage to the vascular tissues supplying the brain can occur (Omaya and Yarnell cited in Barnsley et al 1994). This is thought to be the result of shearing of the brain in relation to the skull.

Using MRI scanning Davis et al (1991) identified cord damage in 5 out of 14 patients who had sustained a whiplash injury. They all presented with myelopathies and their scans revealed oedema within the cord. Out of these, three made complete recoveries and the other two were observed to make significant improvements. This paradoxically indicates that the results of these injuries are surprisingly transient in nature on a tissue which is formerly assumed to have no healing capacity.

Many sources refer to the involvement of the sympathetic chain in whiplash injuries. Most of these include it in their lists of potential lesions due to the work of MacNab (1971) who showed that the cervical sympathetic chain was damaged during whiplash injury studies using monkeys. There have been no reported findings in the clinical literature of this type of injury in humans. However, it seems reasonable for the sympathetic chain to be a likely contender to be damaged as patients occasionally show symptoms thought to be attributable to the sympathetic nervous system, such as Horner's syndrome (Barnsley et al 1994). There are problems with this type of reasoning as apparent 'sympathetically' mediated symptoms are often seen as epiphenomena that arise as secondary responses to the stress of injury rather than because of direct injury.

The QTF (Spitzer et al 1995) recognise the involvement of neural tissue as they make it a diagnostic criteria to distinguish between Grade 11 and 111 injuries in their classification.

Miscellaneous injuries

Many other injuries are also reported (Box 2). These include odontoid fractures, retropharyngeal/oesophageal bleeds, temporomandibular joint problems and damage to the inner ear. These types of injuries are probably less common and therefore described by only one or two authors with a specific interest in them. However, they are often at the more extreme end of the spectrum and therefore of obvious importance. Several may result in the misinterpretation of symptoms, for example dizziness is often thought to arise in WAD from altered proprioception or vertebro basilar insufficiency, but could also be the result of subtle inner ear trauma.

Discussion

There now appears to be enough data to support the case for the production and presence of a lesion following whiplash trauma. There is also significant evidence to support the notion that of those tissues known to have been damaged, many are very slow to repair and many are known to never return to their former healthy state. Injury to tissues provides the initial stimulus that sets the nociceptive system into action giving rise to the sensation of pain. As time goes on it is normal to expect levels of pain to subside in parallel with tissue recovery. For a significant number of whiplash victims this end point never arrives and they continue to suffer pain that is out of all proportion to evidence which is based purely on the scrutiny of tissue abnormality. 'The level of pain is inconsistent with the evidence for tissue damage' is a common declaration (see Ch.13). Elements of doubt and frustration creep in and many enduring psychological sequelae sadly begin to dominate the clinical presentation of these patients. Integrating modern interpretations of pain mechanisms helps bring about a much needed shift in attention towards the nervous system (see Introductory Essay and Chs 2-5) that is effectively putting an organic back-bone into the horribly frustrating and unhelpful inorganic label. The evidence suggests that pain mechanisms can move or shift as time goes on and the relevance of the tissue lesion diminishes in an inversely proportional way to the relevance of changes in the central nervous system. Central pain mechanisms can be said to start to dominate the clinical picture as chronicity sets in. Clearly, even modest trickles of nociceptive activity from abnormal peripheral tissues and peripheral nerves may have a role to play in maintaining the sensitivity state in some patients. However, this has to be put alongside the likelihood of significant 'trickles' arising as a result of background emotional and cognitive states. This powerfully sets the scene for the need to provide therapeutic elements that address the complete picture—hence the provision of improved health of the tissues in parallel with improved cognitive and emotional well-being and improved overall function that includes a graded early return to work and recreational activities (see Chs 8 & 9, and 13 & 14). It is also a perspective that makes the concept of a problem being either tissue-based or wholly psychogenic in origin fundamentally redundant.

Dualistic thinking, i.e. 'either it's in the tissues, or it's a fault of the mind', applied to the diagnosis and treatment of ongoing pain states is still prevalent. The great desire is to find the tissue/lesion at fault for the patient's pain despite the well known fact that pain and damage have been shown to have a surprisingly tenuous link. It would be irresponsible to suggest that we can completely dispense with the notion of tissue pathology in the management of ongoing pain states; the key is that tissue status is better seen in relation to a much bigger picture (see Ch.2). A modest shift in thinking requires a perspective that encourages improved tissue fitness via active healthy movement and exercise rather than via passive therapy dominated approaches that largely withhold responsibility from the patient and which are being criticised as unrealistic in their rationale and goals (see Chs 12 & 15).

Diagnostic and therapeutic zygapophysial joint blocking

What now follows is an in-depth discussion of the recent zygapophysial joint blocking work published by the group associated with Professor Bogduk. While it is ground-breaking and rigorous scientific work that has to be applauded for helping provide new insights into chronic pain related to whiplash, there are some important criticisms of it that are very pertinent to physiotherapy.

Much of the thrust of Bogduk and co-workers' research can be seen to promote the quest for a single faulty tissue in ongoing whiplash associated disorder (Barnsley et al 1994, Lord et al 1996a, 1996b, Wallis 1997). This quest is understandable for there can be nothing worse than having a condition that the medical profession at large tend to view in a dismissive and derisory way. However, this author feels that it is important that the physiotherapy profession has a broad understanding of the issues and some of the criticisms that can be raised.

Lord et al (1996a) reported that the zygapophysial joint was the source of ongoing pain in around 50% of WAD patients. They used selective blocking techniques to the nerves that innervate the zygapophysial joints to produce this data. It is the opinion of this group that their double blind placebo controlled blocking protocol is specific for zygapophysial joints and therefore is a reliable and scientifically validated diagnostic tool. Hancock (1995) raises some twenty points that he feels require attention before these papers can be considered to offer the answers to the problem. The main point of his criticism focuses on the underlying precept of the work, namely, that it is an excessively surgical perspective (i.e tissue/anatomicaly focused—see Ch. 15). Hancock (1995) feels that this has led to an absence of any physiological (pathobiological) explanation for the pain and makes the case for the pain experienced being an example of secondary hyperalgesia. He proposes that the block may reduce the sensitivity of the system by reducing the input from, what he sees as, a secondary source. In effect the block is eliminating a primary, possibly normal input, but not necessarily the 'real' source of the pain. Hancock (1995) highlights work that shows how muscle blocks (to scalenes) have been shown to reduce tenderness to upper cervical zygapophysial joints. In other words alter the input from any tissue, normal or diseased, and some alteration in symptoms is likely to occur.

Wall (1997 personal communication) is of the opinion that if the circumstances are right then it doesn't matter whether the primary lesion or an area of secondary hyperalgesia are treated—there still may be a resolution of pain. This argument holds in doubt some of the assumptions made by the protagonists of joint blocking diagnostic techniques. Hancock (1995) also warns that the blocking work only focuses on the joints as a source of lasting pain in whiplash and remarks that even if they did confirm the joint as the site for pain production it only explains around 50% of the patients who report post whiplash injury pain. The response to this criticism makes worthwhile reading (see Bogduk 1995). It argues that the lack of acceptable studies identifying other tissues as a reliable source of pain means that so far the zygapophysial joint is the only proven cause of ongoing pain.

If the criticisms of the work by Hancock (1995) and opinions of Wall (1997, personal communication) are taken on, the wise stance should be to view the conclusions with a healthy scepticism. The bottom line is that if the technique can significantly and enduringly relieve a large proportion of chronic post whiplash pain then it may ultimately be worth while.

It is questionable whether one can truly placebo control and 'double blind' such a trial (the above groups used intra-articular injection of saline which they suggest has no direct effects on the joints). All invasive placebo techniques carry an 'active' component due to the direct physical effect on the body and subsequent influence on the central nervous system and brain. The studies discussed used a previous block to identify those patients who were suitable to go into their experimental group. This methodology is likely to enhance the placebo, as the 'selected' group would have benefited from the first block and therefore would have expected that further intervention would be helpful. Expectation is known to enhance the placebo response markedly (see Wall 1994). Whilst Bogduk and co-workers would argue that this is negligible as all the patients entering the study had shown a previous positive response to a block, there still remain questions over the use of this procedure as a screening tool in this type of study. Hancock (1995) raised the point that there may be differences in the physical/ psychological make up of the patients who were included in the study and those omitted, thus adding bias to the experimental group.

The placebo response is known to habituate i.e. lessen in effect with time (see Wall 1994). In some of these studies the patients required a series of blocks. This could indicate that the need for repeated blocks shows a weakening or failure of the placebo response. Additionally, all of the patients used in these studies had received previous treatment and were referred to the authors' specialist clinic. This in itself could mean that the patients entering the study would be expecting to receive 'better' care and therefore would be likely to respond accordingly to this 'better' treatment as a result. This is a point raised by Raja (1997) in his article on the use of joint blocks as a diagnostic tool. He suggests that this effect could undermine the validity of the results from studies using these criteria.

Despite this type of criticism the same workers (Barnsley et al 1994, Lord et al 1996a) have used the information gathered from their studies to legitimise the use of radiofrequency neurotomy in the same type of patient and have concluded that the technique is superior to placebo (Lord et al 1996b). This procedure involves the use of radiowaves to cause heating, secondary to molecular oscillation within the nerve, causing thermal coagulation and therefore destruction of the nerve innervating the culpable joint. The reader should note the recently published work of Slappendel et al (1997). They showed that there was no difference between a group of patients treated with temperatures of 67°C (damage producing) and 40°C (non damaging), both groups having significant reductions in pain. What is striking is that the patients in their study (both damage producing and non damaging groups) were told that it was a last ditch therapy; they received diagnostic local anaesthetic blocks prior to treatment and were aware that they were being used for research purposes, all of which were likely to influence the potential outcome of the effect of the treatment received.

This discussion highlights the immense problems inherent in trying to establish a tissue/ structure as a source of pain. Clearly it is not easy, but this has not deterred the making of powerful and provocative statements:

> This calls into question the present nihilism about chronic pain, that proclaims medical therapy alone to be ineffectual, and psychological co therapy to be imperative.
>
> Co-therapy may be useful if medical therapy cannot provide complete relief of pain, but is redundant if psychological distress disappears when pain is relieved.
> (Wallis et al 1997)

They continue by stating that:

> These results should influence physicians to pursue an organic diagnosis of cervical zygapophysial joint pain in patients with chronic neck after whiplash injury.

The inherent dangers of this way of thinking should be clear. This rather top-heavy tissue based approach, legitimised by stubbornly blinkered reasoning, could lead to chronicity as clinicians repeatedly attempt and fail to treat all potential tissue lesions before finally changing their tack (giving up) to focus on chronically accumulated and stubbornly entrenched disability that could have been overcome earlier or prevented from happening in the first place (see Chs 12 & 15). The approach is also likely to put pressure on the clinician to coldly 'find the cause' of the patient's distress so that it can be blocked/ treated and therefore 'cured', rather than promoting a focus on the most favourable conditions for natural recovery (see Ch. 7). It is my opinion that the approach suggested by Wallis et al (1997) is not only unrealistic and unfair to the patient but also to the therapist and the currently available resources.

These therapies are aimed at inputs to the nervous system only, and in the long run could well be futile in those patients where the pain mechanisms have shifted to reside predominantly in the pathways and processing systems of the CNS (see Chs 2-5 for further details of the mechanisms involved). As Wall (1996) laudably says in relation to neurosurgical treatment of persistent pain:

The long term results are very disappointing in their failure to produce a selective analgesia. The short-term results are always encouraging in their apparent success, which later fades.

A similar message may well apply here.

Many clinicians are rightly wary of taking on the findings of Bogduk's group as a therapeutic principle; nevertheless, this work serves as a powerful stimulus and challenge to rethink the current management status of WAD. In the first instance it gives powerful organic credibility to patients who suffer ongoing pain following whiplash injury, but in the second, it appears to strive to wipe out the accruing evidence that focuses on alterations in central nervous system processing and the powerful role of psychosocial factors in the maintenance of disability and suffering in chronic pain. It enforces a rethink of the role of tissues in ongoing pain states and, most importantly, it is a challenge for opponents of the view to present their data.

Conclusion

There is good evidence to show that varying types and degrees of lesion exist in WAD. Most of these are difficult to diagnose (especially via clinical testing). Many are slow to repair and are therefore potentially persistent 'inputters' to the central nervous system. There is good evidence (see Chs 2-5) that such post-injury scenarios can be partly responsible in leading to and maintaining ongoing pain states. We should avoid falling into the trap of believing that all we have to do is 'cure' the lesion and all will be well, or that we should leave these people alone as they will heal with time. We need to make use of the information presented to help with our clinical reasoning and our approach to the management of these challenging yet interesting patients. It is my opinion that we, as clinicians, need to change the focus of our therapies in the light of this information and should move away from purely tissue based approaches, driven by dualistic thinking, to treatments that encompass a broader biopsychosocial approach in the management of the WAD patient.

REFERENCES

Barnsley L, Lord S, Bogduk N 1994 Whiplash injury. Pain 58:283–307

Boden S D, McCowin P R, Davis D O, Dina T S, Mark A S, Weisel S 1990 Abnormal magnetic resonance scans of the cervical spine in asymptomatic subjects. Journal of Bone and Joint Surgery (Am) 72:1178–1184

Bogduk N 1986 The anatomy and pathophysiology of whiplash. Clinical Biomechanics 1(2):92-101

Bogduk N 1995 Reply to Hancock. Letter to Editor. Pain 61(2):490–491

Cohen M L 1996 Arthralgia and myalgia. In: Campbell J N (ed) Pain 1996: an updated review. IASP Press, Seattle

Crowe H E 1928 Injuries in the cervical spine. Paper Presented at the Western Orthopaedic Association. San Francisco

Davis S J, Teresi L M, Bradley W G, Ziemba M A, Bloze A E 1991 Cervical spine hyperextension injuries: MR findings. Radiology 180:245–251

Deng Y C 1989 Anthropomorphic dummy neck modeling and injury considertions. Accident Analysis and Prevention 21:85–100

Fricton J R 1993 Myofascial pain and whiplash. Spine: State of the Art Reviews 7:403–422

Galasko C S B, Murray P M, Pitcher M, Chambers H, Mansfield S, Madden M, Jordan C, Kinsella A, Hodson M 1993 Neck sprain after road traffic accidents: a modern epidemic. Injury: 24(3):155–157

Hamar A J, Gargan M F, Bannister G C, Nelson R J 1993 Whiplash injury and surgically treated cervical disc disease. Injury 24(8):549–550

Hancock J 1995 Comments on Barnsley et al. Letter to the Editor. Pain 61(2):487–490

Jonsson H, Cesarini K, Sahlstedt B , Rauschning W 1994 Findings and outcome in whiplash-type neck distortions. Spine 19(24):2733–2743

Lord S M, Barnsley L, Wallis B J, Bogduk N 1996a Chronic cervical zygapophysial joint pain after whiplash. Spine 21(15):1737–1745

Lord S M, Barnsley L, Wallis B J, McDonald G J, Bogduk N 1996b Percutaneous radiofrequency neurotomy for chronic cervical zygapophysial joint pain. New England Medical Journal 335(23):1721–1726

MacNab I 1971 The whiplash syndrome. Orthopedic Clinics of North America 2:389–403

Maimaris C, Barnes M R, Allen M J 1988 Whiplash injuries of the neck: a retrospective study. Injury 19:393–396

Mayou R, Bryant B 1996 Outcome of 'whiplash' neck injury. Injury 27(9):617–623

Maxwell M 1996 Current physiotherapy treatment for whiplash injury to the neck. British Journal of Therapy and Rehabilitation July 3(7):391–395

McConnell W E, Howard P R, Guzman H M 1993 Analysis of humen test subject kinematics responses to low velocity rear impacts. In: Vehicle and occupant kinematics: simulation and modelling. Society for Automotive Engineers Technical Paper Series 930889

Mendelson G 1995 Psychological and psychiatric aspects of pain. In: Shacklock M (ed) Moving in on pain. Butterworth-Heinmann, Sydney

Noonan T J, Garrett W E 1992 Injuries at the myotendinous junction. Clinics in Sports Medicine 11(4):783–806

Parmar H V, Raymakers R 1993 Neck injuries from rear impact road traffic accidents: Prognosis in persons seeking compensation. Injury 24(2):75–78

Raja S N 1997 Nerve blocks in the evaluation of chronic pain. Anaesthesiology: 86:4–6

Robinson D D, Cassar-Pullicino V N 1993 Acute neck sprain after road traffic accident: a long term clinical and radiological review. Injury 24(2):79–82

Slappendel R, Crul G J J, Braak G J J, Geurts J W M, Booij L H D, Voerman V F, de Boo T 1997 The efficacy of radiofrequency lesioning of the cervical spinal dorsal root ganglion in a double blind randomized study: no difference between 40∞C and 67∞C treatments. Pain 73(2):159–164

Spitzer W O, Skovron M L, Salmi L R 1995 Scientific monograph of the Quebec task force on whiplash associated disorders: redefining whiplash and its management. Spine 20(Suppl):10s–73s

Swartzman L C, Teasell R W, Shapiro A P, Mc Dermid A J 1996 The effect of litigation status on adjustment to whiplash injury. Spine 21(1):53–58

Twomey L T, Taylor J R 1993 The whiplash syndrome: pathology and physical therapy. The Journal of Manual and Manipulative Therapy 1(1):26–29

Wall P D 1993 The mechanisms of fibromyalgia: a critical essay. In: Voeroy, H, Merskey H (eds) Progress in fibromyalgia and myofascial pain. Elsevier, Amsterdam 53–59

Wall P D 1994 The placebo and the placebo response. In: Melzack R, Wall P D (eds) Textbook of pain 3rd edn. Churchill Livingstone, Edinburgh

Wall P D 1996 The mechanisms by which tissue damage and pain are related. In: Campbell J N (ed) Pain 1996: an updated review. IASP Press, Seattle

Wallis B J, Lord S M, Barnsley L, Bogduk N 1996 Pain and psychological symptoms of australian patients with whiplash. Spine 21(7):804–810

Wallis B J, Lord S M, Bogduk N 1997 Resolution of psychologicl distress of whiplash patients following treatment by radiofrequency neurotomy: A randomised, double-blind, placebo controlled trial. Pain 73(1):15–22

Yeung E, Jones M, Hall B 1997 The response to the slump test in a group of female whiplash patients. Australian Journal of Physiotherapy 43(4):245–252

2

The mature organism model

LOUIS GIFFORD

Introduction

The Mature Organism Model (MOM) (see also Gifford 1998) has been developed as a teaching tool to help clinicians *and patients* reach a broader understanding of pain, appreciate it in a biological context, and ultimately manage it better. A fundamental feature of the model is the placement of pain into the discipline of stress biology. Stress biology is concerned with the physiological mechanisms and behavioural strategies that enable organisms to survive, or to maintain their homeostasis (Weiner 1991). Thus, pain can be viewed as a single perceptual component of the stress response whose prime adaptive purpose is to powerfully motivate the organism to alter behaviour in order to aid recovery and survive.

The perspective and principles proposed in the MOM are essentially Darwinian in nature (for example, see Nesse & Williams 1994, Williams 1996) in that it views the human body (or any living organism's 'body') as a very sophisticated vehicle that carries and looks after our genes. Hence our bodies can be viewed as *survival machines* in which the genetic material that enables us to replicate lives (Dawkins 1989). The animal and plant kingdoms contain a remarkable variety of replicating survival machines (for example, see Dawkins 1996).

In a simple single celled animal, like an amoeba, it is fairly plain that in order for it to survive it must have some mechanism of sampling its immediate environment, assessing or 'scrutinising' what it finds, and then reacting/ responding in accordance with whether it finds the environment advantageous or threatening. Thus, it may move towards an area which contains food or a possible mate or move away from areas that contain toxins or predators. For many organisms the physiological essence of this sample—scrutinise—respond pathway is chemical; chemicals are sampled from the environment via chemical receptors which then initiate cascades of internal biochemical processes whose end result is an appropriate survival reaction or behaviour—a 'motor' response. Note that higher animals have evolved sophisticated sense organs that are capable of conveying remarkably detailed environmental information via the medium of light sound and smell. Even so, the information received is still converted into meaningful information for 'scrutiny' via chemical activity.

Survival of an organism also involves the capacity to sample itself. There is a need for a system that is able to monitor the health of the organism's own body and provide an appropriate recovery response should damage occur. For a single celled animal, this may mean the activation and conveyance of chemical messengers from the damaged area to the nucleus, the activation of appropriate genes in nuclear DNA and hence the production of new protein products for transport back to the damaged area to complete the repair process. In higher, larger and more complex animals the underlying mechanisms are fundamentally the same. It is just that more sophisticated communicating and coordinating systems have evolved that are capable of producing far more complex responses. The vertebrate central nervous system/brain is a prime example.

In thinking about ourselves, our own bodies and brains, as sophisticated machines bent on survival and maintaining homeostasis, it helps if the CNS/brain is viewed as a central *scrutinising* centre, or stress response coordination centre, that continually *samples* (consciously and 'unconsciously') the outside environment, its own body and relevant past experiences (the brain samples 'itself'), and then *'acts'*, or *outputs*, on what it finds, to the best advantage for its body and the vital genes it contains (Fig. 2.1).

'Actions' can be broadly divided into:

1. **Overt behavioural responses.** For example, when injured we demonstrate subsets of 'illness' behaviours (Fordyce 1984, Pilowsky 1986, Waddell et al 1993, Pilowsky 1995a, 1995b), which may be useful—hence adaptive, or of no use whatsoever—hence maladaptive. Other examples of behavioural 'actions' that maintain homeostasis include food seeking when levels of vital energy diminish and activities like shivering, putting an extra jumper on and switching on the heating when the temperature drops. It should be evident that our behaviour contains elements of conscious decision as well as being driven by robust unconscious reflex mechanisms and drives (see Plotkin 1994). What must be accepted is that these unconscious reflexes are keenly influenced by the decisions and thoughts produced in the conscious brain. The fact that I may have a pain and appropriate muscle spasm preventing movement of my neck is quickly overridden if for some reason movement is essential to survival or I strongly desire to move it normally.

2. **The less obvious but highly complex physiological processes that are a necessary response to environmental and bodily changes.** These also allow a chosen behaviour to occur, or are a homeostatic response to the behaviour.

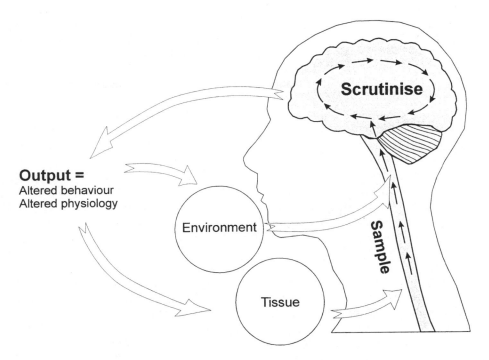

Fig. 2.1 Staying alive—homeostasis and the mature organism model. This figure represents the fundamental pathways into and out of the brain/CNS that are required for bodily survival. (From Gifford L S 1998 Pain, the tissues and the nervous system: a conceptual model. Physiotherapy 84(1):27-36, with permission)

The biological systems that may be involved in producing the behavioural or physiological 'response' to any given threat to our homeostasis include: the somatic motor system, the autonomic nervous system, the neuroendocrine system, and the immune system. Thus, physical injury may alter the activity of all these systems. A key facet of the CNS/brain is that it provides the essential co-ordinating role. Note that these systems will also be activated to produce positive responses to favourable situations and environments.

The biological systems involved in 'sampling' largely involve afferent sensory neural pathways but the slower and more primitive circulatory communicating systems should not be forgotten. Interestingly, the immune system is now being viewed not only as an effector system—for example in fighting off invading pathogens or by facilitating repair of damaged and worn tissues—but also as a sensory afferent system that receives information from the environment and other parts of the body. Thus, the immune system has similar capability as the CNS/brain, in that it samples—scrutinises—acts. What is also interesting is that strong afferent and efferent links exist between the brain and the immune system and so one system's activities can powerfully effect the other, even up to, or from, the psychological/behavioural level (see Sternberg & Gold 1997).

The young organism is naive, it has a relatively 'empty' brain and central nervous system *in terms of environmental and physiological experiences* (but see Mithen 1996). As the organism ages it matures and its CNS/brain 'fills-up' with mindful and physiological experiences on which it can draw to aid in its quest for survival and reproductive success. The naive human organism is strongly dependent on its parents for survival. As it matures it becomes progressively more independent, until it is capable of reproducing and having offspring which are in turn dependent on it. In these terms, maturity is all about getting to know the environment and learning how to act within it to one's bodily and genetic advantage. The process of maturation is also about the brain getting to know its own survival machine and how to use it. Simply, this can be regarded as a progression from naiveté, where the CNS/brain houses only a few innate but vital *sample—scrutinise—action* pathways, to maturity, where layers of *sample—scrutinise—action* experiences are imprinted into the system and which can be drawn upon if needed later. Thus, as the system matures it slowly gets 'filled' with meaningful new interconnections and pathways that can be considered the biological representations of past experience (Kandel et al 1995). Physiological and environmental experiences are thus stored as 'memories' during 'learning' and are capable of being 'recalled or remembered' when needed (Rose 1992, Gross 1996, LeDoux 1998). Along with physical maturation, learning, memory and recall, in the broadest sense, are the fundamental neurobiological processes that take the naive organism from being grossly dependent on its parents, to being fully independent and capable of rearing children.

Figure 2.1 schematically illustrates the mature organism, its connections to the environment via the sense organs and to its own body. Inputs produce outputs which can alter the environment and the body, they are sampled again and so on in a perpetual manner. All life, from the minutest single celled organisms right up to the complexities of the multicellular human-being depend on this continuous *sample—scrutinise—response—re-sample* capability in order to survive.

Injury and pain in the context of the MOM

Consider a situation in which someone is innocently sitting in their car waiting to pull out of a junction when a large truck hits them from behind. The impact is so heavy that the recipient is jerked violently forward and back. The situation takes on a dramatic turn physiologically and behaviourally. Figure 2.2 includes a representation of just this—the perceived events in the environment and the damage to the tissues. The brain receives information about it all, scrutinises it and reacts accordingly. In turn, physiological responses in the body go into red alert to produce stress response subsets appropriate to the situation the brain finds itself in (Cannon 1929, Selye 1978, Gray 1987, Sapolsky 1994, Gifford 1997). This may or may not involve the perception of pain.

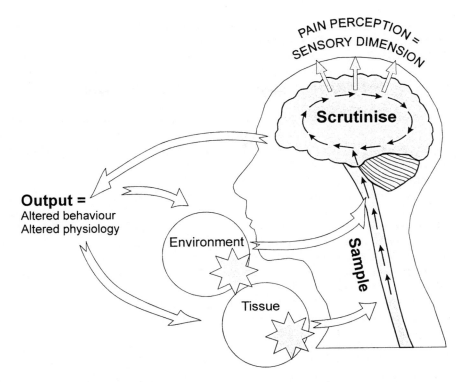

Fig. 2.2 Injury and the mature organism model: a possible initial stage. (From Gifford L S 1998 Pain the tissues and the nervous system: a conceptual model. Physiotherapy 84(1):27–36, with permission)

Part of the CNS/brain response/output may be to actually prevent nociceptive messages from impinging on consciousness (Fields & Basbaum 1989, Fields & Basbaum 1994). For instance, if the injured persons' life was under severe threat they would be unlikely to feel any pain. The issues of bodily survival (classically involve freeze, fight or flight) take priority over the perception of pain and its concomitant illness behaviour (Gray 1987). Thus, whether we feel pain at the time of injury is very variable and largely a product of the circumstances as assessed by our brain (for example, see Beecher 1946, Melzack et al 1982, Blank 1994).

Perhaps we should not forget that pain, like the appreciation of colour, is ultimately a perceptual quality whose neuronal correlates are somewhere in the CNS/brain (Edelman 1992, Crick 1994, Adolphs & Damasio 1995, Backonja 1996, Wall 1996, Koch 1997).

The sensation of acute pain is the conscious signal of a physical threat whose major purpose, in parallel with producing the biologically linked emotional reaction of fear and/or anger, is to motivate and bring about an alteration in our behaviour in order to further our chances of recovery and survival (Wall 1979, MacLean 1990). Thus, acute pain from injury and the classic instantaneous behaviour patterns that are found across all cultures may be viewed as being 'adaptive' biologically well ingrained in our systems, and hence difficult to consciously modify. Later on, pain helps us to become physically vigilant and avoid use of the injured part, our whimpering and distress attract support from others and our general demeanor demands care and respect from anyone venturing too close without undue care (Walters 1994). Seen in this way, pain adaptively drives recuperative behaviour (Wall 1979).

Figure 2.3 adds another component to the MOM that introduces the possibility of a degree of flexibility of response. The brain samples itself before creating a behaviour. For example, it samples relevant past experience, knowledge and beliefs and mixes this in with its appraisal of the current situation. This sampling includes knowledge of past successful behaviours in similar situations, as well as successful behaviours related to us or observed in others. Adventure stories and the rather sickening attraction many of us have to investigate accidents or read about other people's mishaps may well have great survival advantages! What any one individual has stored in their brain's filing cabinets of experience is a reflection of the culture and society they were brought up in, their relative age, and the life experiences they have had. In comparison to the naive organism the mature organism has a large number of behavioural strategies to choose from. It is worth reflecting that as a result of

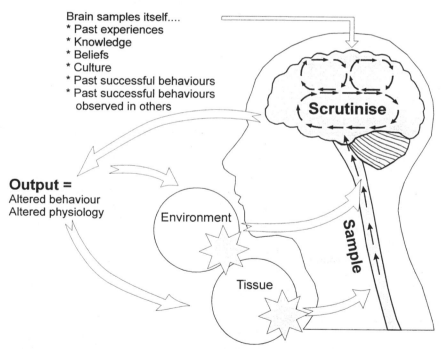

Fig. 2.3 Injury and the mature organism model, showing the brain sampling itself and how the contents of our brains that represent such attributes as experience, beliefs and culture will influence the output system activity. (From Gifford L S 1998 Pain the tissues and the nervous system: a conceptual model. Physiotherapy 84(1):27-36, with permission)

the great variety of options provided by modern complex societies (should I go to the doctor? to the chiropractor? to the casualty department? to my aromatherapist? etc.) the more difficult it becomes for the individual to make a secure choice—and that doubt promotes anxiety.

The message is that along with the powerful effects resulting from the inputs being sampled and reflexly scrutinised from the damaged tissues, our current thoughts and feelings about the situation that we find ourselves in, as well as the thoughts and attitudes of those around us, will all have a marked influence on the degree of pain, our illness behaviour and the level of suffering (see Fordyce 1986, Jensen et al 1991, Skevington 1995, Turk 1996).

Figure 2.4 highlights the importance that the current thoughts and feelings a person suffering pain may have on the outputs of the brain. Most therapeutic approaches usually consider pain in a single **sensory dimension** (Fig. 2.2): i.e., the perception of where the pain is located, the quality and type of pain, its intensity and the way it behaves over time. However, pain has been considered in terms of three dimensions for quite along time (see Melzack & Casey 1968, Melzack 1986): i.e., the **sensory dimension** as described; the

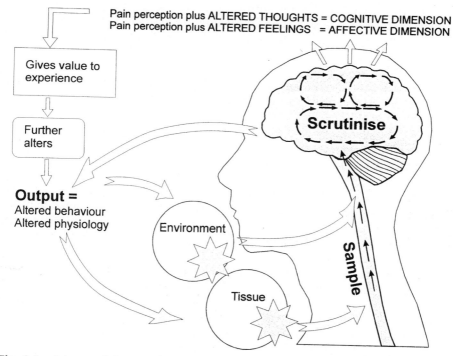

Fig. 2.4 Injury and the mature organism model. As a result of tissue sampling, environment sampling and self sampling, the brain/CNS produces appropriate thoughts and feelings. These perceptual outputs of the brain give value to the injury experience and hence further influence the activity of the physiological and behaviourally related output systems involved in survival and recovery. (From Gifford L S 1998 Pain the tissues and the nervous system: a conceptual model. Physiotherapy 84(1):27-36, with permission)

cognitive dimension, which recognises that pain alters our thoughts; and the **affective dimension** recognising that for every pain we have there is some kind of emotional reaction.

Consider again the car accident described earlier. One minute the individual was happily minding their own business, the next minute they've been rudely shunted forwards by the vehicle behind. They have altered their feelings (shocked and anxious, perhaps increasingly angry—affective dimension), altered their thoughts ('What am I going to do now? I'd better ring my neighbour to take me to the casualty, and I'm not that keen on going there, they haven't a very good reputation according to the newspapers and some ex-patients I know'—the cognitive dimension), and they feel a building throbbing pain in the neck, shoulder and back of head (sensory dimension).

These three dimensions represent three levels of integrated higher neural processing relating to consciousness that are largely responsible for an individual's behaviour pattern. Clearly, our thoughts and feelings about a given situation are the fundamental processes that give it value. Value means that if the individual sees the experience as very important, then something must be done, and the experience is worth giving attention to, focusing on (Wright 1994) and remembering for future use. Emotions are vital to providing experience with value and hence motivation to act (Melzack & Casey 1968, Damasio 1995) and are largely determined by our thoughts and beliefs as well as being reflexly triggered in novel and unexpected situations (LeDoux 1993, 1994, 1998).

The classic emotional centres that reside in the more primitive limbic brain and associated areas are very powerfully linked to the areas of the major brain output systems—for example, the neuroendocrine system via the hypothalamus and pituitary glands; the sympathetic system via the hypothalamus and locus coeruleus in the brain stem and the somatic motor system via the motor cortex (Chrousos & Gold 1992, Brown 1994, Chapman 1995, Chrousos et al 1995). The powerful links between the neuroendocrine and sympathetic systems and the immune system are also well recognised (see below). The important clinical implication is that if we can change the way a person feels emotionally, by for instance changing their knowledge and beliefs about their problem or situation, we can beneficially change activity in the output systems (Bandura et al 1985, Bandura et al 1987, O'Leary et al 1988). This does not just mean bringing about changes in observable behaviour but also changes in autonomic, neuroendocrine and immune activity. The simple concept of 'mind influencing matter' is very much a scientific reality (for excellent overviews see Sapolsky 1994, Martin 1997, Sternberg & Gold 1997).

Figure 2.5 illustrates that a new experience is put into memory in the CNS/ brain for future reference (Rose 1992, Kandel & Hawkins 1993, Kandel et al 1995). Note that the Figure includes the possibility of a pain memory (see the discussion in Ch. 4), but will also include a 'memory' of the successful and not so successful behaviours, cognitions and emotions that were used and the concurrent physiological reactions required pertinent to the experience (Skevington 1995). In other words, if a similar experience happens later in

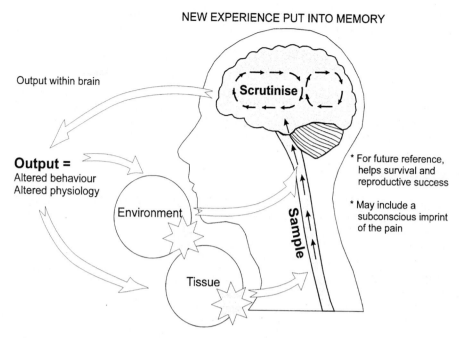

Fig. 2.5 The mature organism model. Illustrates the retention of the incident in memory and proposes that this may include a neural representation of the pain.

life, our behaviour and physiological reactions to it may well be more efficient since the pathways responsible for it originally do not need to be newly established, merely rekindled. This is an example of how the organism gets 'cleverer' at survival as it matures and gains more experiences to add to its wisdom.

One would imagine the perfectly adapted organism to only 'record' events and experiences that were of significance or of great value to survival and replication (Sylwester 1995). However, it is also possible that many environmental and physiological events may be recorded detrimentally in some cases (Kandel et al 1995). Man's unique consciousness has the ability to think about the value he puts on events and experiences and may well consciously or unconsciously prejudice the maladaptive 'over' retention of many unhelpful experiences. Pain in all its dimensions is of course a prime example. The 'recording' of unhelpful experiences and related maladaptive physiological processes is perhaps the price we pay for being endowed with this rather remarkable recording capability (discussed at length in Butler & Gifford 1999). On the other hand, a cynical view could argue that given the present cultural climate, over-focusing and constantly attending to pain and adopting a disabled role may be relatively advantageous and hence biologically adaptive (see Ch. 15). Problems arise when the interface between malingering, and the present cultural norms that condition us to allocate blame and seek compensation are brought into the equation. It is very much a Darwinian notion that says 'get as much as you can for the least possible effort'. Perhaps before allocating blame, we should recognise that while overt selfishness is ethically offensive, it is biologically well ingrained and therefore very much a part of the makeup of the selfish gene and life's very success (see Wright 1994).

The MOM provides a biological perspective on which the effects of injury and pain can be more broadly rationalised. Chapters 3, 4 and 5 take a personal look at the science and clinical relevance of pain mechanisms and relates them back to the MOM (see also Gifford 1997, Gifford 1998).

REFERENCES

Adolphs R, Damasio A R 1995 Consciousness and neuroscience. In: Bromm B, Desmedt J E (eds) Pain and the brain: from nociception to cognition. Raven Press, New York 83–97

Backonja M-M 1996 Primary somatosensory cortex and pain perception. Yes sir, your pain is in your head (part 1). Pain Forum 5(3): 171–180

Bandura A, O'Leary A, Taylor C B et al 1987 Perceived self-efficacy and pain control: Opioid and nonopioid mechanisms. Journal of Personality and Social Psychology 53:663–571

Bandura A, Taylor C B, Williams S L et al 1985 Catecholamine secretion as a funtion of perceived coping self-efficacy. Journal of Consulting and Clinical Psychology 53:406–414

Beecher H K 1946 Pain in men wounded in battle. Annals of Surgery 123:96–105

Blank J W 1994 Pain in men wounded in battle: Beecher revisited. IASP Newsletter Jan/Feb: 2–4

Brown R E 1994 An introduction to neuroendocrinology. Cambridge University Press, Cambridge

Butler D S, Gifford L S 1999 (In press)The dynamic nervous system. NOI Press, Adelaide

Cannon W B 1929 The wisdom of the body. Physiological Review 9:399–431

Chapman C R 1995 The affective dimension of pain: A model. In: Bromm B, Desmedt J E (eds) Pain and the brain: from nociception to cognition. Raven Press, New York 283–301

Chrousos G P, Gold P W 1992 The concepts of stress and stress system disorders. Overview of physical and behavioral homeostasis [published erratum appears in JAMA 1992 Jul 8;268(2):200]. Journal of the American Medical Association 267(9):1244–52

Chrousos G P, McCarty R, Pacak K et al (eds) 1995 Stress. Basic mechanisms and clinical implications. Annals of the New York Academy of Sciences vol 771: Stress, basic mechanisms and clinical implications The New York Academy of Sciences, New York

Crick F 1994 The astonishing hypothesis. The scientific search for the soul. Touchstone Books, London

Damasio A R 1995 Descartes' error. Picador, London

Dawkins R 1989 The selfish gene. Oxford University Press, Oxford

Dawkins R 1996 Climbing Mount Improbable. Viking, London

Edelman G 1992 Bright air brilliant fire. On the matter of the mind. Penguin Books, London

Fields H L, Basbaum A I 1989 Endogenous pain control mechanisms. In: Wall P D, Melzack R (eds) Textbook of pain. 2nd edn. Churchill Livingstone, Edinburgh 206–217

Fields H L, Basbaum A I 1994 Central nervous system mechanisms of pain modulation. In: Wall P D, Melzack R (eds) Textbook of pain. 3rd edn. Churchill Livingstone, Edinburgh 243–257

Fordyce W E 1984 Behavioural science and chronic pain. Postgraduate Medical Journal 60:865–868

Fordyce W E 1986 Learning processes in pain. In: Sternbach R A (ed) The psychology of pain. 2nd edn. Raven Press, New York 49–65

Gifford L S 1997 Pain. In: Pitt-Brooke (ed) Rehabilitation of movement: Theoretical bases of clinical practice Saunders, London 196–232

Gifford L S 1998 Pain, the tissues and the nervous system: A conceptual model. Physiotherapy 84(1): 27–36

Gray J A 1987 The psychology of fear and stress. Cambridge University Press, Cambridge

Gross R D 1996 Psychology. The science of mind and behaviour. Hodder & Stoughton, London

Jensen M P, Turner J A, Romano J M et al 1991 Coping with chronic pain: a critical review of the literature. Pain 47:259–283

Kandel E R, Hawkins D H 1993 The biological basis of learning and individuality. Mind and brain. W H Freeman, New York 40–53

Kandel E R, Schwartz J H, Jessell T M (eds) 1995 Essentials of neural science and behavior. Prentice Hall, London

Koch C 1997 Computation and the single neuron. Nature 385:207–210

LeDoux J 1993 Emotional memory systems in the brain. Behavioural and Brain Research 58

LeDoux J E 1994 Emotion, memory and brain. Scientific American June 32–39

LeDoux J 1998 The Emotional Brain. The mysterious underpinnings of emotional life. Weidenfeld & Nicolson, London

MacLean P D 1990 The triune brain in evolution: Role in paleocerebral functions. Plenum Press, New York

Martin P 1997 The sickening mind. Brain, behaviour, immunity and disease. Harper Collins, London

Melzack R 1986 Neurophysiological foundations of pain. In: Sternbach R A (ed) The psychology of pain. 2nd edn. Raven Press, New York 1–24

Melzack R, Casey K L 1968 Sensory, motivational, and central control determinants of pain: A new conceptual model. In: Kenshalo D (ed) The skin senses. C C Thomas, Springfield 423–443

Melzack R, Wall P D, Ty T C 1982 Acute pain in an emergency clinic: latency of onset and descriptor patterns related to different injuries. Pain 14:33–44

Mithen S 1996 The prehistory of the mind. Thames and Hudson, London

Nesse R M, Williams G C 1994 Evolution and healing. The new science of Darwinian medicine. Phoenix, London

O'Leary A, Shoor S, Lorig K et al 1988 A cognitive-behavioural treatment for rheumatoid arthritis. Health Psychology 7:527–544

Pilowsky I 1986 Psychodynamic aspcets of the pain experience. In: Sternbach R A (ed) The psychology of pain. 2nd edn. Raven Press, New York 181–195

Pilowsky I 1995a Pain, disability, and illness. Pain Forum 4(2):126–128

Pilowsky I 1995b Spine update: Low back pain and illness behavior (Inappropriate, maladaptive, or abnormal). Spine 20(13):1522–1524

Plotkin H 1994 Darwin machines and the nature of knowledge. Penguin, London

Rose S 1992 The making of memory: From molecules to mind. Bantam Press, London

Sapolsky R M 1994 Why zebras don't get ulcers. A guide to stress, stress-related diseases, and coping. Freeman, New York

Selye H 1978 The stress of life. McGraw Hill, New York

Skevington S M 1995 Psychology of pain. John Wiley & Sons, Chichester

Sternberg E M, Gold P W 1997 The mind-body interaction in disease. Scientific American Special Issue: Mysteries of the Mind June: 8–15

Sylwester R 1995 A celebration of neurons. An educator's guide to the human brain. Association for Supervision and Curriculum Development, Alexandria

Turk D C 1996 Biopsychosocial perspective on chronic pain. In: Gatchel R J, Turk D C (eds) Psychological approaches to pain management Guilford Press, New York 3–32

Waddell G, Newton M, Henderson I et al 1993 A fear-avoidance beliefs questionnaire (FABQ) and the role of fear-avoidance beliefs in chronic low back pain and disability. Pain 52:157–168

Wall P D 1979 On the relation of injury to pain. Pain 6:253–264

Wall P D 1996 The mechanisms by which tissue damage and pain are related. In: Campbell J N (ed) Pain 1996—An updated review. Refresher course syllabus IASP Press, Seattle 123–126

Walters E T 1994 Injury related behaviour and neuronal plasticity. International review of neurobiology 36:325–426

Weiner H 1991 Behavioural biology of stress and psychosomatic medicine. In: Brown M R, Koob G F, Rivier C (eds) Stress. Neurobiology and neuroendocrinology .Marcel Dekker, New York 23–51

Williams G C 1996 Plan and purpose in nature. Weidenfeld & Nicolson, London

Wright R 1994 The moral animal: Why we are the way we are. Abacus, London

3

Tissue and input related mechanisms

LOUIS GIFFORD

Introduction to pain mechanisms

The standard way in which pain mechanisms are viewed is broadly linear in aspect. For example, an acutely twisted ankle or whiplashed neck involves tissue damage. The tissue damage creates inflammation which leads to the sensitisation of nerve endings in the damaged tissues. As a result of this 'nociceptive' pain mechanism, increased numbers of impulses are relayed into the CNS resulting in enhanced sensitivity to movements and mechanical forces with or without ongoing discomfort. This is linear in that it has a clear start (tissues) and a clear end (brain). The resultant thinking is: pain is the result of tissue mechanisms and nociception—therapy should therefore be focused on the tissues as well as at preventing excessive impulse activity being generated from the relevant nociceptors.

Appreciating that for every input to the CNS/brain there is likely to be some form of scrutinising and some form of response/output leads us from a linear mode of thinking to a circular 'Mature Organism Model (MOM)' mode. Not only that, the discussion in Chapter 2, whereby the brain samples itself and the ongoing events in the environment occurring at the same time as it receives information from the damaged tissues, should make us realise that an individual's psychology (their thoughts and feelings) is brought into play in all injury related situations and painful experiences, whether acute or chronic. Linear descriptions of pain mechanisms may be preventing our thinking reaching beyond the sensory dimension of pain or into the biological mechanisms involved in outputs back to the tissues and environment. If we really think about it, there are two easily accessible therapeutic input points: via the tissues where it hurts, and via the brain where all the integrative processing of information goes on. One influences the other. Since a wealth of recent literature is indicating the far superior strength of psychosocial factors over physical factors in determining satisfactory outcome and functional recovery following the onset of a pain complaint (see Ch.15 and the Introductory Essay), it behoves us to think again as to how and where therapeutic inputs should be targeted. A balanced attitude is obviously necessary. What we have to accept is the fantastic sophistication of biology that should make us discard the notion that it is always going to be possible to fix a pain passively via the pure tissue or the 'bodily' effects of pills, surgery, manipulation, or any passive therapy. It is perhaps far wiser to be involved in helping to establish the best possible conditions for natural recovery (Wall 1989). This appears to involve a parallel and well balanced focus on restoration of best possible tissue health/return of function in parallel with a recognition of and focus on relevant cognitive and affective factors. These issues are explored in many of the chapters in this book.

Pain mechanisms have been usefully categorised into five separate classes for manual therapists (Butler 1994, Jones 1995, Gifford & Butler 1997). The current mechanisms in general use and their descriptions are detailed (for more detailed discussion see Gifford 1997, Gifford & Butler 1997).

1 **Nociceptive mechanisms**. Here pain is primarily derived from nociceptive activity in the target tissues of the nervous system. This can involve any musculoskeletal tissue that has a nociceptive innervation, for example: disc, bone, joint, ligament, tendon and muscle tissues. Nociceptive mechanisms may relate to mechanical forces, and/or to the chemical environment of the nociceptors, for example inflammation, ischaemia or the presence of catecholamines (adrenaline and noradrenaline). In the clinic, labelling a particular tissue as the 'source' of the pain is in effect stating that the pain mechanism is nociceptive.

2 **Peripheral neurogenic mechanisms**. This relates to pain generated from abnormal impulse generating sites in the axons and cell bodies of peripheral nerve fibres/neurons. Acute nerve root pain and carpal tunnel syndrome are examples of classic neuropathies that have a predominantly peripheral neurogenic pain mechanism. Injury to peripheral nerve tissue is highly likely in whiplash injury (see Ch. 1).

3 **Central mechanisms**. Following tissue injury, nociception and/or peripheral nerve injury, plastic changes in the CNS/brain result in alterations in processing of afferent information. For example, normal non-noxious movements and standard physical tests on undamaged tissues may provide inputs that get centrally processed in terms of pain. A second perspective is that the CNS/brain may spontaneously generate neural activity that results in pain—without necessarily any reference to peripheral inputs from the tissues. This central generation of pain can be viewed as a 'pain memory' (see Ch. 4).

4 **Sympathetic/motor mechanisms**. This category recognises that activity in the sympathetic and motor systems may enhance pain secondary to a peripheral sensitising process (e.g. nociceptive and peripheral neurogenic).

There may be nothing wrong with these output systems for them to generate pain (see Ch. 5).

5 **Affective mechanisms**. This category accepts the potential of negative and unhelpful emotions and mood states to give rise to pain, or more likely, to be an integral part of the pain problem with many potential repercussions (see Ch. 4)

In order to integrate these mechanisms into the MOM some additions and alterations in terminology need to be made (Fig. 3.1).

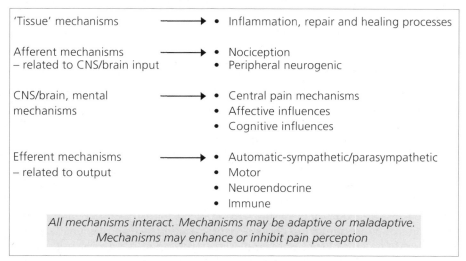

Fig. 3.1 Pathobiological mechanisms related to pain perception and physical and mental/psychlogical dysfunction.

First, note that the term pathobiology is used in order to shift the focus from a rather compartmentalised pain mechanism thinking to a broader concept that analyses all mechanisms and processes from the perspective of the tissues, where injury begins, to then involve the sampling, processing/scrutinising, output systems in every clinical case every time.

Secondly, note that processing/scrutinising involves affective and cognitive processing and thus brings pscychosocial factors into the clinical equation every time. Thus, tissue injury, as in the acute stages of whiplash (see Ch. 1), involves not only tissue damage and the activation of nociceptors, but also:

- the transmission of information to the CNS/brain;
- the multilevel scrutinising and processing of that information in parallel with personally relevant recalled information; and finally
- the production of a response appropriate to the individual—physiologically and behaviourally.

Even though tissue damage and subsequent nociceptor activity can be seen as a dominant mechanism in acute pain, the individual imposes unique affective and cognitively derived neurobiological influences onto the tissue derived processing activity and hence produces a unique output/response to it. All mechanisms are involved in every pain state, however, in some pain states a particular pain mechanism may dominate. Thus, pain arising from an acutely inflamed joint may be 'physiologically' dominated by tissue and nociceptive mechanisms, whereas chronic pain associated with whiplash may be predominantly characterised by maladaptive central/processing mechanisms alongside maladaptive affective and cognitive features.

The rest of this chapter discusses tissue mechanisms and mechanisms relating to 'input' into the CNS/brain. Chapter 4 looks at CNS/brain/mental or 'scrutinising' mechanisms and Chapter 5 at mechanisms relating to output.

Tissue mechanisms

A consideration of the types of tissues injured (see Ch. 1) and their healing capacity is vital. It is necessary to integrate knowledge of healing times of various tissues in parallel with the best conditions required for best recovery. This is a massive topic and one that requires greater scrutiny (see Butler & Gifford 1999). There are some basic facts that need to be fully acknowledged.

Tissue injury is traditionally divided into a 3 phase time-dependent process that leads to recovery. The phases are, *inflammation, fibro-proliferation/repair,* and *remodelling.* Further, there are three types of healing: healing by *regeneration* whereby lost and damaged tissues are replaced with tissue that has similar functional and morphological characteristics; healing by *repair,* where damaged and lost tissue is replaced by granulation tissue that eventually matures to form a scar; and healing by *contraction.* All three components probably play a role in all recovery processes, which one dominates depends on the tissue injured. Thus, removal of 70% of the liver elicits a healing reaction dominated by regeneration, and the outcome is a normal liver in a matter of days. Injury to the oesophagus may result in an exuberant proliferation of myofibroblasts, excessive wound contraction, and contracture. A wound on the anterior tibial surface, where the skin's attachment to the periosteum prevents contraction, forces healing almost exclusively by repair, and a large scar results (Martinez-Hernandez & Amenta 1988).

An important message is that most injuries of the musculoskeletal system heal predominantly by repair (scarring), not by regeneration, and this means that *these tissues are very unlikely to ever be the same again.* This is a fundamental fact that is not at all well accepted—by medicine, by the allied health professionals who deal with rehabilitation, or the general public. The tendency is to believe that medicine has the tools to fix a given problem when the reality is far from this.

It can be argued that a degree of maintained sensitivity in previously damaged but repaired (scarred) tissues is of adaptive (protective) value since the tissues may be weaker or more vulnerable to further damage. Thus, a degree of end range sensitivity or modest discomfort in prolonged positions may well be an adaptive legacy that helps to prevent further injury to a weak and biomechanically compromised tissue. Having said that, the nervous system's role in maintaining an adequate modest protective sensitivity appears to be very open to individual variation and not always easy to control. Two people who suffer exactly the same injury may have quite different long-term outcomes. It seems that there is a homeostatic balancing act going on that can be easily unbalanced and if unbalanced long enough is very difficult to adequately reestablish in a more adaptive and functional way.

Chronic pain and excessive ongoing tissue sensitivity following whiplash are excellent examples of how homeostatic information processing mechanisms may overcompensate and be maintained in a maladaptive state. Thus, tissues may remain exquisitely sensitive and unnecessarily painful long after a reasonable healing time. The sensitivity state is out of all proportion to the likely state of the tissues or their needs. In fact, due more to lack of use than significant damage, it is likely that the excessive sensitivity helps maintain the tissue in a weaker state than they otherwise would be. Clinically it can be very helpful to direct patients attention away from a 'pain equals tissue damage' model towards one focusing on strengthening tissues that have had prolonged underuse. For this to occur the patient needs to be convinced that excessive sensitivity is a problem in its own right and that it is not necessarily an honest reflection of tissue damage.

It is conceivable that even healed but scarred tissues, once more extensible and strong, may send positive biological messages to the nervous system that enable a downshift in its sensitivity. If the nervous system is constantly sampling tissues that are weak, inextensible and little used it will logically tend to want to remain sensitised. By contrast, if the tissues become fitter, the system's overall need to remain sensitive and vigilant may be far less.

It is hoped that if readers can go along with this they will appreciate the need for changes in tissue health in parallel with changes in patient beliefs, attitudes and feelings towards their tissues and their pain (see Chs 11, 13, & 15).

The disc is a good example of a tissue that, once damaged, is unlikely to heal well. In fact the literature indicates that injured discs are prone to degenerate more rapidly than they otherwise would with the passage of time. For example, Osti et al (1990) investigated the effects of surgically producing a 5 mm long and 5 mm deep cut in the anterolateral aspect of young and otherwise normal lumbar discs of sheep. They lesioned 3 discs in each of 21 sheep. Overall the experiment revealed that the lesion lead to a progressive *failure* of the *inner* annulus which occurred between the 4th and 12th month in the majority of animals. As early as the first 1-2 months there was evidence of nuclear degeneration, nuclear displacement, the presence of clefts and the early loss of definition between the outer nucleus and inner annulus in several of the discs. These features were present *in all discs examined at 12 months*. Moderate narrowing of the disc space was observable in most discs by 8 months and was moderate or marked in all discs by 18 months. Osteophytes were apparent in some after 4 months and in all discs by 8 months. Marked changes over the whole length of the end-plates were also observed. Unhappily, what this is saying is that once a disc annulus is damaged the whole disc and its end-plates degenerates further and really quite rapidly.

Against this rather dismal prospect is the more hopeful and well known finding that many people with degenerate tissues and clear evidence of tissue pathology and abnormality are perfectly healthy and complain of little or no pain (see Ch. 15). Far better to view injury-related 'degeneration' as an unfortunate but thoroughly adaptive process.

The use of carefully controlled loading at an optimal time during repair of injured ligaments and tendons has wide support since it undoubtedly promotes healing (for references see Buckwalter 1995, Buckwalter 1996). Tensile loading of damaged tendon tissues appears to cause the repair cells and matrix collagen fibrils to line up parallel to the axis of tension (Liu et al 1995). Lack of tension leaves the repair tissue cells and fibres disoriented. Loading may also alter the rate of tendon repair. For example, three weeks following injury, surgically repaired tendons treated with early mobilisation had twice the strength of repaired tendons treated with immobilisation (Gelberman et al 1982). This is a very useful piece of information that can be given to early whiplash patients to help them understand the need for early and progressive movement.

The following important information is taken directly from Goodship et al (1994):

> The initial haphazard arrangement of collagen fibres is modified as functional loading is restored, resulting in a return toward parallel alignment of fibers. It has been suggested that immobilization of collagenous structures results in a decrease in mechanical strength that is never regained on remobilization. These facts would suggest that complete rest may be contraindicated except in the very early period after injury and controlled exercise should be introduced in a progressive manner from an early stage. Application of physical stimulation includes specific exercise regimes and the use of physiotherapy, particularly in the early stages, to provide low levels of loading and cause fluid dispersion.

A comment here is that passively moving a patients neck with grade II or III mobilisations for 2–3 minutes 3 times a week during a treatment session is likely to be wholly inadequate. Consider too that some passive techniques in some patients may involve a great deal of fear/anxiety/tension by the patient that may be a factor in actually exacerbating and maintaining the pain. Far better that the patients convincingly learn the underlying principles, and then apply regular movement themselves (see Ch. 7).

Input/sampling mechanisms

The CNS/brain samples the state of damaged tissues primarily via the nociceptive system . Tissue damage alters the chemical environment of the nerve terminals of nociceptors and as a result sensitises them so that their firing capability becomes dramatically increased (Schaible & Grubb 1993, Levine & Taiwo 1994, Schmidt et al 1994). This equates to ongoing discomfort, due to the continued spontaneous firing of sensitised nociceptor populations, as well as to increased sensitivity to movement, touch/palpation and postures. Thus, gentle movements, gentle pressure on the tissues or sustained postures cause nociceptors to fire far more easily and for far longer than normal. Inputs that normally do not hurt or cause discomfort now easily hurt and cause pain to continue for a while after their cessation (see Gifford 1997).

In addition to nociceptive input there is now much evidence to support the importance of tissue—CNS/brain communicating links via the immune and hormonal systems (De Souza 1993, Rivier 1993, Udelsman & Holbrook 1994, Watkins et al 1995, Pennisi 1997). Thus, damaged tissues, and immune cells in damaged tissues, release chemical messengers (e.g. cytokines and prostaglandins) that are sampled by the CNS at specific sites. These sites may be in areas of the brain which specifically sample the blood's contents, for example the tuber cinereum of the hypothalamus, the pineal gland, and the area postrema of the caudal fourth ventricle (Westmoreland et al 1994, Sternberg & Licinio 1995, Watkins et al 1995), or at specific peripheral nerve terminals in the periphery. For example, an important blood sampling route may be via visceral afferent neuron terminals in the liver (Pennisi 1997, Sternberg & Gold 1997). These then relay into the CNS via the vagal nerve (Watkins et al 1995). Since the liver screens the blood and lymph for toxins, pathogens and pro-inflammatory chemicals like cytokines, it is well disposed for processing and then relaying this information on to the brain for further scrutiny.

These sampling sites, in parallel with incoming nociceptor pathways are directly linked to major processing and output centres in the limbic brain that have been shown to be capable of strongly influencing our illness behaviour (Watkins et al 1995, Maier & Watkins 1996). Thus infection, tissue damage like whiplash perhaps, and other bodily threats are dealt with in ways that stubbornly dictate a required behavioural response with its associated mood states. Our psychological state may be quite firmly dictated by the state of our body. It is little wonder that following a severe and disturbing accident many people become withdrawn, passive, moody, angry, worried and frightened— for the biological determinants of these behaviours are well entrenched and are very difficult to over-ride. Of most concern here is understanding the merger from this adaptive early stage to its chronic maladaptive maintenance so often seen in many physiotherapy outpatient departments.

In whiplash actual damage may occur to the sampling pathways (see Ch. 1). Thus, injury to peripheral nerve tissues may result in abnormal or perverted function of the sensory nervous system conduits (Devor 1994, Gifford 1997). This proposal can be expanded to include the ascending sensory tracts in the cord and brainstem which may well be damaged in some whiplash injuries.

Since it is vital for survival that the CNS/brain maintains contact with its 'body' it is little wonder that quite potent homeostatic mechanisms come into play to try to restore contact and maintain the pathways. Thus, when peripheral nerve fibres are injured, related populations of cells in the spinal cord may dramatically enhance their sensitivity, expand their receptive fields, make new and often inappropriate connections, and become spontaneously active to try and compensate for the loss (Woolf et al 1992, Woolf 1994, Woolf & Doubell 1994). Similarly, the surviving proximal remains of severed neurones may upregulate their sensitivity (Devor 1994). Unhappily, this may occur not just at the damaged zone but along the axon to include the cell body. Adjacent normal peripheral neurones may even upgrade their sensitivity, too (Devor 1994). The message here is that damage to vital linking systems/sampling pathways can have devastating consequences when viewed at biological levels looking at maladaptive neural reactivity and plasticity. Thus, thinking in terms of 'peripheral' input mechanisms only, it seems that there is a far greater potential for a maladaptive response if the nervous system is injured than if the target tissues alone suffer injury.

Injury to peripheral nerve is known to take time to generate a response. For instance, $A\delta$ fibres that are injured may remain totally silent for the first day or two after injury, but then slowly increase their spontaneous activity over the following two weeks. C fibres tend to increase activity as the A fibres decrease theirs (Devor 1994). This may be several weeks after the original injury. Think of the unfortunate whiplash patient who for the first few days feels stiff and sore (nociceptive mechanism due to tissue damage likely), but some days or weeks later starts to develop weird symptoms in odd places (peripheral neurogenic mechanism with central mechanism repercussions). Not only is it strange and worrying to the patient it also gets seen as the first signs of malingering by many unenlightened health professionals. This type of knowledge is hugely useful in helping the patient understand the mechanisms of their pain as well as helping to validate their pain experience.

REFERENCES

Buckwalter J A 1995 Activity vs. rest in the treatment of bone, soft tissue and joint injuries. Iowa Orthopaedic Journal 15(42):29–42

Buckwalter J A 1996 Effects of early motion on healing of musculoskeletal tissues. Hand Clinics 12(1):13–24

Butler D S 1994 The upper limb tension test revisited. In: Grant R (ed) Physical therapy of the cervical and thoracic spine. Clinics in Physical Therapy. Churchill Livingstone, New York

Butler D S, Gifford L S 1999 (In press) The dynamic nervous system. NOI Press, Adelaide

De Souza E B 1993 Corticotropin-releasing factor and interleukin-1 receptors in the brain-endocrine-immune axis. Role in stress response and infection. Ann N Y Acad Sci (27):9–27

Devor M 1994 The pathophysiology of damaged peripheral nerves. In: Wall P D, Melzack R (eds) Textbook of pain. 3rd edn. Churchill Livingstone, Edinburgh 79–100

Gelberman R H, Woo S L-Y, Lothringer K et al 1982 Effects of early intermittent passive mobilisation on healing canine flexor tendons. Journal of Hand Surgery 7(2):170175

Gifford L S 1997 Pain. In: Pitt-Brooke (ed) Rehabilitation of movement: theoretical bases of clinical practice. Saunders, London 196–232

Gifford L S, Butler D S 1997 The integration of pain sciences into clinical practice. Hand Therapy 10(2):86–95

Goodship A E, Birch H L, Wilson A M 1994 The pathobiology and repair of tendon and ligament injury. Vetinary Clinics of North America: Equine Practice 10(2):323–349

Jones M 1995 Clinical reasoning and pain. Manual Therapy 1:17–24

Levine J, Taiwo Y 1994 Inflammatory pain. In: Wall P D, Melzack R (eds) Textbook of pain. 3rd edn. Churchill Livingstone, Edinburgh 45–56

Liu S H, Yang R S, Al-Shaikh R et al 1995 Collagen in tendon, ligament, and bone healing. A current review. Clinical Orthopaedics and Related Research 318(78):265–278

Maier S F, Watkins L R 1996 Proinflammatory cytokines and specific immune function. Pain Forum 5(4):234–236

Martinez-Hernandez A, Amenta P S 1988 Basic concepts in wound healing. In: Leadbetter W B, Buckwater J A, Gordon S L (eds) Sports induced inflammation. Clinical and basic science concepts. American Academy of Orthopaedic Surgeons 55–101

Osti O L, Vernon-Roberts B, Fraser R D 1990 Anulus tears and intervertebral disc degeneration: An experimental study using an animal model. Spine 15(8):762–767

Pennisi E 1997 Tracing molecules that make the brain-body connection. Science 275:930–931

Rivier C 1993 Effect of peripheral and central cytokines on the hypothalamic-pituitary-adrenal axis of the rat. Annals of the New York Academy of Sciences 697:97–105

Schaible H-G, Grubb B D 1993 Afferent and spinal mechanisms of joint pain. Pain 55(1):5–54

Schmidt R F, Schaible K M, Heppelmann B et al 1994 Silent and active nociceptors: structure, functions and clinical implications. In: Gebhart G F, Hammond D L, Jensen T S (eds) Proceedings of the 7th World Congress on Pain, Progress in Pain Research and Management. IASP press, Seattle 213–250

Sternberg E M, Gold P W 1997 The mind-body interaction in disease. Scientific American Special Issue: Mysteries of the Mind June: 8–15

Sternberg E M, Licinio J 1995 Overview of neuroimmune stress interactions. In: Chrousos G P, McCarty R, Pacak K et al (eds) Annals of the New York Academy of Sciences vol 771: Stress, basic mechanisms and clinical implications The New York Academy of Sciences, New York 364–371

Udelsman R, Holbrook N J 1994 Endocrine and molecular responses to surgical stress. Curr Probl Surg 31(8):653–720

Wall P D 1989 Introduction. In: Wall P D, Melzack R (eds) Textbook of pain. 2nd edn. Churchill Livingstone, Edinburgh 1–18

Watkins L R, Maier S F, Goehler L E 1995 Immune activation: the role of pro-inflammatory cytokines in inflammation, illness responses and pathological pain states. Pain 63:289–302

Westmoreland B F, Benarroch E E, Daube J R et al 1994 Medical neurosciences. Little Brown, Boston

Woolf C J 1994 The dorsal horn: state-dependent sensory processing and the generation of pain. In: Wall P D, Melzack R (eds) Textbook of pain. 3rd edn. Churchill Livingstone, Edinburgh 101–112

Woolf C J, Doubell T P 1994 The pathophysiology of chronic pain—increased sensitivity to low threshold Ab-fibre inputs. Current Opinion in Neurobiology 4:525–534

Woolf C J, Shorland P, Coggeshall R E 1992 Peripheral nerve injury triggers central sprouting of myelinated afferents. Nature 355:75–78

4

The 'central' mechanisms

LOUIS GIFFORD

This chapter addresses the central mechanisms that follow on from tissue damage, nociception and peripheral nerve injury (peripheral neurogenic mechanism). Its major purpose is a clinical perspective and the reader should refer to the cited references for more details of the sometimes complex biology.

There are several areas of focus: *Alterations in processing* deals with the known dynamic changes that occur in central nervous system pathways following tissue damage, nociception and peripheral nerve injury. *Pain memory,* focuses on the potential for ongoing barrages of impulses, that may be derived from tissue or peripheral nerve damage, to actually form an imprint or memory trace in the CNS/brain. Hence the potential for a 'pure' central mechanism whereby pain is actually a result of central nervous system neuronal activity that has become independent of the target tissue origins. Last, the *affective and cognitive mechanisms/dimensions* integrates the more conscious aspects of 'processing' into the clinical picture.

Alterations in processing

The central nervous system is capable of altering its sensitivity state very quickly and very easily. Following tissue injury or peripheral nerve injury, there is an increased impulse discharge of all sensory afferents which results in increased input into the dorsal horn of the spinal cord (see Dubner & Basbaum 1994, Woolf 1994). This barrage of afferent impulses impinges on second order neurones in the dorsal horn and electrochemically alters their sensitivity state too. Thus, dorsal horn cells (second order cells), many of which transmit onwards to higher centres, become increasingly excitable in the first few hours following tissue injury. This central sensitisation has several repercussions:

1   Dorsal horn second order cells alter their responsivity

Dorsal horn neurones that formerly only responded to inputs from nociceptors may start to respond to inputs from other fibre types too. Thus an Aβ fibre, which normally transmits impulses in response to non-noxious inputs like light touch and joint movement, now becomes capable of driving or stimulating neurones in the central nervous system that ascend to areas of the brain to produce pain sensations (Dubner & Basbaum 1994, Woolf & Doubell 1994). These Aβ fibres innervation fields may be in quite normal and undamaged tissues. This means that mechanical stimuli like light touch, gentle joint movement, palpatory pressures, performing neurodynamic tests like the upper-limb tension test or slump test, can produce pain from tissues that may be perfectly normal. This phenomenon is known as *secondary hyperalgesia* and amounts to a false positive for the tissues under scrutiny when tenderness is detected or standard physical 'differentiating' tests reproduce pain (Gifford 1997). The fact that it is a false positive for the tissues under scrutiny does not mean that the pain is not real, or is non-organic or psychosomatic in any way.

Clinically it is often the case that acute sprains and strains produce marked and widespread tenderness and most tissues under test easily provoke pain. Think of the acute back strain where tests of the SI joint, the lumbar spine, the SLR and Slump and PKB may be acutely positive, or a sprained and swollen knee joint where the whole area has become tender to palpate and all movements and tests hurt. Identifying a culpable specific faulty structure is often extremely difficult. However, several days later, when the acute inflammatory phase has settled it is common to find that this widespread hypersensitivity, or hyperalgesia, diminishes to become far more focused on the actual tissues that were originally injured or that need to maintain protective sensitivity. Sensitivity that actually relates to the damaged tissues is termed *primary hyperalgesia* and is thus a true positive—the tissues under test that hurt *are* abnormal (for a full discussion of hyperalgesia and allodynia see Gifford 1997).

In more devastating injuries, especially where peripheral nerves have been injured to some degree, ongoing enhanced tissue sensitivity may continue for a long time in a great many tissues. Clinically the problem of tissue labelling based on reproduction of pain and the discovery of hypersensitivity has to be interpreted very carefully. Knowledge of secondary hyperalgesia helps us understand the potential for widespread enhanced sensitivity, but it leaves us with a clinical dilemma—is the sensitivity adaptive and therefore protective, or is it maladaptive and preventing adequate functional rehabilitation? We can only confidently address this if we have better knowledge of issues like tissue healing time, tissue strength while healing and the physical needs of injured tissues in general. Widespread mechanical hypersensitivity may well be highly adaptive in the first days after a whiplash, it certainly is not after a few weeks/months or one or two years.

2   Dorsal horn cells enhance their responsivity to nociceptors

Not only do dorsal horn cells come to fire far more volleys of impulses following an injury, they also fire for a long time after the peripheral stimulus stops. Further, if the peripheral stimulus is repeated over and over these cells fire more and more every time—a phenomenon known as wind-up (Dubner & Ruda 1992, Dubner & Basbaum 1994).

In clinical terms if I were to extend my neck back until it hurt, one nociceptor in the tissues stretched might hypothetically fire 5 impulses into the dorsal horn and be relayed on as 7 or 8 impulses by second order neurones—enough to make me feel discomfort and enough to stop me pushing further perhaps. If I actually sprained the neck tissue, in the next few hours the relevant dorsal horn cells would receive a building afferent barrage in parallel with building tissue inflammation, and hence become sensitised. Now, extending the neck back very gently initiates say 15 impulses from the sensitised nociceptor, the dorsal horn cells respond by producing 60 impulses in the first few milliseconds and the volley continues thereafter for seconds if not minutes. Hence, a nasty pain far earlier in range that goes on for some time after. Keep repeating the movement and the volleys build and build with a proportionate exacerbation of the pain.

3   Dorsal horn cells increase their receptive fields

A receptive field is the area of tissue that an individual neurone will respond to when an appropriate stimulus is given. It could also be said to be the area of tissue that a given neurone 'looks after' (Thacker, pers comm). Thus, an individual C fibre, whose terminal branches may be in the skin overlying the neck, may have a receptive field with a diameter of, say 15 mm. Perhaps the best way to understand a receptive field is to imagine looking down the neurone in question and 'viewing' the tissues it supplies. In order to view a single second order dorsal horn cell's receptive field it is necessary to 'look down' many individual afferent neurones, since many afferent neurones terminate on a single dorsal horn cell. There is thus a marked convergence of input onto the one cell. In this way a single dorsal horn cell's receptive field may be quite large, perhaps as much as the skin over the whole of one side of the lower neck. Dorsal horn cells are actually physically connected to many thousands of arriving neurones but many of the connections may be inactive or silent under normal conditions. When conditions change, as in injury, many of the sub-threshold or 'sleeping' connections wake up and become active. Hence, the receptive field increases in size. It is as if we are looking down a viewfinder that in normal conditions reveals a relatively limited view, but in injury conditions the viewfinder is capable of marked expansion to incorporate a great number of tissues not otherwise 'seen'.

The following are examples from the literature that show how vast a single dorsal horn cell's receptive field can be:

- Gillette et al (1993) showed that *individual* second order cells in the dorsal horn of spinal segments L4-5 of the cat have receptive fields in the back/hip/leg that included both skin and deep somatic tissues innervated through both the dorsal (back/hip) and ventral (leg/ventral spine) rami (Gillette et al 1993). Dramatically, many of the cells were found responsive to stimulation of many different somatic tissues including skin, muscles, facet joint capsules, ligaments, dura, intervertebral discs and periosteum. It is important to realise that the CNS is largely incapable of making an accurate map of many of the body's tissues, especially the deeper ones, and that what we perceive in terms of sensation as a result of a noxious stimulus to an individual deep tissue may well be very different to what we would logically expect.
- In association with chronic experimental arthritis in rats, Grubb et al (1992) have demonstrated receptive field expansion of second order neurones normally only associated with the ankle joint, to increase in size to include the thigh, the tail, abdomen and the contralateral leg.
- While the potential size of an individual dorsal horn neurone's receptive field is striking, it is important to realise that this expansion is controlled by powerful ongoing, or 'tonic', descending inhibitory currents from higher brain centres (Schaible & Grubb 1993). These workers have shown massive increases in single neurone receptive field sizes in cats where descending inhibitory currents were prevented by using cold blocks on the spinal cord. The fact that descending inhibitory currents may be influenced via conscious mechanisms adds weight to the potential maladaptive influence that emotional and cognitive states may have on neuronal intracellular relationships.

The messages from all this for whiplash are useful in that they help to explain the often widespread sensitivity and pain that are beyond the traditional dermatome/myotome boundaries set down in textbooks and rather dogmatically adhered to by much of medicine (including physiotherapy.) The reality of the standard textbook is perhaps light-years away from the reality of the patient, and the patient suffers because of this. A reasoned understanding of pain mechanisms validates the reality of ongoing unrelenting and often untreatable chronic post-whiplash pain. It also enables a reasonable speculative leap that links the complexities of reductionist biology with an individual's psychological state. Thus, worsening pain and an often massive spread of tenderness into multiple tissues can be tied in with an interaction of early low level biological 'tissue input' related neural plasticity, as well as with unhelpful emotional and cognitive responses that so often accompany these types of injury. Both 'inputs' ultimately interact to bring about the plasticity changes. The danger of making links like this is that it can easily be translated into a focus on the fault lying with the patient and issues of personal weakness, blame and inability to cope that are so disparaging. Perhaps the skill of the therapist is to provide the correct level of input to enhance the ability to cope—physically and mentally (see Ch.7).

Finally, it would also seem reasonable to presume that every individual, being genetically unique, and having had a unique life experience, will at any given time, have an established sensitivity variability capacity. Thus, as a result of the combined biological effects of inheritance and past and current experience, some individuals may be more predisposed to entering a highly sensitised pain states than others.

4   Dorsal horn cells may become spontaneously active

This concept relates to the pain memory issues discussed in detail below. Importantly, spontaneous activity of a cell, that as far as the brain perception networks are concerned represents huge tissue receptive fields, means that we can perceive pain when nothing untoward is wrong or happening in the tissues. The concept of a pain memory expands this to move beyond the dorsal horn population of cells to incorporate integrated networks of cells that represent the pain but that need no, or very little, peripheral input to activate them.

Pain memory

The proposal is that many, probably all, ongoing pains have a major component of their pain source within the central nervous system in the form of a somatosensory memory or imprint (see Katz & Melzack 1990, Melzack 1991a, Melzack 1991b, Flor et al 1995, Melzack 1995, Basbaum 1996, Hill et al 1996, Melzack 1996). This is **not** the same as suggesting that the pain is non-organic or 'functional'. What it is doing is suggesting a firm physiological basis to ongoing pain, whose roots are in the biology of memory and synaptic efficacy (e.g. Dudai 1989, Rose 1992, Kandel & Hawkins 1993, Meller & Gebhart 1993, Kandel et al 1995, Pockett 1995).

The concept of a somatosensory memory is not new, especially in relationship to the understanding of post amputation phantom limb pain (Katz & Melzack 1990, Hill et al 1996). All that is required is a shift in view to see that any powerful or ongoing nociceptive input into the central nervous system (CNS) may leave an imprint, or central representation of the pain. Three examples follow, the first two from the work of Lenz et al (1994, 1995, 1997):

1   The first example involves a 69-year-old woman who was undergoing an operation to implant a deep brain-stimulating electrode for treatment of chronic leg and perineal pain secondary to arachnoiditis. Her previous history involved nine years of exertional angina that had been treated via angioplasty and had been stabilised. At the time of the operation she reported having not had an angina episode for two months. During the operation specific sites in the thalamus were identified and stimulated using microstimulation techniques and the awake patient reported feeling angina of exactly the same location and quality as normally experienced during an attack. Further, the researchers were able to turn the angina pain on and off using the stimulator. The angina could even be reproduced in the

presence of nitroglycerin, a vasodilatory drug normally self administered by the patient to relieve angina. The authors pointed out that performing the exact same stimulation techniques in the same areas of other patients, but who did not have a history of angina, failed to reproduce any symptoms.

2   In another patient, thalamic electrical stimulation evoked intense pain in the peroneal region. On stimulation at one thalamic site the patient responded that she 'thought she was having a baby'. At a second site the stimulation reproduced pain experienced during sexual intercourse. As in the first example, intense pain experiences had left their mark.

The current general view, only recently challenged, is that electrical stimulation of the brain *does not* produce pain. All that is reported are perceptions like music, pictures, tingling and odours, but rarely the elicitation of pain (Basbaum 1996). It is notable that until recently, all the electrical stimulation studies of the brain had only been done on asymptomatic healthy people. What is now apparent is that previous pains can be reproduced in stimulation studies of subjects who have a significant past pain history. They appear to have a 'pain memory', albeit a subconscious one.

3   This example relates to a female patient (from Hill et al 1996) who had had a below knee amputation because of recurrent infection of a leg wound over a two year period. During this time she had suffered much pain following infection, multiple surgeries and damage to her popliteal nerve. The most distressing pain experienced was evoked by the treatment procedure carried out on the open drainage site on the calf, which had to be cleaned and re-packed twice daily. During this time the patient was very distressed, not only by the pain, but also by the prospect of having to have the wounds dressed regularly. In order to manage the procedure as comfortably as possible she was administered both diazepam and morphine prior to the treatment. For additional pain relief, a mixture of nitrous oxide and oxygen was also self administered during the procedure. When even this did not alleviate her pain the decision was made to amputate.

Subsequent to the amputation she experienced phantom limb pain of two kinds: that which was ongoing, experienced only in the distal parts of the limb, and infrequent episodes which remarkably resembled some of the pre-amputation pains associated with the open drainage site. Triggers to this second pain were recorded by the researchers (Hill et al 1996) and varied from more physical antecedents, like a stump abscess problem, after receiving a new prosthesis, and during a flu virus; to more cognitive/emotional ones, such as following a discussion of her pre-amputation experience with a friend and while watching a television drama which showed an individual with a leg injury being given nitrous oxide and oxygen to relieve pain.

If this analogy with memory holds some truth, then there are several important clinical messages:

- Memories are hard to get rid of (Connolly & Tully 1996) and if ongoing pain has a large memory component it may be beyond any tool/therapy we presently have. Certainly even the most dramatic brain surgeries for ongoing pain states appear to fail repeatedly (Gybels & Sweet 1989) and have been strongly criticised (Wall 1995, Wall 1996). Adequate management in the acute stage that recognises the biopsychosocial, and hence neurobiological impact of injuries like whiplash is probably the best hope at this time (Ch. 7).

- Treatments and approaches which tend to focus the patient on pain and on the alleviation of their pain need serious inspection. There has been a helpful shift in focus in the literature to restoration of physical function in parallel with strategies that positively address the patients' negative or unhelpful thoughts and feelings (Caudill 1995, Harding & Williams 1995, Cohen & Campbell 1996, Gatchel & Turk 1996, Harding 1997) (see also Chs 8, 9, 13, & 14 in this text). The emphasis is to address the dimensions of suffering and the physical dysfunction, and the focus is far less on pain ablation or relief, especially in the ongoing pain situation. It seems likely that the long held focus on the concept of an 'irritable' pain state, and hence on damaged or inflamed tissues (e. g.Brown 1828, Buckwalter 1995, Maitland 1986), has held back the functional restoration of many patients with ongoing pathologically benign pain states (see Ch. 15 and Zusman 1997).

- One very useful message is that hurt does not necessarily equal harm. A far better message for the patient is to view the tissues as being 'deconditioned' rather than damaged.

- Another aspect is the need to integrate diagnosis of pain mechanisms rather than over-focusing on tissue based diagnosis (Gifford 1997, Gifford & Butler 1997, Gifford 1998, and Introductory Essay to this volume). If a tissue is thought to be at 'fault' by the patient (and the therapist) then it is hardly surprising that the patient and therapist are going to fear doing anything that causes more pain—it adds to the problem of hurt equals harm (see also Chs 12 & 15, and Zusman 1997).

- Memories can be put into subconsciousness but dragged back up if given the right cues. Some memories and experiences may, if given great significance, stay continuously in our consciousness, rather like an annoying tune or nagging worry tends to. If this goes on for long enough it becomes very distressing and in some ways could be seen as a mental 'habit' that may be extremely hard to overcome.

- Many clinicians may be inadvertently helping to keep pain in consciousness by over-focusing on the relief of pain, on pain response during treatments and afterwards by actively getting the patient to pay great attention to post-treatment pain behaviour. From a patient's perspective, over focusing on pain, expecting pain, being vigilant for the pain, giving great value to pain, worrying about it, being frustrated by it, or being in fear or anxious about it…may all help to maintain its presence in consciousness *and its neurobiological underpinnings.*

- A nice example from a recent article in the journal *Pain* provides splendid evidence that if patients can be helped to accept their pain better, then they are likely to report 'lower pain intensity, less pain-related anxiety and avoidance, less depression, less physical and psychosocial disability, more daily uptime, and better work status' (McCracken 1998).
- Successful cognitive behavioural approaches to pain management steer patients away from a focus on pain and pain related behaviour and towards positive functional achievements (see Harding & Williams 1995, Klaber-Moffett & Richardson 1995, Harding 1997, Klaber-Moffett & Richardson 1997).

For ongoing pain states, the simple statement 'close the pain gate to consciousness by focusing less on the desire for pain changes and pain relief and more on functional achievements and helpful thinking', may be a useful way for clinicians to understand the shift in emphasis by pain management and cognitive behavioural approaches. Perhaps *de*focusing on pain is a new skill that needs to be taken on—by us primarily and as a consequence by the patient. A wise action approach might be initially to seek to understand the pain, the nature of the disorder, the tissue status, the spread of tenderness/ hyperalgesia, and the level of suffering and disability (requiring a degree of focus on pain during assessment)—but subsequently to defocus on it for management purposes (see Chs 8 & 9). A warning is that merely telling the patient not to focus on their pain is likely to be very unhelpful since it is an incredibly difficult thing to do when pain has firmly established itself or when pain is very severe.

Arguments about giving less emphasis to pain, like this, need to be made with caution. We need to recognise that significant pain in the acute stages of a disorder is a major predictor of chronicity (Dworkin 1997). For example, Reid et al (1997) found that workers who report intense pain (greater than 7 on a 0–10 scale) during the first two weeks of their problem were more likely to be on sick leave two months after injury. The clear message is for early and effective pain control—which may be a combination of pharmacological and non-pharmacological interventions. Relaxation techniques, loan of TENS machines and graded exercises may be more worthwhile than passive therapies alone, since they encourage independence and control by the patient rather than total reliance on visits to a therapist. Fordyce (1992) warns us that adequate pain control must take place in a therapeutic setting that does not overlook many other key issues that affect performance. We should not get carried away by overfocusing on just one thing—the alleviation of pain and single modality treatments. Pain has multifactorial components which requires a multifactorial approach (see Preface).

Patients in pain are often disparaged or accused of malingering if they are seen to be capable of normal movements one moment, yet when asked to perform a test movement another moment demonstrate quite remarkable pain behaviour and verbalise a strong pain complaint. A biological perspective of this apparently 'inconsistent' phenomenon tends to view it as *consistent* with mechanisms that work in favour of survival. Thus, pain inhibiting systems (pain gates to consciousness closed) operate quite powerfully when the organism is occupied and focused on some important task. At times of little threat/safety these inhibitory systems are relaxed, pain returns and consciousness is reflexly 'requested' to spend some time attending to the area containing pain—a very adaptive mechanism for acute injury. Having continuous pain and continuously being forced to adopt tissue protective movement patterns and behaviours is just not consistent with survival. We are designed to heal while we move and function, but alongside this there are powerful tissue-friendly pain mechanisms that dictate the need for rest/altered behaviour whenever it can be achieved safely. If you think about it, modern humans are far safer for far longer than our ancestors ever were. We may have too much time that allows too much focus, and too much conflicting evidence that may promote too much concern.

By focusing patients on their pain or by repeating movements that have been associated with the onset of pain many times before we simply trigger the opening of 'pain gates' to consciousness. It would be far better if the inconsistent behaviours and complaints frequently associated with chronic pain, and usually viewed as evidence of malingering, are wisely viewed as maladaptive since they have gone on for far too long.

The affective and cognitive mechanisms/ dimensions

How our thoughts and feelings not only influence the way in which we perceive pain but also influence the outputs of the brain that powerfully govern recovery control systems and our behaviour has already been discussed (Ch. 2).

There are many problems with misguided day to day clinical application of psychological and psychiatric theory to pain states, in particular when a patient's thoughts and feelings are over-focused on *as the reason for their pain problems* (see Chs 8, 9, 10, 13 & 14). An appropriate stance is that:

1   Low or depressed mood, and other maladaptive alterations in psychological function that are commonly found in ongoing pain states are largely *the result of the pain* state rather than the cause of pain (For a review of psychological factors in chronic pain see Gamsa 1994a & b, Banks & Kerns 1996, Gatchel 1996.) Patients can happily accept this; what they cannot accept, and what most rational investigative science cannot accept either, is that their emotions or their 'mind' are *wholly* causative or blameworthy for their pain state, or maintaining it for reasons of gain (for a good overview see Mendelson 1995, Banks & Kerns 1996; see also Ch. 10).
    On the other hand, it would be wrong to dismiss this notion entirely. It is recognised that ongoing low mood, depression, or psychologically stressed

states cause alterations in sympathetic, neuroendocrine and neuroimmune function, and, that people who are in low spirits adopt unhealthy behaviours that lead to deconditioned tissues (Martin 1997). Thus, unhealthy behaviours, like doing little exercise, increased use of mood enhancing drugs, poor diets, or insufficient sleep, all contribute to a weakened physical and mental capacity to cope. It may well be that an individual's capacity to cope is severely 'physiologically' strained by ongoing psychological and associated behavioural factors, and that stresses that normally would have little impact actually do precipitate problems that are otherwise adequately dealt with. Again, the adverse psychology is not the sole prime cause, but it may well add to the plethora of potential predisposing factors that weakens the natural stability and strength of the tissues and our homeostatic 'coping' mechanisms (e.g. see Gatchel, 1996). Hence,

2 Low or depressed mood and other maladaptive alterations in psychological function powerfully influence the health of the body and hence the perception of pain (see Figures 4.1 and 4.2). In terms of the Mature Organism Model, the CNS/brain senses that its 'body' is weak/vulnerable and that its capacity for recovery may be compromised. It thus allows minor or modest injuries and the subsequent nociceptive/input events, that would otherwise be dealt with quite adequately utilising subconscious physiological processing, or only modest awareness, to be given a highly significant status and hence give rise to a pain state of great significance.

Figures 4.1 and 4.2 emphasise the circular, and forward and back interactions between psychology, behaviour and tissue health that have important implications for management. The starting point can be anywhere on the circle (Fig. 4.2) since one state feeds off the other, and the best approaches are likely to be those that address them all together.

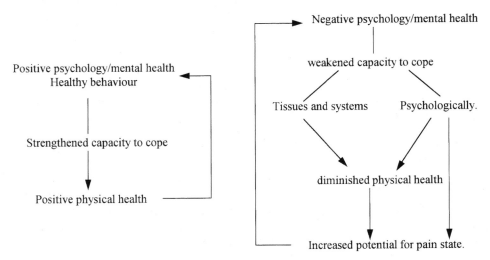

Fig. 4.1 The influence of 'psychological state' on tissue healing

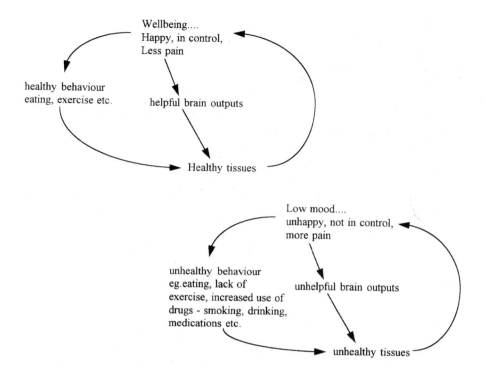

Fig. 4.2 Diagrams to show patients the interactions of positive and negative mood states with behaviour and tissue health.

The 'affective' pain mechanism still stands and is in use today to help clinicians in their evaluation of factors involved in their patients pain states (Gifford & Butler 1997). It is by no means perfect for two reasons:

1 The affective 'pain' mechanism, in isolation, implies that the emotions are a *primary* source of pain. This is obviously dangerous in the evaluation of pain that is 'physical' in character, in history and in nature. However, to most open-minded people, it is reasonable to link pain with emotions like sadness, grief, anger, disgust, extreme anxiety, and even love, for it can 'physically' and 'mentally' hurt when you are deeply emotional (e.g. see Cassell 1991, Morris 1991, Damasio 1995). Problems arise when a psychological component is used and viewed in terms that disparage and suggest hysteria or even dishonesty and malingering.

2 By only using the word 'affective' it unfortunately omits the 'cognitive' dimensions and factors discussed. Thoughts influence feelings and the interaction of thoughts and feelings influence the perception of pain, the health of the body as well as determining behaviour patterns.

It may be a wise and open-minded step to rename this category 'psychological/mental processing mechanisms' and leave it at that.

REFERENCES

Banks S M, Kerns R D 1996 Explaining high rates of depression in chronic pain: A diathesis-stress framework. Psychological Bulletin 119(1):95–110

Buckwalter J A 1995 Activity vs. rest in the treatment of bone, soft tissue and joint injuries. Iowa Orthopaedic Joornal 15(42):29–42

Basbaum A I 1996 Memories of pain. Scientific American: Science and Medicine Nov/Dec: 22–31

Brown T 1828 On irritation of the spinal nerves. Glasgow Medical Journal 1:131–160

Cassell E J 1991 The nature of suffering and the goals of medicine. Oxford University Press, New York

Caudill M A 1995 Managing pain before it manages you. Guilford Press, New York

Cohen M J M, Campbell J N (eds) 1996 Pain treatment centres at a crossroads. A practical and conceptual reappraisal. IASP Press, Seattle

Connolly J B, Tully T 1996 You must remember this. The Sciences May/June: 37–42

Damasio A R 1995 Descartes' error. Picador, London

Dubner R, Basbaum A I 1994 Spinal dorsal horn plasticity following tissue or nerve injury. In: Wall P D, Melzack R (eds) Textbook of pain. 3rd edn. Churchill Livingstone, Edinburgh 225–241

Dubner R, Ruda M A 1992 Activity-dependent neuronal plasticity following tissue injury and inflammation. Trends in Neuroscience 15:96–103

Dudai Y 1989 The neurobiology of memory. Oxford University Press, Oxford

Dworkin R H 1997 Which individuals with acute pain are most likely to develop a chronic pain syndrome? Pain Forum 6:127–156

Flor H, Elbert T, Knecht S et al 1995 Phantom-limb pain as a perceptual correlate of cortical reorganization following arm amputation. Nature 375:482–484

Fordyce W E 1992 Opioids, pain and behavioral outcomes. JAPS J 1:282–284

Gamsa A 1994a The role of psychological factors in chronic pain I. A half century of study. Pain 57:5–15

Gamsa A 1994b The role of psychological factors in chronic pain. II. A critical appraisal. Pain 57:17–29

Gatchel R J 1996 Psychological disorders and chronic pain. Cause and effect relationships. In: Gatchel R J, Turk D C (eds) Psychological approaches to pain management. Guildford Press, New York 33–52

Gatchel R J, Turk D C (eds) 1996 Psychological approaches to pain management: A practitioner's handbook. Guildford Press, New York

Gifford L S 1997 Pain. In: Pitt-Brooke (ed) Rehabilitation of movement: Theoretical bases of clinical practice. Saunders, London 196–232

Gifford L S 1998 Pain, the tissues and the nervous system: A conceptual model. Physiotherapy 84(1):27–36

Gifford L S, Butler D S 1997 The integration of pain sciences into clinical practice. Hand Therapy 10(2):86–95

Gillette R G, Kramis R C, Roberts W J 1993 Characterization of spinal somatosensory neurons having receptive fields in lumbar tissues of cats. Pain 54:85–98

Grubb B D, Stiller R U, Schaible H G 1992 Dynamic changes in the receptive field properties of spinal cord neurons with ankle input in rats with unilateral adjuvant-induced inflammation in the ankle region. Experimental Brain Research 92:441–452

Gybels J M, Sweet W H 1989 Neurosurgical treatment of persistent pain. Karger, Basel

Harding V 1997 Application of the cognitive-behavioural approach. In: Pitt-Brooke J (ed) Rehabilitation of movement: Thoretical bases of clinical practice. W B Saunders, London

Harding V, Williams C d C 1995 Extending physiotherapy skills using a psychological approach: Cognitive-behavioural management of chronic pain. Physiotherpay 81(11):681–688

Hill A, Niven C A, Knussen C 1996 Pain memories in phantom limbs: a case study. Pain 66:381–384

Kandel E R, Hawkins D H 1993 The biological basis of learning and individuality. Mind and brain. W H Freeman, New York 40–53

Kandel E R, Schwartz J H, Jessell T M (eds) 1995 Essentials of neural science and behavior. Prentice Hall, London

Katz J, Melzack R 1990 Pain 'memories' in phantom limbs: review and clinical observations. Pain 43:319–336

Klaber-Moffett J A, Richardson P H 1995 The influence of psychological variables on the development and perception of musculskeletal pain. Phyisotherapy Theory and Practice 11:3–11

Klaber-Moffett J A, Richardson P H 1997 The influence of the physiotherapist-patient relationship on pain and disability. Physiotherapy Theory and Practice 13(1):89–96

Lenz F A, Gracely R H, Hope E J et al 1994 The sensation of angina can be evoked by stimulation of the human thalamus. Pain 59:119–125

Lenz F A, Gracely R H, Romanoski A J et al 1995 Stimulation in the human somatosensory thalamus can reproduce both the affective and sensory dimensions of previously experienced pain. Nature Medicine 1(9):910–913

Lenz F A, Gracely R H, Zirh A T et al 1997 The sensory-limbic model of pain memory. Pain Forum 6(1):22–31

Maitland G D M 1986 Vertebral manipulation. Butterworth, London

Martin P 1997 The sickening mind. Brain, behaviour, immunity and disease. Harper Collins, London

McCracken M L 1998 Learning to live with pain: acceptance of pain predicts adjustment in persons with chronic pain. Pain 74(1):21–27

Meller S T, Gebhart G F 1993 Nitric oxide (NO) and nociceptive processing in the spinal cord. Pain 52:127–136

Melzack R 1991a Central pain syndromes and theories of pain. In: Casey K L (ed) Pain and central nervous system disease: The central pain syndromes. Raven Press, New York 59–64

Melzack R 1991b The gate control theory 25 years later: new perspectives on phantom limb pain. In: Bond M R, Charlton J E, Woolf C J (eds) Proceedings of the VIth World Congress on Pain Elsevier, Amsterdam 9–21

Melzack R 1995 Phantom-limb pain and the brain. In: Bromm B, Desmedt J E (eds) Pain and the brain: From nociception to cognition. Raven Press, New York 73–82

Melzack R 1996 Gate control theory. On the evolution of pain concepts. Pain Forum 5(2):128–138

Mendelson G 1995 Psychological and psychiatric aspects of pain. In: Shacklock M (ed) Moving in on pain. Butterworth-Heinemann, Chatswood 66–89

Morris D B 1991 The culture of pain. University of California Press, Berkeley

Pockett S 1995 Spinal cord synaptic plasticity and chronic pain. Anesthesia and Analgesia 80:173–179

Rose S 1992 The making of memory: From molecules to mind. Bantam Press, London

Reid S, Haugh L D, Hazard R G et al 1997 Occupational low back pain: recovery curves and factors associated with disability. Journal of Occupational Rehabilitation 7:1–14

Schaible H-G, Grubb B D 1993 Afferent and spinal mechanisms of joint pain. Pain 55(1):5–54

Wall P D 1995 Pain in the brain and lower parts of the anatomy. Pain 62(3):389–390

Wall P D 1996 The mechanisms by which tissue damage and pain are related. In: Campbell J N (ed) Pain 1996—An updated review. Refresher course syllabus. IASP Press, Seattle 123–126

Woolf C J 1994 The dorsal horn: state-dependent sensory processing and the generation of pain. In: Wall P D, Melzack R (eds) Textbook of pain. 3rd edn. Churchill Livingstone, Edinburgh 101–112

Woolf C J, Doubell T P 1994 The pathophysiology of chronic pain—increased sensitivity to low threshold Ab-fibre inputs. Current Opinion in Neurobiology 4:525–534

Zusman M 1997 Instigators of activity intolerance. Manual Therapy 2(2):75–86

5

Output mechanisms

LOUIS GIFFORD

Introduction

Output mechanisms can be divided into: somatic motor, autonomic, neuroendocrine, neuroimmune, and descending pain control systems. There may well be others to consider.

Output activity is governed by multiple level CNS/brain processing of inputs from the environment, inputs sampled from the body, inputs derived from previous experiences (memory), and current conscious appraisal of the situation (see Ch. 2). Thus all physiological levels, including the physiological processing that goes on concerned with activities of the mind, are involved in governing CNS/brain output. It is well established that the way we think and feel alters our behaviour and our muscle tone, changes autonomic and neuroendocrine activity, and alters the immune system's responsivity. Activity in all these systems may influence the level of pain perceived and the degree of function obtained directly or indirectly.

Somatic motor

Our response to threat is to change our behaviour. Pain is frequently a component of physical threat and by its very nature demands a change in behaviour. Behaviour is a motor response; what we do when we are in pain, the way we move, the way we talk, the postures we adopt, the quality and range of movements we display when examined, the grunts and groans made, are all motor responses that convey protection to the part concerned and convey information to others. Humans as social animals have evolved behavioural patterns that convey powerful messages to others to help us (or to avoid us!). Fundamentally, help means talking and touching—input via mind and input via body; but how much talking and touching and the way in which it is done are hugely variable. In this respect, every individual's requirements are different and are ultimately an expression of the culture and beliefs and knowledge of a given individual.

At a more 'physiological' level, adaptive motor responses are governed by reflex activities—hence protective reflexes, increased or decreased tone (Mense 1997) of muscles that surround or are capable of influencing the hurting part, and alterations in patterns of movement. But, again, tonal changes and alterations in reflex postures and movement patterns can be overcome or altered once the mind intervenes. 'If we pick up a hot cup of tea in an expensive cup we are not likely simply to drop the cup, but jerkily put it back on the table, and *then* shake our hand (Melzack & Casey 1968).'

Patients with chronic whiplash related pain not uncommonly have markedly restricted and jerky movement patterns when performing active movements in examination and focusing on them. In some situations where it is possible to alleviate patients' fear of damage and instruct regarding the positive nature of normal smooth movement, it is often the case that given simple help and guidance better range and better quality of movement can quickly be achieved (see Chs 7, 8, 9, 13 & 14).

Prolonged maladaptive or inappropriate muscle activity should be considered as a mechanism that can add to the discomfort of the tissues via increased nociceptive drive (Ohrbach & McCall 1996). The following is an interesting example of the indirect influences that there can be on the behaviour of pain. Herta Flor and colleagues (Flor et al 1991, Flor et al 1992, Birbaumer et al 1995), using electromyographic (EMG) measures, have shown that subgroups of chronic pain patients show markedly increased muscular activity and tension when they are in pain *and* when they are exposed to personally relevant stressful situations. The increase in muscular response was found to be localised to the site of pain and maintained for a prolonged period when compared to healthy controls. They also noted that patients with pain exhibit a reduced capacity to consciously perceive and voluntarily regulate their levels of muscular tension.

In any pain state there may be an increased muscle response which may well add to the barrage of afferent impulses that help maintain the pain state, the often multiple pain mechanisms responsible, and the levels of perceived pain (see Ohrbach & McCall 1996, Flor & Turk 1996 for an excellent critical overview of current theories).

Clinicians are advised to review a recent report by Mense (Mense 1997) who challenges the age old 'vicious circle' notion that pain leads to muscle spasm and hence more pain. If the primary source of nociception and pain is from a muscle the evidence suggests that its EMG activity is actually decreased, not increased. Thus...

> The pain-spasm-pain concept is not substantiated by critical analysis. Strong arguments against this concept are that very commonly the painful muscle (even though it may feel tense) shows no EMG activity and that in animal experiments inhibition of the motor neurons supplying the painful muscle is a much more common finding than excitation (Mense 1997).

This makes blatant adaptive sense—if you injure a muscle, going into spasm is likely to make matters much worse; far better to turn the muscle off, not on. Mense (1997) goes on to argue that increased tone will occur only if there is a strong descending fascilitatory command.

It is important not to take from this the message that increased tone does not occur; the discussion only relates to primary injury to muscle. Clearly in chronic pain states, or in acute nocicepiton that has its origins in joint injury, the response mustered may be quite different. This has already been noted in chronic pain patients from the discussion of the work by Flor and colleagues above.

According to Mense (1997) joint injury may well be accompanied by *increased* muscle tone and/or heightened reflex sensitivity. Preventing joint movement, slowing it down or even abruptly stopping it as soon as it occurs may be a very protective reaction for freshly injured joint tissues. Problems arise when this process out-lasts its biological usefulness. The role of cognitively derived descending fascilitatory/inhibitory commands links the acute well ingrained 'reflex' responses that prevents movement of the injured part to the much longer termed maladaptive maintenance of the reflex. For example if an individual is under the impression that rest is vital and that any pain is a signal to stop moving then a degree of consciously derived facilitation of reflexes concerned with the protective maintenance of 'no movement' will be kept up. Perhaps the long term result is that the tonal changes and inhibitory reactions to movement become subconsciously ingrained as a form of 'habit' or 'learned reflex'. Recall that Flor et al (1991, 1992) noted that some patients with chronic pain exhibit a reduced capacity to consciously perceive and voluntarily regulate their levels of muscular tension. From a chronic pain management perspective this is all strongly persuasive for the inclusion of relaxation techniques and the gradual and progressive relearning of relaxed and comfortable movement patterns and posturing. New 'good' habits need to be laid down on top of biologically well ingrained 'bad' ones. In the language of conditioning, the unhelpful reflex response needs to be 'extinguished'.

From the acute perspective rehabilitation requires progressive restoration of function in parallel with relevant information related to the best conditions for adequate healing.

Autonomic

In terms of pain and the broad topic of stress biology, the major focus of attention and investigation as far as the autonomic nervous system is concerned, has been on the sympathetic system. Little attention has been given to the role of the parasympathetic system in injury, pain states, and repair and healing mechanisms. When science starts to turn its attention towards understanding the mechanisms of natural healing, the parasympathetic system should receive more attention.

The activity of the sympathetic nervous system has been singled out as a primary factor in many severe and intractable pain states for quite some time (for a good current overview see Janig & Stanton-Hicks 1996).

There are two major points of discussion:

First, that the sympathetic nervous system is likely to be activated/influenced more intensely than would be normal in *all* pain states. This does not mean that it necessarily has a direct role to play in producing or enhancing the immediate perception of pain.

Second, that the sympathetic nervous system's efferent (secretory) activity, in a small but significant patient group, can be a significant mechanism that is responsible for enhancing and maintaining pain (for an overview of this mechanism see Campbell 1996, Gifford 1997).

1   It is the opinion here that the sympathetic system has a role to play in all pain states that result in suffering, simply because pain is unpleasant, is biologically interpreted as a threat to the organism, and hence will always activate this system to a greater or lesser degree. Activation of the sympathetic nervous system is strongly linked to threatening events that precipitate a feeling of anxiety and stress and that alter mood states (Chrousos & Gold 1992, Sapolsky 1994, Chrousos et al 1995). The most notable role of the SNS is in physiologically preparing the organism for the more or less instinctive reactions of freeze, fight or flight that are so important to survival. If you really think about it this is a very potent example of a psychosomatic reaction—the largely cognitive assessment by the CNS/brain (psycho) of the danger, followed by the appropriate physiological (somatic) adjustments in preparation for survival action/inaction (Weiner 1991).

Spare a thought for the sympathetic nervous system activity of the whiplash patient with ongoing pain who is frequently in low mood and is often subjected to unpleasant experiences—including physiotherapy, physical examinations and techniques! Pressing thumbs into hypersensitive tissues, performing techniques that produce further pain, putting patients in odd and often threatening postures and positions during techniques and testing, especially when novel and done with little explanation or care and skill, are surely powerful sympathetic nervous system activators. Therapists are urged to consider frequently that the CNS/brain may well be processing a very potent 'threat' message resulting in powerful physiological (and behavioural) 'threat' blunting responses, that includes sympathetic activation. A good example is a whiplash patient positioned for the first time in long-sit slump position, with their head in flexion, and their trunk in flexion plus side flexion plus rotation with the therapist eagerly digging their thumbs into a sore and stiff 5th or 6th rib angle. It might be fine for a patient who has come expecting to be tied in knots and who has been given an adequate explanation of the procedure, but for many people the position and technique are uncomfortable and unpleasant, potentially worrying and of great cause for alarm—even with a reasonable explanation. Patients often look as if they understand and believe in what you are doing, but underneath they may be very uncertain. It is important that as therapists we should always consider ourselves as representing a potential biological threat to any given patient. It is not uncommon for patients to demonstrate abnormal sweating, skin flushing and to report nausea when undergoing tests in examination. Therapists are urged to consider far more than the mechanical features of the sympathetic system and to avoid unreasonable labeling of a 'sympathetic' component to a problem based on responses such as those mentioned. A male physiotherapist performing a SLR or upper limb tension test on a semi-undressed, young, shy, female patient suffering from unexplained and unrelenting post whiplash symptoms, regardless of the discomfort produced, may be a very unpleasant experience that adds to the sympathetic activity already generated by the pain and the anxiety of the first consultation.

Ongoing SNS overactivity (or altered activity—it may become dulled/dysregulated in its response), as the result of the ongoing negative consequences of pain, may well have further unhelpful consequences for the immune and neuroendocrine systems and hence may have far reaching effects on such things as general health, healing responses and the metabolism and circulation of the tissues of the body. The speculative assumption is that ongoing altered sympathetic activity may have far-reaching detrimental and accumulative consequences on the health of the individual and hence have some influence, all be it relatively *indirect*, on the level of pain and the resultant impairment/dysfunction.

2   Although the SNS may be considered to be involved in all pain states, it is only in a few where symptoms are distinctly linked to its *direct* activity.
The concepts of sympathetically maintained pain (SMP) and reflex sympathetic dystrophy (RSD) have come under much scrutiny and criticism of late (see Stanton-Hicks et al 1995, Campbell 1996, Haddox 1996, Janig & Stanton-Hicks 1996). The overwhelming message is that presentations that appear to have much in common and which are lumped together for the sake of clinical utility, often have multiple and quite different underlying mechanisms.

As far as the role of the SNS is concerned in any pain state, the determining factor as to its relevance is the relief of pain (or a single aspect of the pain) by a local anaesthetic block of the sympathetic ganglia that serve the painful area. Since there is no definitive way to diagnose SMP on the basis of signs and symptoms or clinical history, diagnostic blocking of relevant sympathetic nerves, or the blocking of receptors on nociceptors that are responsive to noradrenaline secreted by sympathetic nerve terminals in the painful area, are the only tools available (see Campbell 1996). The fact that many pain states, that are commonly labeled as being SMP or RSD in the clinic, show no response to sympathetic blocking/receptor blocking, has lead to the introduction of the term 'sympathetically independent pain' or SIP (Campbell et al 1993).

Just because a patient's affected limb may be either warmer or substantially cooler, show more profound sweating response, or show atrophic changes *does not* denote that a patient has a direct sympathetic mechanism to the pain state.

One finding of significance to the non-invasive testing and diagnosis of the sympathetic mechanism is that all patients with SMP, proven by analgesic block, demonstrate cooling hyperalgesia, whereas only 50% of patients with SIP demonstrate this phenomena. In the laboratory, sensitivity to cooling is tested by placing a drop of acetone on the painful area (see Campbell et al 1993). The only clear clinical assumption that can be made is that if patients indicates that cooling the painful area has little impact on their pain they are unlikely to have a sympathetic mechanism to their pain! However, Campbell (1996) suggests that the following two factors are the *only* strong indicators of suspicion of a sympathetic mechanism: the painful area has to be in the extremity or face, and there must be cooling hyperalgesia. He specifically emphasises that the more classic features: oedema, atrophic changes, temperature changes, abnormal sweating, or other dystrophic changes, are *not* included.

A fundamental aspect believed to be at the heart of understanding the role of the SNS in pain is that there is no evidence of anything being actually wrong with the sympathetic system. The crux of the matter is that SNS *normal* secretions of noradrenaline/adrenaline can activate sensitised nociceptors or sensitised damaged neurones and cell bodies of peripheral nerves and hence cause pain. The latest research findings suggest that the abnormality lies in the cell walls of nociceptors and damaged neurones which have been shown to be capable of acquiring enhanced noradrenaline sensitivity in animal models (e.g. see Janig & Stanton-Hicks 1996). The key issue is that in order for a neurone to be sensitive to noradrenaline/adrenaline there have to be specific receptors for these chemicals in the cell wall. These receptors are called adrenoreceptors.

A wise stance to adopt is to accept the fundamental role of the SNS in all pain states and that, to a greater or lesser degree, its secretions may be involved in the production and maintenance of nociception/pain from within the tissues where the pain is felt and which are mechanically hypersensitive. No two pain syndromes are the same, have the same mechanism participation and the same participation from one moment to the next. What needs to be accepted, especially in difficult syndromes like the ongoing pain states following whiplash, is that sympathetic activity is most easily modified by the thoughts and feelings an individual is having regarding their current situation and that the more novel and threatening an environment or thing is perceived to be, the more potent is the ensuing SNS response.

Neuroendocrine

The sympathetic nervous system can be seen as a strong effector system that is subservient to the whims and needs of higher mental processing (this ultimately means bodily and genetic survival). If the needs of survival are to run away, the appropriate sympathetic activity ensures that the appropriate tissues have the capacity to perform. The neuroendocrine system has a similar close relationship with the mind/consciousness, yet unlike the very rapidly acting SNS, its responses, since it acts on its target organs via the circulation, are naturally far slower and less focused.

The relationship between mental and physical stress and alterations in the activity of the hypothalamus-pituitary-adrenal (HPA) 'axis' has been the focus of a great deal of research since Hans Selye pioneered the scientific scrutiny of the 'stress response' in the 1930s (Selye 1978, Sapolsky 1994). When something stressful happens, or you think a stressful thought, the hypothalamus secretes corticotrophin releasing factor which in turn causes the release of adrenocorticotrophic hormone (ACTH) from the pituitary into the blood. Within a few minutes ACTH arrives at the adrenal cortex and triggers the release of the steroid hormone glucocorticoid.

A major role of glucocorticoid is to work in parallel with the sympathetic system to provide the best conditions for an adequate response to threat. It thus helps provide suitable levels of energy for the activities desired and required as well as substantially inhibiting any processes that may be unnecessarily utilising vital energy stores. Hence such things as the inhibition of glucose uptake from the blood, the suppression of growth and repair processes, and the inhibition of inflammation and of the immune system's activities. Efficient energy mobilisation and provision 'at all costs' is its strong characteristic, hence mobilisation of glucose from fat stores and the catabolic break down of muscle commonly associated with prolonged exposure to glucocorticoids.

The adaptive nature of this classic stress response is apparent when considering conditions, cultures and environments where the major stressors or threats are physical in nature and are quickly dealt with. However, the stresses of modern cultures and societies are far removed from those of our ancestral environment in that most are ongoing, are not physically life threatening and are far harder to adequately deal with. Ongoing pain and the ongoing mental and physical 'stress' which can accompany it is an example of a situation that has the potential to cause an ongoing stress response. Ongoing stress may ultimately precipitate maladaptive changes in neuroendocrine responsiveness. For example, some whiplash patients are classified as demonstrating post-traumatic-stress disorder (see Ch. 10) and this condition is being shown to demonstrate subtle but persistent alterations in HPA axis responsiveness (Yehuda 1997).

The important point is that maladaptive neuroendocrine responsivity may well have detrimental effects on tissue health and its recovery mechanisms, and hence may have an indirect influence on nociceptor activity and pain perception.

Neuroimmune

The close links of the immune system to the brain, the SNS and neuroendocrine system have already been discussed. Traditionally immune system activities are tied to identifying antigens, making antibodies and fighting pathogens. However, a close look at the processes of inflammation and repair, the sensitisation of nociceptors, and the relaying of information from damaged areas to response centres like the liver and brain, reveal a much more complicated system than has previously been thought. Not only is the immune system known to act at the tissue physiological level but it is also now known to have quite powerful influences on our mood states, on our behaviour patterns and even our sensitivity to pain (Watkins 1994, Watkins et al 1995, Pennisi 1997). In turn, our mood states, our mental well-being, or simply our 'stress' levels, can influence the immune system's responsiveness and reactivity (see Ader et al 1991, Stein & Miller 1993, Sternberg & Licinio 1995, Stratakis & Chrousis 1995, Martin 1997). The interplay between the brain, the mind and the immune system is, not surprisingly, very complex. The main mediators of control are via the neuroendocrine HPA system and the sympathetic nervous system which innervates immune organs and plays a part in regulating inflammatory reactions throughout the body (Sternberg & Gold 1997). Links between the immune system and the CNS/brain are mediated via the cytokine messenger system (see Ch. 3).

Many patients with ongoing pain states have high levels of distress, depressed mood and depressive symptoms (e.g. see Banks & Kerns 1996). The recognition that whiplash/road traffic accident victims can go on to suffer post-traumatic stress disorder (PTSD) is strengthening (see Ch. 10), and the sciences of psychoneuroimmunology and psychoneuroendocrinology are firmly linking the influences of the mind and body to each other. Statements like: 'The popular belief that stress exacerbates inflammatory illness and that relaxation or removal of stress ameliorates it may indeed have a basis in fact' (Sternberg & Gold 1997), are helping the merger and better balancing of physical and psychological approaches to the complex problems that surround ongoing illnesses and pain complaints like those following whiplash trauma. The neuroimmune system is yet another example of an output mechanism that ultimately feeds back to the tissues and hence influences their health status, and the potential for ongoing nociceptor activity.

Descending pain control systems

In the psychology and stress literature the term 'stress induced analgesia' is commonly used (e.g. Gray 1987). It recognises that injury in the presence of acute threat may not produce any feeling of pain at the time, as pain would merely hinder any physical activity needed to escape the threat (McCubbin 1993, Blank 1994, Fields & Basbaum 1994).

The important point is that the CNS/brain has a system that permits a 'choice'—between allowing nociceptor messages to produce the sensation of pain, or preventing them from doing so (Fields & Basbaum 1989, 1994). In the standard linear way of thinking about nociceptive messages ascending to the higher centres this is merely seen as a system that can prevent or promote the stream of nociceptive information and hence prevent or promote the perception of pain. However, taken from the viewpoint of the Mature Organism Model the CNS/brain can be seen to be acting in the first instance as a receiver of information—via nociceptor flow from the tissues, but also from inputs whose origins stem from the environment; and secondly, as a processor that says 'OK nociceptive message = damage, but big life threat here—dampen flow of nociceptor traffic, ignore pain, activate behavioural strategies that are likely to result in survival...' While the gating out of pain can be scientifically reduced to subconscious processing involving hypothalamus and brain stem inhibitory circuitry, the bigger picture involves conscious scrutinising, the influence of emotions and subsequent output to these centres too. One message is that the reflex activity of the pain control systems are strongly influenced by more rostral processing. A problem for those who are in pain is that access to it is not at our beck and call.

A further point is that how much we perceive our body is extremely variable. It is well known that focusing on some activities or tasks cuts out awareness of many bodily sensations. For example when under pressure at work we may well continue with a particular task for quite a long time being unaware that our bladder is full, yet as soon as the work pressure is removed the feeling of urgency becomes all to apparent! To a large extent what we perceive is influenced by the value we put on an experience or sensation. Consider the difference between the way in which we perceive or focus on a pain in the back of the head following a drinking binge compared to one which suddenly appears for no apparent reason and gets worse and worse. Or following a whiplash accident, when several weeks later pain starts to appear in the arm, head and thorax for no apparent reason. Pain that is not diagnosed convincingly or is not properly validated by medicine is often the source of much concern and anxiety; sometimes it precipitates anger. Thus, our focus of attention and the value we give to a sensation or experience may help to enhance its significance and hence its neurobiological imprint within our nervous system. As already discussed, therapists must be alert to the dangers of continually focusing on pain and its behaviour in the clinical setting—we could well be inadvertently promoting its retention (Byl & Melnick 1997).

Conclusions

The aim of Chapters 2–5 has been to introduce the reader to the science of pain mechanisms and the broader biological and clinical repercussions in terms of the whole organism. The striking feature of the phenomenon of pain is that, on the one hand, it is remarkably complex yet, on the other, it is only a small part of the full picture relative to bodily insult like whiplash.

It can be argued that ongoing whiplash pain has to be more than a tissue lesion like a sore or arthritic zygapophysial joint or an annular tear in a disc (see Ch. 1). An acceptance of the complex biology of pain, and the poor healing potential of nearly all the tissues injured requires a modest shift in therapeutic emphasis from 'fix' and 'relieve' to best possible physical and mental functional recovery. This incorporates carefully graded return of physical health within a realistic time-frame of recovery, the recognition of cognitive and affective influences on pain and behaviour, and their powerful physiological influence on the many output pathways of the brain. Changing the way individuals see their problem, what they believe, what they feel and how they move does more than alter their perception of the pain and their illness behaviour. If current literature is to be believed, positive or 'helpful' psychological states look as if they have healthy biological effects at many physiological levels too.

The incorporation of pain mechanism analysis into physiotherapy diagnostic protocols and clinical reasoning is becoming ever more important (Gifford & Butler 1997, see also Introductory Essay). Hopefully these chapters have presented material that will encourage a broader and more helpful analysis of the pain our patients are suffering.

REFERENCES

Ader R, Felten D L, Cohen N (eds) 1991 Psychoneuroimmunology. 2nd edn. Academic Press, San Diego

Banks S M, Kerns R D 1996 Explaining high rates of depression in chronic pain: A diathesis-stress framework. Psychological Bulletin 119(1):95–110

Birbaumer N, Flor H, Lutzenberger W et al 1995 The corticalization of chronic pain. In: Bromm B, Desmedt J E (eds) Pain and the brain: From nociception to cognition. Raven Press, New York 331–343

Blank J W 1994 Pain in men wounded in battle: Beecher revisited. IASP Newsletter Jan/Feb: 2–4

Byl N N, Melnick M 1997 The neural consequences of repetition. Clinical implications of a learning hypothesis. Journal of Hand Therapy 10(2):160–174

Campbell J N 1996 Complex regional pain syndrome and the sympathetic nervous system. In: Campbell J N (ed) Pain 1996—An updated review. Refresher course syllabus. IASP Press, Seattle 89–96

Campbell J N, Raja S N, Meyer R A 1993 Pain and the sympathetic nervous system: connecting the loop. In: Vecchiet L, Albe-Fessard D, Lindblom U et al (eds) New trends in referred pain and hyperalgesia. Elsevier, Amsterdam 99–108

Chrousos G P, Gold P W 1992 The concepts of stress and stress system disorders. Overview of physical and behavioral homeostasis [published erratum appears in JAMA 1992 Jul 8;268(2):200]. Journal of the American Medical Association 267(9):1244–52

Chrousos G P, McCarty R, Pacak K et al (eds) 1995 Stress. Basic mechanisms and clinical implications. Annals of the New York Academy of Sciences vol 771: Stress, basic mechanisms and clinical implications. The New York Academy of Sciences, New York

Fields H L, Basbaum A I 1989 Endogenous pain control mechanisms. In: Wall P D, Melzack R (eds) Textbook of pain. 2nd edn. Churchill Livingstone, Edinburgh 206–217

Fields H L, Basbaum A I 1994 Central nervous system mechanisms of pain modulation. In: Wall P D, Melzack R (eds) Textbook of pain. 3rd edn. Churchill Livingstone, Edinburgh 243–257

Flor H, Birbaumer N, Schulte W et al 1991 Stress-related EMG responses in patients with chronic temporomandibular pain. Pain 46:145–152

Flor H, Schugens M M, Birbaumer N 1992 Discrimination of muscle tension in chronic pain patients and healthy controls. Biofeedback and Self Regulation 17:165–177

Flor H, Turk D C 1996 Integrating central and peripheral mechanisms in chronic muscular pain. An initial step on a long road. Pain Forum 5(1):74–76

Gifford L S 1997 Pain. In: Pitt-Brooke (ed) Rehabilitation of movement: Theoretical bases of clinical practice. Saunders, London 196–232

Gifford L S, Butler D S 1997 The integration of pain sciences into clinical practice. Hand Therapy 10(2):86–95

Gray J A 1987 The psychology of fear and stress. Cambridge University Press, Cambridge

Haddox J D 1996 A call for clarity. In: Campbell J N (ed) Pain 1996—An updated review. Refresher course syllabus. IASP Press, Seattle 97–99

Janig W, Stanton-Hicks M 1996 Reflex sympathetic dystrophy: A reappraisal. IASP Press, Seattle

Martin P 1997 The sickening mind. Brain, behaviour, immunity and disease. Harper Collins, London

McCubbin J A 1993 Stress and endogenous opioids: Behavioral and circulatory interactions. Biological Psychology 35:91–122

Melzack R, Casey K L 1968 Sensory, motivational, and central control determinants of pain: A new conceptual model. In: Kenshalo D (ed) The skin senses. C C Thomas, Springfield 423–443

Mense S 1997 Pathophysiologic basis of muscle pain syndromes. An update. Physical Medicine and Rehabilitation. Clinics of North America 8(1):23–53

Ohrbach R, McCall W D 1996 The stress-hyperactivity pain theory of myogenic pain. Proposal for a revised theory. Pain Forum 5(1):51–66

Pennisi E 1997 Tracing molecules that make the brain-body connection. Science 275:930–931

Sapolsky R M 1994 Why Zebras don't get ulcers. A guide to stress, stress-related diseases, and coping. Freeman, New York

Selye H 1978 The stress of life. McGraw Hill, New York

Stanton-Hicks M, Janig W, Hassenbusch S et al 1995 Reflex sympathetic dystrophy: changing concepts and taxonomy. Pain 63:27–133

Stein M, Miller A H 1993 Stress, the immune system, and health and illness. In: Goldberger L, Breznitz S (eds) Handbook of stress. Free Press, New York 127–141

Sternberg E M, Gold P W 1997 The mind-body interaction in disease. Scientific American Special Issue: Mysteries of the Mind June: 8–15

Sternberg E M, Licinio J 1995 Overview of neuroimmune stress interactions. Implications for susceptibility to inflammatory disease. In: Chrousos G P, McCarty R, Pacak Ket al (eds) Annals of the New York Academy of Sciences vol 771: Stress, basic mechanisms and clinical implications. The New York Academy of Scinces, New York 364–371

Stratakis C A, Chrousis G P 1995 Neuroendocrinology and pathophysiology of the stress system. In: Chrousos G P, McCarty R, Pacak Ket al (eds) Annals of the New York Academy of Sciences vol 771: Stress, basic mechanisms and clinical implications. The New York Academy of Scinces, New York 1–18

Watkins A D 1994 Hierarchical cortical control of neuroimmunomodulatory pathways. Neuropathology and Applied Neurobiology 20:423–431

Watkins L R, Maier S F, Goehler L E 1995 Immune activation: the role of pro-inflammatory cytokines in inflammation, illness responses and pathological pain states. Pain 63:289–302

Weiner H 1991 Behavioural biology of stress and psychosomatic medicine. In: Brown M R, Koob G F, Rivier C (eds) Stress. Neurobiology and neuroendocrinology. Marcel Dekker, New York 23–51

Yehuda R 1997 Sensitization of the hypothalamic-pituitary-adrenal axis in posttraumatic stress disorder. In: Yehuda R, McFarlane A C (eds) Psychobiology of postraumatic stress disorder. The New York Academy of Sciences, New York 57–75

6

Physiotherapy management of whiplash injuries: a review

MICHAEL A THACKER

Introduction

Many accounts of the treatment of Whiplash Associated Disorder (WAD) propose a management programme that involves rest, soft collar, and non-specific physiotherapy. Although it may be inappropriate to extrapolate from one area of the spine to another, it appears that WADs parallel the findings regarding chronicity found in the lumbar spine. One such finding is that the efficacy of traditional physiotherapy is still very much unproven. This chapter is a review of the recent literature relevant to the treatment and management WAD. Some personal comments have been included.

The Quebec Task Force (QTF) (Spitzer et al 1995) reviewed available literature on the treatments employed by physical therapists in the management of the WAD patient. The review makes fascinating reading and the reader is urged to consult this report for more detail. Box 1 summarises the treatments they reviewed and the key indicates the efficacy and validity of each modality.

It is striking that in the QTF (Spitzer et al 1995) report only two commonly employed physiotherapy modalities have been shown to have any effect—exercise and mobilisation techniques. One must also recognise that the effects demonstrated for these modalities are short term only.

Influenced by the publication of the QTF, Maxwell (1996) conducted an evaluation of physiotherapy management of WAD in Great Britain. She sent questionnaires to 20 randomly selected departments. Eighteen departments responded and a total of 72 questionnaires provided the actual data reported. Senior 1 physiotherapists formed 43% of the total, whilst 28% were Senior 2 physiotherapists. The remainder were either managers with some clinical input or junior physiotherapists.

Box 1 The treatment modalities cited by the QTF (Spitzer 1995)—with an indication of their efficacy

---

Treatment Modalities cited in the Quebec Task Force Report

Collars -ve
Rest -ve
Cervical pillows *
Manipulation ?
Mobilisation +ve ?
Exercise +ve
Traction *
Postural alignment *
Spray and stretch *
TENS *
PEME ?
Electrical stimulation *
U/S *
Heat (SWD, laser, ice) ?
Surgery *
Intra articular injections (anaesthetic & steroid) ?
Sterile water injections ?
NSAID /analgesics +ve
Psychosocial interventions *
Acupuncture *

*   denotes that the report found no acceptable studies using/indicating this modality in the treatment of whiplash associated disorders.

?   indicates a question over methodology.

A-ve   indicates that there have been negative long term effects reported for these modalities.

A+ve is not an indicator of any long term benefit; rather, all of the above modalities with A+ve have been shown only to have a short term effect.

Maxwell (1996) looked at referral patterns, treatment approaches, and how patients were classified (many aspects will be discussed in the following account.) Her conclusions make interesting reading.

Maxwell maintains that the main purpose of the clinical examination is 'to localise accurately the anatomical site which is involved'. In the light of what much of pain science is saying, this may be a difficult if not an impossible task. The statement is also an example of the domination of the tissue specific way of thinking we have all been schooled in (see Introductory Essay, Chs 1-5 and 15).

Maxwell (1996) comments that physiotherapists draw on a large range of techniques and interventions and puts this as a positive aspect of our management approach. Laudably, she highlights the controversy surrounding the efficacy of these techniques.

Physiotherapy modalities

Collars

Nearly all non-specific regimens for the management of whiplash patients endorse the use of soft cervical collars with the aim of immobilising the cervical spine and making the patient more comfortable (they often form the first part of a management triad including collars, rest and 'physiotherapy'). There is much evidence that soft collars are incapable of immobilising the neck (Colachis et al 1973, Fisher et al 1977, Johnson et al 1977) and their overall utility has been strongly questioned (Spitzer et al 1995).

The QTF (Spitzer et al 1995) found no studies that looked directly at collar effectiveness or efficacy in WAD patients. Most studies use collars (seldom alone) as controls for the comparison of more active therapies. In nearly all cases they have been shown to *delay* recovery in terms of pain rating (Mealy et al 1986, Mckinney 1989, Mckinney et al 1989, Borchgrevnik et al 1998). The QTF (Spitzer et al 1995) conclude that collars do not 'restrict the range of motion of the cervical spine. Collars may promote inactivity, which can delay recovery in patients with WAD.'

Twomey and Taylor (1993) have suggested that immobilisation for a few days post injury should help to reduce effusion and haemorrhage, and therefore support their limited use.

The wearing of a collar can be viewed as a form of illness behaviour in that it helps warn others to approach with care, it demonstrates that something is wrong, and it attracts potentially useful attention and sympathy. In the short term this may be viewed as an adaptive form of behaviour and therefore 'normal'. However, if the patient retains the collar for too long, its use can be viewed as maladaptive since it no longer serves any long-term healthy purpose.

Rest

While not a specific 'modality', rest is often the second recommendation in the standard management triad. The QTF (Spitzer et al 1995) found no studies looking at the effectiveness of rest alone. Based on convincing messages from the broader literature they recommend that prolonged periods of rest are detrimental to recovery from WAD. For example, it has been shown that bed rest in the management of low back pain should be avoided if at all possible and, where this is not possible, rest should not exceed 4 days (Waddell et al 1996).

The concept of rest as being imperative to allow tissue healing has little scientific basis; in fact early movement is essential following injury to promote an adequate repair process (e.g. Akeson et al 1987, and Ch. 3). This is supported by McKinney et al (1989) who found that an assessment and an appropriate exercise programme given by a physiotherapist was as effective as out-patient physiotherapy. Significantly, they found that recovery is delayed in the region of one month in patients advised to rest when compared to those who were encouraged to mobilise early. One comment here is that being guided by pain irritability concepts and focusing the patient on the behaviour of their pain in order to assess the efficacy of passive therapy, may be a significant factor holding back an adequate and regular exercise programme. Skilled initial screening for significant 'red flags' is obviously an essential prerequisite that requires a modest focus on pain behaviour.

A final point is that we must avoid singling-out and totally condemning rest; it is an instinctive behaviour in the face of pain, and it does ease discomfort. Short but regular rest periods as part of an overall management strategy that includes progressive restoration of normal activities and normal movements is a more helpful and realistic perspective (see Ch. 7).

Passive activation*

Manipulation

Manipulation is often reported as being contraindicated in the early stages of whiplash. It is probably for this reason that no studies have looked at its effects in this phase. However, the QTF (Spitzer et al 1995) cited one study that looked at the effects of manipulation in the later stages of whiplash on patients who had pain and a cervical movement discrepancy of 10° or more. The findings showed that any improvements made following manipulation lasted for less than 5 minutes! Barnsley et al (1994) also reported that there were no data to support the use of manipulation.

Woodward et al (1996) demonstrated that chiropractic adjustments of the neck together with PNF and ice in chronic WAD patients was beneficial in 26 out of 29 patients (93%). This trial was published after the QTF report but would have failed their criteria for inclusion as it was not controlled and the patients were not randomly assigned. The authors also fail to comment on anything but the manipulation component of the treatment given. This overlooks the potential for the other modalities to have been the 'active' component. They omit to include how the patients were asked to consent to the study. For instance, could there have been some aspect of suggestion that would have biased their outcomes?

Maxwell (1996) identified that Grade V manipulations were the least performed manual therapy techniques in her study of physiotherapy clinical practice in Great Britain. She highlighted the need for further research into manipulation and concluded that she could see no reason why manipulation should not be used as long as the patient was properly screened. This is an excellent example of the difficulties therapists face in trying to establish good practice in the light of the paucity of research. In the present climate, perhaps the best recommendation is to avoid interventions that potentially harm even though there may be powerful anecdotal and historical evidence for their efficacy (see Introductory Essay).

---

*   This is my own terminology—it includes both manipulation and mobilisation and any other technique where the patient is moved passively.

Maxwell's (1996) opinion is in direct conflict with that of Twomey and Taylor (1993) who recommend that manipulation of patients who have suffered a whiplash injury should not be performed. Their cadaveric studies indicate that manipulation could lead to damage to the annulus and, in turn, to long term disc degeneration. Although speculative, this would tie in with modern research findings of disc degeneration.

Clinicians are urged to consider two important issues relating to pain relief using potentially tissue damaging techniques:

1 That the more impressive the procedure the more powerful the placebo effect (see Introductory Essay). Skilled manipulation and surgery are good examples. Finneson (1969, quoted by Wall 1994) in his book on surgery for pain said: 'Surgery has the most potent placebo effect that can be exercised in medicine'. Just as in surgery, Grade V manipulation could well be relieving pain but at the same time be producing unnecessary tissue damage.

2 The production of pain during treatment relieves pain (reviewed in the context suggested here by Melzack, 1994). Thus, powerful pain relief can be produced regardless of the potentially devastating effect a procedure may have on the tissues.

Passive mobilisation

Again there is a lack of good research in this area and most of the better work reviewed uses mobilisations combined with other interventions.

McKinney et al (1989) found that mobilisations including those advocated by Maitland and Mckenzie in combination with passive modalities, analgesics and collars (physiotherapy group) showed greater improvements after 3 weeks than those receiving therapy which included rest, analgesics and collars (rest group). Interestingly, the improvements noted were the same as those for the 'self management' group of patients who received advice on posture, early activation, a programme of home exercises, analgesics and a collar. Participants were instructed to gradually tail off the use of the analgesics and the collar. Follow-up 2 years later revealed that there was no difference in the outcome of the rest and physiotherapy group but that *the self management group had a significantly superior outcome*. These findings are in line with similar short term improvements shown by the work of Mealy et al (1986) who compared Maitland mobilisations, in conjunction with passive modalities and advice to rest for 2 weeks using a soft collar and analgesics.

This evidence indicates that mobilisation may offer short term benefits which are time dependent. As yet there is no evidence for any long term benefits for these modalities. Barnsley et al (1994) state that there is no indication for passive mobilisation in chronic WAD patients.

These results are interesting when viewed alongside Maxwell's (1996) findings. Maxwell (1996) identified that Maitland type mobilisations were the most commonly performed hands on therapy by physiotherapists. She argued that this was useful since it concurred with the finding that most of her responders thought that posterior arthro-ligamentous structures were those most commonly injured.

The reasoning error is that intervention is based on a belief that a damaged structure is the main problem rather than considering the physical finding in a clinical reasoning model that includes an understanding of pain science (see Introductory Essay).

Traction

Although Maxwell (1996) found that over 40% of her respondents used traction (the percentage was roughly the same for manual and mechanically delivered methods) there are no data validating its use in the treatment of WAD (Spitzer et al 1995). Weinberger (1976) has warned against the use of high poundage (10–30lbs) intermittent traction in the treatment of the WAD patient. He felt that such treatment may lead to the exacerbation and prolongation of symptoms although he failed to offer any real reasons for his statements.

Exercise

The QTF (Spitzer et al 1995) report found no studies that looked at the effects of exercise in isolation. Some of the studies that showed beneficial outcomes have included exercise as a core component of treatment. The QTF (Spitzer et al 1995) recommends: 'active exercise as part of a multimodal intervention strategy may be beneficial in the short and long term.' They suggest that further work is still needed to corroborate this.

Twomey and Taylor (1993) also recommend that exercise be included in the management programme of the WAD patient. They offer a physiological explanation for this. In doing so they highlight the controversy about when movement should begin and suggest that 'early, gentle movement would seem the most logical approach given current information…'.

Maxwell (1996) makes no comment on the use of exercise as part of the management strategies of a large number of her responders. Forty percent reported that they use exercise alone, whilst around 70% would appear to use it together with manipulation and mobilisation. An interesting inquiry would be to examine which component of their treatment therapists thought to be the most effective. Often, exercise is said to 'maintain the improvements that were made in the therapy sessions'. The informed literature is starting to indicate that this is not the case and that exercise, advice and information may be the most powerful tools of therapy (Klaber-Moffett & Richardson 1997, Wittink et al 1997).

This is hugely encouraging for traditional physiotherapy values whose roots lie in rehabilitation, education and the implementation of therapeutic exercise. Exercise is a component that is used successfully in the management of other soft tissue injuries as well as in the management of chronic pain states (Brennan et al 1994, Davis et al 1992, Lockett and Campbell 1992). It forms a major part of most pain management protocols and helps to prevent ongoing inactivity

(Linton 1996, Linton et al 1990, Linton and Bradley 1996). In whiplash, the importance of early active exercise and of providing information is promoted by Mealy et al (1986) and McKinney et al (1989) and more recently by Borchgrevnik et al (1998) (see Chs 7-9).

The issues regarding the scientific evaluation of exercise that Butler raises in his Introductory Essay are of great significance here.

Postural alignment and advice

Spitzer et al (1995) found no acceptable trials studying the effect of advice or postural alignment in isolation on WAD patients.

Borchgrevnik et al (1998) compared the outcomes of two randomly assigned groups of WAD patients (intervention occurred within 14 days of the whiplash incident). One group were given time off work and prescribed a cervical collar, and the other encouraged to act as normal, i.e. to continue to engage in pre injury activities. Both groups were given instructions for 'self training' (unfortunately they do not give specifics) of the neck and a short course of NSAIDs. Both groups showed significant reductions in pain at twenty four weeks but the *'act as usual' group showed significantly better results in terms of subjective symptoms, including pain localisation, pain during daily activities, stiffness, memory and concentration, and also in terms of visual analogue pain measurements and headache intensity.*

This work supports the earlier findings of McKinney et al (1989) who demonstrated superior outcomes for WAD patients treated with self performed training of neck movements, than for groups treated with supervised physiotherapy or an initial period of rest.

Similar effects have been shown elsewhere in the spine. Indahl et al (1995) showed better outcomes for an approach to treatment that viewed low back pain as a self limiting condition and treated it with recommendations for light mobilisation when compared to conventional therapies that included hands on treatments.

Added together these findings shows a powerful role for patient advice and encouragement, especially when initiated early in the management regimen.

In view of the above, the findings of Maxwell's (1996) study are encouraging as a majority of her respondents reported that they included advice or specific alignment exercises as part of their management regimen.

Electrotherapy

TENS and interferential

Although TENS and interferential are commonly prescribed for pain relief there were no studies found that looked at their effects on WAD patients (see also Spitzer 1995). Maxwell (1996) found that TENS and interferential were commonly used by physiotherapists for the treatment of WAD.

Despite this lack of research, TENS can be seen as a useful adjunct to therapy since it is a device which allows patients to feel that they have some independent control over their condition and it does not require a therapist to apply. It can be particularly useful in the early stages of the condition and may well help to promote self management and the better acceptance of the need to perform regular active movements (see Ch. 7). This of course requires a good level of communication between the therapist and the patient.

Pulsed shortwave; pulsed electromagnetic currents

There has only been one study (Foley-Nolan et al 1992) that attempts to establish the effect of pulsed electromagnetic currents on WAD patients. These researchers placed a shortwave delivery device in a soft collar and compared the effects with a group that just wore a plain collar. The study ran for twelve weeks. The patients in each group could, after 4 weeks, choose to include physiotherapy, including hands on and exercise therapies. At four weeks the treatment group showed greater improvements in terms of increase range of movements and less pain than the control group. The use of analgesics was also less in the treatment group. At four weeks approximately half of each group added physiotherapy into their regimen. Following this the control group improved more rapidly so that at the completion of the study the outcomes were the same for each group.

There are no studies looking at the effects of more traditional application of pulsed shortwave, although it was shown to be a popular modality in Maxwell's study (1996).

Other forms of electrotherapy have not been studied in WAD patients. Thus, as yet there is no evidence of efficacy, despite common usage, for ultra sound, laser, hot packs, shortwave diathermy, or ice (see Maxwell 1996).

Acupuncture

The QTF (Spitzer et al 1995) found no studies that assessed the effects of acupuncture. Su and Su (1988) attempted to look at the effects of traditional Chinese acupuncture on 55 patients suffering chronic pain following previous whiplash injuries. Unfortunately their study is full of flaws and therefore the results suggesting that a remarkable 91% of patients showed significant improvement cannot be accepted as real proof of efficacy for this modality. Although acupuncture has been shown to be effective in the management of pain, the exact mechanisms of its action remain under debate (see Melzack 1994)

Discussion

This review highlights the paucity of basic research into the treatment of WAD patients and Maxwell's (1996) study shows that many of the therapies are commonly employed in physiotherapy clinical practice. The clearly disturbing message is that if one were to follow the strict criteria of evidence-based practice, there is little justification for almost all of the passive modalities currently in use. While we are not yet restricted in our freedom to choose our therapeutic interventions, it may not be that far away. There is mounting pressure from the powerful evidence-based practice movement to implement only those treatments that have proven efficacy (for a useful discussion of the place of evidence based practice see Butler's Introductory Essay).

A major professional challenge is that what we see and interpret as positive responses and outcomes in the clinic just do not seem to tally with the bulk of scientific evidence that is reviewed here. An important point is that we should not feel guilty or angry about the way we have been operating or the way in which we have been schooled. New knowledge is challenging our practices and beliefs as well as challenging us to learn more about injury and pain and the biology of human interactions. If this can be accepted we can come to better understand the ways in which people mend and the ways in which mending can be influenced by therapies. This does involve subtle, and for many, welcome changes to the way we currently practice.

The following are two examples of findings and statements from the literature that on first reading are very challenging (see also Ch. 15 re low back pain).

First, Feine and Lund (1997) reviewed the literature (1980-1997) on the use of physical therapy and physical treatment modalities in the management of chronic musculoskeletal pain using strict inclusion criteria. They make several points:

- No specific therapy had long term efficacy greater than placebo.
- Only 7 out of 22 trials showed the overall treatment to be superior to placebo.
- Treatment was always better than no treatment.
- The more therapies included in the management package the better the outcomes.

They concluded that: 'it seems patients are helped during the period that they are being treated with most forms of physical therapy. However, most of these therapies have not been shown to be more efficacious than placebo.'

The second example relates more specifically to WAD. Robinson and Cassar-Pullicino (1993) reviewed the results of neck sprain following a road traffic accident and commented:

At final review, no patient was still receiving treatment; this reflected the little or no effect on the long term outcome as described by the patients, rather than any success that could be attributed to the treatment received.

These examples highlight two important issues that are notoriously side-stepped. The first is the placebo effect and the second is the 'regression to the mean' phenomenon.

1 It is vital that we take on and understand the full positive meaning and positive implications of the placebo effect (Butler's Introductory Essay is

essential reading). It is an error of reasoning to assume that if a therapy is successfully targeted at a specific tissue it means that the mechanism of the therapy is wholly at the tissue/nociceptive level or that the mechanism responsible for the positive effect was tissue based too. Every therapeutic encounter, however tissue specific, has to be considered in the light of the whole organism and all its relevant biological processing mechanisms (see Ch. 2).

2   All conditions have natural histories and patterns of presentation. These generally involve periods where the patient's symptoms are bad, and periods where they are much less troublesome, even without treatment (Deyo 1993). The fact is that ongoing symptoms naturally fluctuate in their intensity. Deyo (1993) remarks that patients tend to seek help when symptoms are at their worst, but that if left alone most will regress to some average or more typical and bearable level of intensity. He views this phenomenon as being analogous to the statistical concept of regression to the mean, one which he feels most clinicians are unfamiliar with. Deyo (1993) also points out that we tend to examine patients when they are at their worst, yet assess the outcome of our intervention at a subsequent point when things have improved. This leads most clinicians to naturally assume that the change noted is due entirely to their therapies. The error is that it ignores the natural history and the normal fluctuating nature of symptoms. This may be especially so in ongoing pain states including those suffering from WAD.

Deyo (1993) remarks that few therapists are willing to pay much attention to non specific effects of their interaction with patients. These include, attention, empathy, communication and the 'non physiotherapy' aspects of touch, all of which have been shown to positively affect outcomes (see Adams 1997). These positive effects may in turn be erroneously interpreted as being the direct tissue specific physiological consequence of the modality employed. We are all getting to know that ultrasound needs a human being to apply it for it to be successful, and many have heard the evidence that ultrasound works just as well whether the machine is on or off—so long as the patient and therapist believe that it is on (see Wall 1994). Another point of consideration is that localised therapies can often abolish pain and tenderness instantly. This finding is often taken as unequivocal evidence that the targeted tissue was faulty. As Wall (1993) remarks on this effect, '...it is very unlikely that the basic cause is a local histological-biochemical change since the time course of relief of such pathological changes is in the realm of hours to days'. The more acceptable explanation of this type of phenomenon lies in changes in CNS processing systems which have to take into account the influence of the perceptions, thoughts and feelings of the patient. As Butler rightly says, 'the brain is on all the time' (see Introductory Essay).

Where does all this place current physiotherapy practice? The messages are clearly that physiotherapy interaction does generally help patients at the time; but when our treatment modalities are individually scrutinised there is little efficacy for them, and for longer term and chronic conditions outcomes are not at all encouraging. It is worth reminding ourselves that we are not alone here. No profession or treatment approach has the answer so far in chronic pain (although cognitive behavioural therapy, CBT, that includes functional restoration programmes may have something positive to offer—see other chapters in this book). Certainly much medical practice has no evidence of efficacy (spinal fusion, for example) and there is little evidence to support or refute the interventions of any interested group. The reader is advised to review Butler's Introductory Essay.

Conclusion

All the authors in this book are united in their purpose of helping clinicians involved in the treatment of WAD and other broadly similar pain states to facilitate a change in focus. The overwhelming message is that the biomedical and pain-relief oriented approach to recovery is of limited value even in the acute stages of management. One critical aspect of the biomedical perspective is that it helps to perpetuate the tissue-focused, modality-specific approaches to treatment and patient-perceived 'cure' that are really not serving the community with pain that well (see Ch. 7). The encouraging signs are that issues raised from many years of well evaluated CBT treatments and research are being integrated into modern physiotherapy practice (see Chs 7, 8, 9, 11 & 13). Hopefully the outcomes for both therapist and patient will be improved substantially.

REFERENCES

Adams N 1997 Psychological factors in patient—practitioner interactions. In: Adams N (ed) The psychophysiology of low back pain. Churchill Livingstone, Edinburgh

Akeson W H, Amiel D, Woo L-Y 1987 Physiology and therapeutic value of passive motion. In: Helminen H J, Kiviranta I, Tammi M, Saamanen A-M, Paukkonen K, Jurvelin J (eds) Joint loading. John Wright, Bristol

Barnsley L, Lord S, Bogduk N 1994 Whiplash injury. Pain 58:283–307

Borchgrevink G E, Kaasa A, McDonagh D, Stiles T C, Heraldseth O, Lereim I 1998 Acute treatment of whiplash neck sprain injuries. Spine 23(1):25–31

Brennan G P, Shultz B B , Hood R S 1994 The effects of aerobic exercise after lumbar microdiscectomy. Spine 19:735–741

Colachis S C, Strohm B R, Ganter E L 1973 Cervical spine motion in normal women: radiographic study of the effects of cervical collars. Archives of Physical Medicine and Rehabilitation 54:161–169

Davis V, Fillingham R, Doleys D, Davis M 1992 Assessment of aerobic power in chronic pain patients before and after a multi-disciplinary treatment program. Archives of Physical Medicine and Rehabilitation 73:102–106

Deyo R 1993 Practice variations, treatment fads, rising disability. Do we need a new clinical paradigm? Spine 18(15):2153–2162

Feine J S, Lund J P 1997 An assessment of the efficacy of physical therapy and physical modalities for the control of chronic musculoskeletal pain. Pain 71(1)5–23

Fisher S V, Bowar J F, Awad E A, Gullickson G 1977 Cervical orthosis effect on cervical spine motion: roentgenographic and goniometricmethod of study. Archives of Physical Medicine and Rehabilitation 58:109–115

Foley-Nolan D, Moore K, Codd M, Barry C, O'Connor P, Coughlan R J 1992 Low energy high frequency pulsed electromagnetic therapy for acute whiplash injuries. Scandinavian Journal of Rehabilitation Medicine 24:51–59

Indahl A, Velund L, Reikeraas O 1995 Good prognosis for low back pain when left untampered. Spine: 20(4):473–477

Johnson R M, Hart D L, Simmons E F, Ramsby G R, Southwick W O 1977 Cervical orthoses—a study comparing their effectiveness in restricting cervical motion in normal subjects. Journal of Bone and Joint Surgery (Am) 59:332–339

Klaber-Moffett J A, Richardson P H 1997 The influence of the physiotherapist-patient relationship on pain and disability. Physiotherapy Theory and Practice 13:89–96

Linton S J 1996 Early intervention for the secondary prevention of chronic musculoskeletal pain. In: Campbell J N (ed) Pain 1996: an updated review. IASP Press, Seattle

Linton S J, Hellsing A L, Anderson D 1990 A controlled study on the effects of early intervention on the acute musculoskeletal pain problems. Pain 54(3):353–359

Linton S J, Bradley L J 1996 Strategies for the prevention of chronic pain. In: Turk D C, Gatchel R J (eds) Psychological approaches to pain management. Guilford Press, New York

Lockett D M, Campbell J F 1992 The effects of aerobic training on migraine. Headache 32:50–54

Maxwell M 1996 Current physiotherapy treatment for whiplash injury to the neck. British Journal of Therapy and Rehabilitation July 3:7:391–395

Mealy K, Brennan H, Fenelon G C 1986 Early mobilisation of acute whiplash injuries. British Medical Journal 292:656–657

Melzack, R 1994 Folk medicine and the sensory modulation of pain. In: Wall P D, Melzack R (eds) Textbook of pain 3rd edn. Churchill Livingstone, Edinburgh 1209–1217

McKinney L A 1989 Early mobilisation and outcome in acute neck sprains. British Medical Journal 299:1006–1008

McKinney L A, Dornan J O, Ryan 1989 The role of physiotherapy in the management of acute neck sprains following road traffic accidents. Archives of Emergency Medicine 6:27–33

Robinson D D, Cassar-Pullicino V N 1993 Acute neck sprain after road traffic accident: a long term clinical and radiological review. Injury 24(2):79–82

Spitzer W O, Skovron M L, Salmi L R 1995 Scientific monograph of the quebec task force on whiplash associated disorders: redefining whiplash and its management. Spine 20(Suppl):10s–73s

Su H C, Su R K 1988 Treatment of whiplash injuries with acupuncture. Clinical Journal of Pain 4(4):233–247

Twomey L T, Taylor J R 1993 The whiplash syndrome: pathology and physical therapy. The Journal of Manual and Manipulative Therapy 1(1):26–29

Waddell G, Feder G, McIntosh A, Lewis M, Hutchinson A 1996 Low back pain evidence review. Royal College of General Practitioners, London

Wall P D 1993 The mechanisms of fibromyalgia: a critical essay. In: Vocroy H, Merksey H (eds) Progress in fibromyalgia and myofascial pain. Elsevier, Amsterdam pp 53–59

Wall P D 1994 The placebo and the placebo response. In: Wall P D, Melzack R (eds) Textbook of pain 3rd edn. Churchill Livingstone, Edinburgh

Weinberger L M 1976 Trauma or treatment? The role of intermittent traction in the treatment of cervical soft tissue injuries. Journal of Trauma 16:377–38

Wittink H, Hoskins-Michel T, Cohen L J, Fisherman S M 1997 Physical therapy treatment. In: Wittink H, Hoskins-MichelT (eds) Chronic pain management for physical therapists. Butterworth-Heinemann, Boston

Woodward M N, Cook J C H, Gargan M F, Bannister G C 1996 Chiropractic treatment of chronic 'whiplash' injuries. Injury 27(9):643–645

7

Minimising chronicity after whiplash injury

VICKI HARDING

The literature on chronic pain *prevention* following whiplash injury is extremely small. However, there is a growing literature on back pain and the common chronic pain syndromes. Although it is wise to be wary of generalising from one form of injury to another, since these have much in common with whiplash injuries it is worth considering applying these approaches *pro tem*. It at least gives us something to begin with until further confirming or refuting evidence has accumulated.

Steven Linton has done much work on chronic pain prevention. He has summarised the important factors involved in the development of chronicity (Linton 1996) and states that serious pathology is not usually believed to cause chronic musculoskeletal pain problems. Instead it is *learning* processes that are important in the development of chronic pain. Patients may learn habits or behaviours in dealing with their pain and its consequences which, whilst appearing helpful to them, may in the long term lead to further problems e.g. avoidance of certain movements and activities. Time is the essential ingredient.

Emotional and cognitive factors are also involved, where fear, anxiety, attributions, beliefs, self-efficacy (confidence) and coping all interact in complex ways in the development of various problems. These can include:

- low levels of physical and social function
- visiting many different doctors and health care professionals in the search for a pain cure
- over-use of medications
- use of 'passive' coping strategies e.g. prolonged rest, hoping and praying the pain will go away
- beliefs that activity causes pain or injury.

It is clear that in the past it was often poor information and fragmented health care that contributed to these behaviours and beliefs.

Pain normally provokes anxiety to some degree, and an especially important process seems to be fear-avoidance (see Chs 11–15). Since physical activity may have set the pain off or may naturally be related to small increases in pain, the fearful patient may quickly learn to avoid a variety of activities. This may be reinforced by information or advice, e.g. if every time patients mention pain or complain of pain, the therapist responds by:

- looking worried/concerned
- suggesting reducing activity or exercise, going slower or increasing rest
- saying 'Well don't do it then'
- looking puzzled or mentioning the doctor.

Box 1 Important potential risk factors—after Linton (1996)

History	★ Is the pain recurrent? ★ Number of previous health-care visits ★ Days absent from work
Duration	★ Duration of current episode ★ Total duration of problem
Pain beliefs	★ Activity increases pain ★ Activity results in injury ★ Work causes pain
Pain behaviour	★ Does the patient tend to use pain behaviour to communicate pain and distress?
Work situation	★ Does the patient experience his/her work as stimulating? ★ Heavy or monotonous work ★ High levels of stress ★ Poor relations with supervisors or workmates
Coping and self-efficacy	★ Does patient have effective coping strategies? ★ Does the patient believe he/she may deal with pain ★ Does the patient have a catastrophic style of thinking
Distress	★ Is the patient distressed?
Depression	★ Low in mood e.g. describes being 'fed up', no belief in future
Obstacles	★ What obstacles does patient perceive are preventing a return to work and normal life?
Self-perception	★ Does patient believe he/she will get better, return to work?
Information deficit	★ Does patient understand the problem properly? (Cause, self-care, activity, prognosis?)
Current pain/ dysfunction	★ High levels of pain or dysfunction

It is not surprising patients become concerned about pain and movement and learn to avoid them. Since 'passive' behaviours like resting, reading, and watching television can be pleasant and associated with little or no pain, these may eventually become the main activities. As a result a basic tenet of secondary prevention is to intervene early to prevent disruption of the patient's normal lifestyle, including work. Being off work may in itself create problems such as dysfunction and depression, since similar problems are noted among the newly unemployed or retired.

The risk factors listed in Box 1 are based on those Steve Linton (1996) identified as important when first seeing a patient.

A difference between whiplash patients and back pain patients is the absence of learning that occurs through having a recurring problem. Linton (1996) describes very well the role that recurrence has in the development of chronic pain syndromes. The whiplash patient may have more than one whiplash of course, and still shares many of the other risk factors.

Management of the acute whiplash injury

On asking a group of chronic whiplash patients attending a pain management programme what was helpful/unhelpful in the acute stage, they reported the following attitudes and behaviours.

Believe us

Kate Treves discusses this in Chapter 10, but it is a point made by so many patients it warrants serious consideration.

Spending time listening to patients, and being seen to believe all they tell you is very valuable. Not listening or believing does not help, and patients sense when their information and their perspective is not fully respected.

Physiotherapists are in a good position here when nothing shows on the X-ray. They can be an important ally of the patient, by confirming the existence of physical signs of injury and in explaining some of the seeming mysteries of pain. It is also worth remembering that if your neurophysiological knowledge is insufficient to provide an explanation of a patient's pain problem, it is still not helpful to disbelieve them. In this situation it is likely that the point of contact to help the patient make changes will have been lost.

The physio said I should exercise through the pain but when I went to the doctor he said to stop if it hurts—it was very confusing

Having a shared model with the patient's doctor really helps, but is not always possible. Good communication is always helpful however, and it is really the physiotherapist's role to teach and inform doctors about what is helpful for patients from the point of view of movement and function.

Tell us/inform us. If only we'd been told that pain doesn't mean damage, and that lying in bed is harmful

This is self-explanatory, but how often is this message put over **explicitly**?

I found it hard to remember everything

It is vital to write things down for patients. Questions like: 'How can I say that so that you'll understand it tomorrow?' are useful. Remember, too, that terms and instructions like *rotate, side bend, flex, elevate your arm/shoulder* are not understood by many patients. It is important to use their words and to become accustomed again to speaking in plain English rather than in jargon.

Patients also complain of poor memory. The more serious injuries can have a contrecoup effect that might be expected to have an effect in the acute stage. Other factors will also be operating, and are discussed in Chapter 10.

I was betrayed, they colluded

Patients can fear that medical and legal people are ganging up against them, so it helps to write down everything the patient tells you about the accident, and what you observe every time you see them. Physiotherapists' notes are likely to provide good quality evidence for litigation, or for persuading a disbelieving doctor or DSS employee in the future.

Physios encouraged me with exercise so much that I over-exercised

More is not necessarily better, and anyone who has worked with dancers or strongly motivated athletes know how over-exercising can be unhelpful. It is also possible to believe a patient is not over-exercising, when the patient thinks s/he is. It is important here to consider the patient's fears and also whether s/he feels in control of the situation. It is possible to make strong recommendations without being dogmatic and without making the patient feel guilty or that you will be displeased if they cannot manage it completely. Generally if patients are not feeling completely in control, urging them on or only giving them reassurance will not work. This needs discussing more broadly with them.

What have we learnt from chronic pain patients?

- **Promote self-management not a passive, you fix-it approach.**
- **Pace exercises and activities to quotas or time, NOT pain (see Ch. 8).**

Fordyce et al in 1986 did a randomised study of acute back pain patients attending casualty. Both groups were given pills and exercises. The 'traditional' group were given pills prn, and exercises with the advice 'let pain be your guide'. The behavioural group were given prescriptions for fixed time intervals and a set number of exercises on a set incremental schedule. At 9 months follow-up, the traditional group showed significant increases in chronicity and impairment, whereas the behavioural group had returned to pre-onset levels of activity. They had exactly the same treatment. How it was presented produced the chronicity.

Lindstrom et al (1992) demonstrated that compared to a control group of usual physiotherapy, a graded activity programme returned patients to work significantly faster and reduced long term sick leave.

- **Encourage medication to be taken time contingently, not to pain (prn).**

In the early days whiplash injury patients need good analgesia. The dosage should prevent breakthrough pain, and the physiotherapist should support patients in this. It is important to bear in mind the role of distress, though that may easily be mistaken for increased pain. Distress should receive its own appropriate treatment; analgesia is not appropriate for distress and may be counterproductive.

Patients therefore need a plan for coping with increased pain that does not include increases in medication. Also, patients should not be encouraged to continue taking analgesics for an acute injury once they are beginning to reach the subacute phase. They need instead to look further at other ways of managing their pain.

- **Patients' beliefs are of paramount importance—don't second guess, and verify what they think or mean.**
- **Pain must not be the whole focus—function and return to work is more important long term.**
- **Make sure that patients work on enjoyable goals and activities.**

These will help raise mood. Pleasurable and exciting activities also provide reinforcement for patients' efforts, as well as being relevant to the quality of life changes they really want to work on. Often patients give up hobbies and interests, and social activities, saving all their energies for work or chores. It is important that these 'quality of life' activities are included in both short and long term goals.

- **Secondary musculo-skeletal problems can be major—work hard at prevention.**

Think about the rest of the body, encouraging patients to work hard at maintaining or improving these other areas. This will help maintain good self efficacy and mood.

- **Keep patients at work if at all possible, even for a small part of the day.**

Encourage them to maintain work habits and work relationships, and make reasonable adaptations to the work place if necessary. More time off work does not increase the likelihood of a successful return to work, quite the opposite.

- **Patients easily come off track at times of increased pain.** They need to have a plan to cope with this and eventually get back on track.

How to manage acute whiplash injury

These methods are based on theories of healing, cognitive-behavioural principles, and my own experience of treating acute whiplash injuries in a London teaching hospital. Further study is needed to demonstrate conclusively their efficacy in whiplash patients. It is also necessary to allow leeway for each individual patient depending on the severity of the accident, the extent and type of injury, and the effect it has had on that individual. Adaptations will be needed for different lifestyles, but the patient needs to be aware that time spent early on will be less disruptive to routines and lifestyles in the long run.

1 See them as soon as possible

Ideally all whiplash patients should be sent to physiotherapy as soon as the appropriate examinations and tests have been done. Department timetables and waiting lists need to adjust so that all acute injuries can be seen immediately from casualty or in casualty. This requires a regular education programme of all new and existing casualty officers as to the importance of early intervention, as well as any other doctors who are likely to need to see acute injuries first. If patients are seen by a physiotherapist really early, then good quality advice can be given that gives patients confidence to continue with an immediate mobilisation approach. My impression is that early intervention generally markedly reduces the overall time and frequency that patients need to be seen, and that the biggest difference can be made if patients are seen and advised before they have slept overnight i.e. the same day.

2 Impart information and listen

Information should be understandable but not oversimplified, and should not frighten patients. Normalise what has happened: 'Damage has been done, you have had a nasty injury, but the healing process has begun already'; 'You have had a big injury, but it won't be like this for ever, there is a lot you can do that will mean it will recover—given time'. Patients may have heard of someone else who has become very disabled following a whiplash. It is necessary then not to deny this but explain it in a way that gives them confidence that they will not end up disabled: 'Some people do do badly—they are not necessarily worse, they are not so well managed'; 'Research shows that the more you move—provided it's gentle, little and often—the better the results'.

Make sure that information does not just go from the physiotherapist to the patient. Again, listen to patients and check that the information you have provided is what they were after and that it relates to their situation. Try not to in any way be dismissive of anything they say, otherwise it may sound as if you don't believe them. If it is important to them, it is important to address it. Patients need reassurance that all the more unusual symptoms they describe such as nausea, dizziness, difficulty swallowing and poor concentration, are usual. If these symptoms are repeatedly mentioned despite information and reassurance, patients need help to learn to reassure themselves. This is more effective in helping patients take responsibility than being sent off for consultations or tests that are unlikely to provide answers and risk worrying or frightening them.

3 Encourage self management

Avoid passive therapies that patients cannot do themselves. Ice, warmth, massage, and TENS are acceptable, as are mobilisations—as long as patients can take over with auto-mobilisations or exercise. It is when passive manipulative techniques are presented as 'putting things back' or given an aura of mystique that patients are harmed by being made dependent or frightened—'The state of my neck is obviously on a knife edge if only people with such skill can keep it together. I'd better not move it in case I put it back out or mess up what the therapist did'. Similarly, magic rays from shiny boxes with flashing lights are not in patients' control. As Thacker has reviewed in Chapter 6, there is little evidence for efficacy and plenty against (see also Butler's Introductory Essay). Most physiotherapists have seen or heard about the beneficial effects of ultrasound with the machine mistakenly switched off!

4 Reduce nociception

Factors that may be responsible for increasing or maintaining nociception include:

- Large movements—rapid, tense, too many.
- Resting or major reduction in activity for the rest of the body.
- Complete immobilisation of the injured part.

Factors that can decrease nociception include:

- Rest—frequent and relatively short, fully supported in the most pain free position and with deliberate work on relaxing muscle tension/spasm. Patients often find they need more pillows than usual, or that one side is preferable to the other. This is absolutely fine for a limited period, after which other positions can very gradually be paced up. Occasionally, patients who have been unable to find a comfortable resting position have remarked that lying prone with several pillows under the chest and their face in the examination couch breathing hole is more comfortable than anything else. It is helpful to give them time to rest in this position for a period at the beginning and the end of treatment and to problem solve with them how they may try this out at home as an alternative rest position. Once more movement returns, this position can often become less comfortable again and needs adaptation, or a change to more usual positions.
- Relaxed gentle oscillating movement little and often—the therapist may help to start with by using mobilisations (e.g. Maitland type) or passive movement to the shoulder joints and cervical spine. This shows patients the amplitude and frequency that is helpful, as well as helping patients to

111

learn to relax. Patients need to be able to perform these at home at least every quarter of an hour during waking hours and whenever muscle spasm and pain build up. At night, patients may be advised to wake themselves 2 hourly in order to get up, walk around, climb some stairs, gently swing the arms and do their neck exercises to minimise the effects of keeping still for too long. This may result in a little less sleep, but patients may not sleep much anyway, and it gives them something purposeful and helpful to do, as well as markedly reducing their overall pain and spasm. Some patients will baulk at doing this; however if they have major problems moving in the morning, it is still well worth promoting. They may agree to try getting up once a night, then agree to twice a night when they see some benefit. Patients do not need to continue waking 2 or 3 hourly for long. After 2 or 3 days they may find it is possible to extend their sleep times gradually as swelling and spasm reduce.

In a few cases, especially where too much time has elapsed between the accident and seeing a physiotherapist e.g. more than a few hours, neck exercises may have to be done initially while lying down with the head supported on a pillow. This routine can then be reinforced by following it with a 10 minute relaxation while still lying. Once this has been performed a few times, some muscle relaxation and reduction in pain will have occurred and patients can be encouraged to do these movements when standing or sitting unsupported. Treating patients this way makes obvious those few who have a missed fracture of the odontoid peg or other serious injury, rather than losing them in the morass of patients where intense muscle spasm due to inappropriate immobilisation has been allowed to build up. The vast majority of whiplash injury patients do not have immediate muscle spasm; this generally appears on waking the next day or after resting. If physiotherapists can get in early and prevent the vicious cycle from getting a hold, most patients will find they have a much easier recovery than has occurred in most cases until now.

- Heat, ice, analgesia (time contingent), NSAI drugs for a limited time period in patients who are tolerant to them, acupuncture, TENS.
- Appropriate use of a collar for cases with very severe muscle spasm—collars can help patients extend their up-time or walking distance by helping them relax their muscles. Linking the collar to function and to muscle relaxation will help reinforce the use of relaxation and not prolonged rest. Physiotherapists need to be absolutely certain that the patient is aware the collar has *not* been prescribed as a support for a 'weak' neck or to stop it moving to allow it to heal. Most patients will have the confidence to manage wearing the collar outdoors. The routine for collar use will be to take it off hourly and do active near full range rotation, side-flexion and chin retraction. Patients need to be aware that the weaning process will begin on the second day after the injury, as fibrous repair begins. It is important that this process is done time-dependently, after discussion, so they put the collar back on when it is time to, not in response to pain. If they are not coping, then the times can be changed to make it more manageable and for the patient to still feel in control.

5 Movement

Use graduated, incremental exercise that is time/repetition contingent rather than pain contingent if at all possible. Don't push, threaten, or frighten. Remember that these patients are not chronic, and the day before were relatively fit, so that other areas need maintaining and efforts should be made to prevent muscle spasm from spreading to other areas as much as possible.

6 The physiotherapist's manner

Be aware of cues and reinforcers. Rather than focusing on symptoms e.g. asking them about pain, paraesthesia, nausea etc. every time, ask them about achievements. This reinforces the message that pain relief is not the only goal.

Don't panic. Unless you suspect major problems, for example cord symptoms and signs, haematoma, missed fracture, etc. then casualty or their doctor are unlikely to be helpful unless you know they will effectively deal with the patient's distress. If you see them very early and they still have major muscle spasm, something may have been missed. Be very careful how you portray any suggested visit to a doctor or request for a test, and only in exceptional circumstances suggest anything more than would normally happen.

It is best not to discharge patients if you do send them to the doctor. Speak to the doctor or write and give it to the patient so that if the doctor wants to stop or change physiotherapy, s/he knows that you would like him/her to speak to you. This helps those incidents when the patient is told 'Well! don't move it then! Stop physio if it's making you worse!'

7 Keep them functioning—back to light work ASAP

While patients are off work, if it has not been possible to maintain them there, get them to mock it up at home in a systematically paced way, and include travelling since travelling is part of work. Liaise with work, the family and the GP wherever necessary.

Do not encourage patients to consider that pain is entirely responsible for putting life 'on hold'. 'This is an injury, and your time off is to help you manage it and treat it optimally.' 'Injuries do heal; it is about taking control.'

Semantics

In low back pain we know what words to avoid: crumbling, slipped discs, degenerative, wear and tear. Unhelpful words for whiplash patients include *serious* and *ripped*. *Torn* needs to be used with care, and is probably worth avoiding, since patients can easily misinterpret it.

More helpful words include *significant*, *big*, *overstretched*, *sprained* and *strained*. *Nasty* is possibly all right since it legitimises their problem and helps them realise you understand, without inducing fear. It is necessary to encourage patients to think in terms of action and recovery such as strengthening, scar tissue flexibility and remodelling, rather than using potentially frightening terms that induce helplessness.

Summary

When addressing tactics for prevention of chronicity, the critical period for intervention is thought to be between 1 and 90 days. However, while early intervention may be necessary, it does not appear to be sufficient to ensure a successful prevention. The content of the intervention is very important, and it is necessary to assess the patient's motives for seeking care:

- concern about the causes of pain and why it continues beyond a few weeks
- fears that activity may cause further injury
- pain relief
- interest in improving function.
- wondering whether the injury may be repaired or healed.

Physiotherapists need to:
- Help the patient better understand and deal with the disorder.
- Sow the seeds of self management especially where pain relief is concerned.
- Maintain everyday activities.

The behaviour of health-care providers may greatly influence how the patient perceives the problem and deals with it.

Treatment should:
- be health-behaviour oriented
- focus on physical and social activities
- concentrate on what the patient should be doing rather than on what they should avoid
- tell patients that it is helpful to the healing process to return to work relatively soon
- teach self care skills such as relaxation and short term pain-relieving rest positions
- include telling the patient that becoming permanently pain-free is unlikely, but this does NOT mean permanently injured or handicapped
- utilise behavioural techniques of operant learning, goal setting and pacing (see Chs 8 & 9).

Patients should feel part of the process, integral in defining the problem, setting goals, selecting treatments and following through with them.

I think we also need to watch that the trend towards chronic pain management does not result in over-exercising and under-treatment in the acute phase. We need to learn from chronic pain but not directly transfer the philosophies and methods to acute pain. They are two different things altogether.

REFERENCES

Fordyce W E, Brockway J A, Bergman J A, Spengler D 1986 Acute back pain: a control-group comparison of behavioral vs traditional management methods. Journal of Behavioral Medicine 9(2):127–140

Lindstrom I, Ohlund C, Eek C, Wallin L, Peterson L, Fordyce W E, Nachemson A L 1992 The effect of graded activity on patients with subacute low back pain: a randomized prospective clinical study with an operant-conditioning behavioral approach. Physical Therapy 72(4):279–93

Linton S 1996 Pain 1996—an updated review: refresher course syllabus. IASP Press, 305–311

8

Management of chronic pain following whiplash injuries

SUZANNE SHORLAND

Introduction

Of all whiplash injuries reported in the literature 15-40% go on to develop some form of chronic pain (Wells 1997). Any attempt at functional recovery and rehabilitation tends to come very late if at all, by which time disability is often severe (Rainville et al 1992). Battie et al (1995) and Wolff et al (1991) showed that the majority of physiotherapists prefer to treat patients with acute pain rather than those with delayed recovery or chronic pain. Since physiotherapists are often apprehensive about treating such severe pain and disability, sadly the outlook for ongoing pain sufferers looks bleak.

Patients with chronic pain following whiplash injuries present to physiotherapists for a variety of reasons. These will include wishing for full recovery of their pain and injury, and wanting to be able to return to all their normal activities.

Chapters elsewhere in this text have shown that for chronic pain syndromes, a pure biomedical approach is proving insufficient. Studies have also shown that there is little direct relationship between chronic pain and disability (Waddell 1987). Instead, it is widely recognised that pain and pain disability are not only influenced by organic pathology, but also by psychological and social factors that act upon the motoric, cognitive and psycho-physiological response systems to pain (e.g. Vlaeyen et al 1995). It has been widely suggested that behavioural or biopsychosocial approaches offer the foundations for a better insight into how pain can be managed once it has become a chronic problem (e.g. Hanson & Gerber 1990).

Self-management principles are important in behavioural and biopsychosocial approaches. The biopsychosocial model of pain naturally recognises not only biological factors, but also cognitive, emotional, behavioural and environmental factors. The role of the clinician within this approach is that of teacher or guide, whose main responsibility is to encourage or assist the patient in learning and making better use of pain self-management skills (Hanson & Gerber 1990). Cognitive-behavioural therapy (CBT) is an example of such an approach and is recognised as an effective therapy that may be used alone or in combination with other therapies for chronic pain (e.g. Williams 1996).

Chronic pain can be successfully managed within interdisciplinary chronic pain management programmes (Flor et al 1992, Fordyce et al 1985). However, these are still a scarce commodity. This chapter will explore the role of the physiotherapist working with post-whiplash chronic pain sufferers on an individual basis, by using the principles physiotherapists use in chronic pain management programmes. The general consensus is that regardless of possible aetiology, individuals with chronic pain are seen as sharing not only many common pathobiological mechanisms (see Chs 2-5) but also, importantly, many cognitive and behavioural features. Consequently, for the purpose of this chapter the term chronic pain will be used to describe sufferers with chronic pain sustained following a whiplash injury.

The medical approach vs. the self management approach

Conventional medical models of pain have tended to present a strictly dichotomous paradigm where pain is viewed as being either physically or psychologically based. The traditional approach of 'let pain be your guide' and seeing pain as a 'warning sign' assumes that pain means ongoing damage. This also assumes that healing is incomplete, or at least, not sufficient to permit resumption of activity. However, it is now very clear that there is no inherent relationship between pain and non-healing, and that rest and non-activity may actually inhibit healing (e.g. Fordyce et al 1986, Melzack & Wall 1996).

A more medical approach tends to suppose that when pain persists, there must be psychogenic or psychiatric explanations. But this has not been shown to be so, or to be helpful. A biopsychosocial model, though, considers the interactive role of biological, environmental, and psychological processes on both pain and disability (e.g. see Feuerstein & Beattie 1995). It defines the patient's problems and provides a template for a more beneficial approach. Its emphasis is on helping chronic pain sufferers to develop their own skills in managing their pain and the consequences of the pain so that they may ultimately improve their quality of life. Table 8.1 compares and contrasts the approaches.

Cognitive-behavioural therapy

Cognitive-behavioural therapy (CBT) is an established management approach developed by clinical psychologists and used by trained practitioners. Cognitive-behavioural therapy for patients with chronic pain focuses on altering

Table 8.1 Comparison of the medical and self-management approaches to chronic pain.

Medical model	Self-management model
Responsibility lies with the healthcare practitioner, who will aim to alleviate the pain	Responsibility lies with the patient. The practitioner acts as a teacher or guide.
The patient is passive, receiving treatment.	Once instructions are given, the management resides with the patient.
More effective with acute injuries. and diseases	Any necessary medical, diagnostic and treatment procedures have been tried.
The primary goal is pain relief, with correct diagnosis and treatment.	The goal is to increase quality of life with pain, not find a cure.
Greater risk of negative side effects.	Very useful for chronic pain.

(Adapted from: Hanson R W, Gerber K E 1990 Coping with chronic pain. a guide to patient self-management. Chapter 3. Guildford Press. New York)

unhelpful thoughts, beliefs or behaviours that may be contributing to the clinical problem. The therapist attempts to help the sufferer control distressing emotions, such as anxiety and depression, by teaching them more effective ways of interpreting and thinking about their experience and helping them to become more aware of maladaptive behaviours. There is evidence that chronic pain causes depression and some chronic pain patients may have been depressed preceding the onset of their pain, but there is no clear evidence that depression causes pain (Magni et al 1994). This is an important feature of cognitive-behavioural therapy, which states clearly that chronic pain is a multifactorial problem where physical, social and psychological factors will all be operating.

Cognitive-behavioural approach

Despite the fact that physiotherapists do not receive cognitive-behavioural therapy training, they still may apply some of its principles within their treatment. This is practised within interdisciplinary chronic pain management programmes where physiotherapists work closely with team members of all disciplines towards the same aims and goals:

Aims and goals

- Exercise regimes to improve general or aerobic fitness and muscle strength (Fordyce 1976, Turner et al 1990).

- Relaxation techniques to reduce muscle tension, facilitate sleep and improve the management of stress (Gil et al 1988, Linton 1986).
- Increasing levels of activity and reducing the frequency of pain behaviours through methods such as goal setting, planned gradual increments in activity and exercise levels, as well as reinforcement of achievements (Fordyce 1976, Keefe 1982, Linton 1986).
- Cognitive therapy to identify and modify maladaptive thinking processes and coping strategies (Philips 1988, Turk et al 1983).
- Reduction of inappropriate pain and mood altering drugs, which are ineffective in managing chronic pain (Gil et al 1988, Philips 1988).

Principles

The cognitive-behavioural principles that are most useful for physiotherapists are:

Pacing: in order that patients break the overactivity-underactivity cycle. Pacing, or quota led rather than pain led, exercise has been shown to be effective in stabilising and increasing exercise activity in physiotherapy (Lindstrom et al 1992, Doleys et al 1982).

Goal setting: this helps physiotherapists to focus on improving function relevant to patients; this is also linked to issues of maintenance, since the focus for patients is to get them back to what they want to do.

Providing patients with good quality information: to affect patients' beliefs and help change behaviour.

Reinforcement: to help patients change unhelpful behaviours and habits to more helpful ones.

Teaching patients helpful coping strategies: those skills that can help patients cope with their pain, especially at difficult times e.g. relaxation, self-use of stretch, exercise and sport, good posture and ergonomics, and planning for pain flare-ups.

Research on the role of the cognitive-behavioural approach in increasing patients' sense of control over their pain is documented in pain management programmes (Fordyce 1976, Turner et al 1990). However, it is suggested that many of the aims and goals for physiotherapists working in isolation from interdisciplinary chronic pain management programmes will be the same. The cognitive behavioural principles outlined will therefore be beneficial when implemented by physiotherapists in order to achieve those same aims and goals. This does not suggest that physiotherapists should become amateur psychologists, but be much more aware that psychological factors are involved and that physiotherapists are in a position to influence those factors related to physical fitness and function.

The remainder of this chapter will focus on some of the strategies used within a CBT approach and how they may be integrated into physiotherapy practice. Some self-management principles have already been discussed in Chapters 7, 13 & 14.

The place of reinforcement

All of us in our lives will respond to reinforcement, albeit in an unconscious way (Harding 1997). Research supporting its use in all therapeutic interactions cannot be passed by (Fordyce 1976), especially when it has been shown to be effective in physiotherapy (Cairns & Pasino 1977).

The use of helpful reinforcement is vital throughout patient assessment and in all subsequent sessions, be they management or treatment focused. Reinforcement is the basis of operant learning, learning being characterised by a lasting change in behaviour or habits (such as relaxing rather than tensing, sitting upright rather than slumped) that will occur if conditions are favourable (Lindstrom et al 1992).

A reinforcer is anything that immediately follows a behaviour/action that leads to a subsequent increase in that behaviour's frequency. Reinforcement can be used to help the patient increase activities that have been avoided or that they are fearful of doing. For example, when a patient agrees to reduce the use of a collar previously worn all the time, s/he may start by removing it for an agreed trial of 30 seconds during the appointment with you. As the collar is removed reinforcement can be given. Interest and eye contact is maintained as the collar stays off, then as the patient completes the 30 seconds you immediately follow this by giving further praise. As the patient subsequently builds on 'collar-off' time, using a systematic plan, you can reinforce this progress. Asking the patient when they last removed the collar can help the patient to become aware of achievement, however little, and begin to self-reinforce. As 'collar-off' time builds, it is important to continue to reinforce each new level of achievement, as well as skills of self-reinforcement, since this will ensure maintenance. It can sometimes be difficult to find things to reinforce. However the physiotherapist can become quite skilled at focusing on achievement and applying reinforcement: for example if the patient tells you they did not achieve the full agreed 'collar-off' time at home, they can be reinforced for taking it off alone without your support. Reinforcement for this is likely to contribute to a sense of achievement that is more likely to be built on, rather than a sense of failure because the next step had been too large. If it seems impossible to find achievement for reinforcement, the journey to the appiontment itself will often provide opportunities for reinforcement (e.g. coping with transport, crowds, walking, sitting on a bumpy bus etc.).

Reinforcement needs to be used with care, as it can be seen as patronising or annoying if overused and performed in an unnatural way. A reinforcer may be the physiotherapist's praise and attention/interest, but not always. Thus, words of praise such as 'well done' and 'good' are not always encouraging for everyone. Specific comments orientated to the patient such as, 'Your neck movement looks looser when you turn', and 'You seem to be using less effort and remembering to sit with good posture' may be much more reinforcing. The role-play below provides a further example of reinforcement.

A role-play example of reinforcement techniques

Physio: Hello, nice to see you. You look a little looser and straighter, your head is moving more freely.

Patient: Oh is it? I feel much more sore than last week.

Physio: So you are moving better, but it is much more painful. Have you any idea why that may be?

Patient: Well, I don't know really, that's why I asked you.

Physio: What particularly makes it sore?

Patient: I think it's some of the exercises. I know they're helping, I'm freer, so I don't want to stop them, but whenever I do that turning exercise to the left, it seems to set off that awful muscle spasm.

Physio: That is a good link you've made between the turning and the spasm. What do you think could help?

Patient: Well, I'm trying to relax, but it isn't easy.

Physio: Relaxing is not an easy thing to do, so it is great that you are able to give it a go. Trying little and often will help it become more natural. Do you want to show me how the turning exercises are going? (Patient attempts to turn.) As you do that what do you feel?

Patient: I am aware my shoulders are tight, I'm trying to relax them.

Physio: Yes great, I can see that. Anything else?

Patient: It's tight round here and that's exactly where it gets sore.

Physio: Its really hard to relax where it's sore. Is there anything else you could try to help relax that area?

Patient: Well, maybe I could do a smaller exercise to that spot to loosen it up, like that nodding exercis.e

Physio: That's exactly right, doing it little and often will help loosen it up and reduce the soreness. It will come eventually.

In the role play the physiotherapist provides prompts that are both reinforcing and help patients to problem solve and find the answers to their concerns. The physiotherapist is then in an ideal position to reinforce the answers and changes patients subsequently make.

Assessment

Many patients' experience a sense of not being believed by health care practitioners and the validity of their pain comes into question (see Ch. 7). If patients feel they are not believed or understood they are likely to find it hard to make changes and progress with your approach, let alone to continue with it upon discharge. Physiotherapists are in an ideal position to help validate patients' pain with up to date information, with their approach, and with non-judgmental understanding. Central to any successful therapeutic relationship is an explicit belief in what patients tell us, combined with the development of agreed strategies to cope with it.

Assessing patients with chronic pain can be challenging, especially if what they tell us does not fit our understanding of pain, or of the expected effects of the injury sustained. At these times it can be easy to make inaccurate and unhelpful judgements concerning patients and their pain. Clinical judgements of symptom legitimacy and treatment expectations should not be based on the complaints and behaviours of patients or the knowledge, experience, attitudes and biases of clinicians. Some referral information can be inaccurate or misleading; it is only at the point of initial assessment that a physiotherapist can determine the complexity and chronicity of patients' pain and its effects on their lifestyle.

Simmonds (1997) states: 'It is important to be aware that if "inappropriate" complaints are an attempt by patients to communicate their suffering and distress, we only add to their emotional distress and pain with our scepticism'. She also rightly asks, 'How should patients complain, and how should they behave?' Also, as pain is such a complex multidimensional experience, the difficulty in describing it succinctly is greater the more chronic it becomes.

Traditionally, when assessing patients with pain, physiotherapists try to identify the severity, irritability and pattern of pain, with specific aims for diagnoses, treatment plans and eventual resolution. When assessing individuals with chronic pain this treatment goal has to be reviewed, since a cure for patients' chronic pain is now unrealistic. Physiotherapists need to be aware of this during assessment, and in order to obtain relevant information, the assessment will need to have a different focus. 'The first consultation can provide a rich ground for helping the patient better understand and deal with the disorder. Above all, the seeds of development of chronic problems or in contrast the seeds of self-management, can be sown here' (Linton, 1996).

Clinicians whose assessment and clinical focus is on finding and fixing a pure physical or tissue origin for the patients pain may, as Linton (1996) has intimated in the quote above, be inadvertently helping to sow the seeds of chronic pain development or maintenance (see Chs 12 & 15). Physiotherapists need to be aware that in order to obtain better and more relevant information the traditional assessment needs some modification. This applies not only to assessment but to patient management too. It is vital that both assessment and patient management/intervention are linked with the same underpinning theme.

The following sections cover some important aspects of a self-management approach assessment, but the physiotherapist needs to be conscious of the integration of these aspects into management approaches.

Previous treatment

Asking about previous treatment is routine for physiotherapists but it is especially valuable when assessing patients with chronic pain. It provides an opportunity for the physiotherapist to gain an insight into patients' perception of treatment and the role of physiotherapy in their future management.

Patients' interpretations of treatment can vary greatly: some may think they were discharged from physiotherapy because exercise was (to the patient) obviously unhelpful, damaging, or making their pain increase. Many patients express confusion as they know that exercise is vital, but are unsure of which exercises to do, how hard they should do them and how often. Previous rapid and unexplained discharge from physiotherapy departments may reinforce the idea that exercise in the presence of pain is damaging and should be avoided. Equally, some patients may have found previous specific modalities of treatment helpful. There may be a tendency for physiotherapists to repeat treatments which the patient reports as having been successful, or to introduce ones which the patient cannot remember receiving. This contradicts the very approach you are trying to utilise—especially since it is now acknowledged that these modalities are ineffective in helping chronic pain patients to manage.

It is extremely important and helpful to spend some time explaining this to the patient: that modern concepts of successfully treating chronic pain have changed to focus on fitness and restoration of function, by using alternative strategies.

Current exercise routine

Enquire if the patient is doing any exercise, stretch or sport. Asking them to show you and explain what they are doing, offers an ideal opportunity to reinforce what they are already managing. You are also being explicit in suggesting that exercises are important and manageable.

If the patient is not doing any exercise, discuss with them why they feel unable to exercise. Many will say they are unsure of what to do, how often and how many. A lot of patients have incorrectly come to believe that exercises are damaging them since they cause increased pain. Problem solve with the patient what would make exercise more manageable. Explaining to patients that it is usually the tension and amount of exercises that patients do that causes flare-ups, not the exercise per se. This will be expanded upon later in the chapter.

Ongoing treatment

As is normal practice, identify if the patient is receiving treatment from anyone else. In an attempt to gain understanding and information patients often seek treatment from many different sources. It is important for the physiotherapist to identify what other models of pain management are operating. It can be advantageous to collude with those that support the ideas of self-management but equally to acknowledge that the patient will find it very difficult to make changes with this approach if other health care practitioners are operating using conflicting approaches.

Patients may need to have your approach explained explicitly, why you use it, and what you expect you can help with. It is then that a patient is in a position to decide if they are ready to take it on board. If they are not, it is not a reflection of your skill, or lack of it, but more that the patient is not in a position, for what ever reason to work with you at this stage.

Pain history

Ask the patient to give a brief history of how their pain started and then developed. The physiotherapist can then identify patterns such as of inactivity, excessive collar use, or periods of overactivity. Ask about previous contacts with surgeons, orthopaedic specialists and other health care practitioners.

Use of a pain chart

Where to start can be sometimes overwhelming when assessing someone with chronic pain. Asking the patient an initial question, which is specific to a possible site of pain, may be helpful. For example: 'Do you have any neck pain?' This may allow you to be systematic and efficient. Chronic pain does not usually involve just the neck or one area, the whole body can be involved and assessment should reflect this.

A primary aim is for the patient to feel satisfied that you understand their pain, where it is and how it affects them. If they are not satisfied they are far less likely to go along with the intended approach or the information you provide.

Patients' understanding of their pain

This is a vital component of the assessment and should not be overlooked. The patients' own understanding of their health and health related problems not only influences their decision to seek professional help but also affects their response to treatment and their reaction to illness and disability. By openly listening and gaining an insight into patients' understanding of their pain condition you are collecting information and not making judgements on it. It is important not to make comments concerning the information you obtain as they may be easily biased by personal values and are anyway of little clinical relevance. Sim (1990) suggests that the physiotherapist should attempt to understand and respect the lay beliefs of their patients.

Since psychological variables, such as distress and maladaptive cognitions (i.e. thoughts and beliefs), are thought to have a potent effect on levels of dysfunction, it is hardly surprising that what the patient comes to learn and understand about their pain can be a significant contributing factor. Maladaptive, or unhelpful, cognitions may be central to many patients' fears about pain and their consequent reluctance to be physically active. For instance, the understandable belief that pain signifies damage is almost bound to end in withdrawal from activities thought to bring it on. Once an understanding of patients' thoughts about what is wrong has been uncovered, the physiotherapist can then sensitively challenge those beliefs by providing more specific, accurate and positive information. A major goal is to help the patient to use the information and go on to feel more confident and less fearful of movement and exercise (see also Chs 12 & 15).

It is worth finding out whether the patient has an informed and accurate understanding of their problem. Many do have a basic, but oversimplified, often unhelpful and confused model of their pain (see Ch. 12 for examples). Many patients eagerly wish for more understanding of their pain and feel some clinicians may not want to burden them with what is perceived as unnecessary and complicated information. Patients need accurate information about the nature and known mechanisms of chronic pain as well as information about the health needs of their tissues. This should involve providing detailed, accurate, easy to understand and relevant information about such things as healing, scar tissue formation, nerve, joint, bone and muscle tissue health.

Asking patients the following questions may be useful in identifying patients' beliefs about their pain and disability:

What do you understand is wrong from what the doctors have told you?

Patients may say they understand a lot, but what they describe usually adheres strongly to a tissue based medical model that really only serves to reinforce their disability (see Part 2 of this book). Patients often admit to not understanding or remembering explanations because they were either too complicated or not written down. Explanations may have been given but did little to adequately address or explain the patient's own anxieties about the pain and its behaviour. Many are given the impression, or actually told, that they will end up in a wheelchair, which has obvious implications for your particular style of approach and the information you may give. Patients vary tremendously in how they interpret information. As mentioned earlier, it is crucial that on initial contact physiotherapists do not try to query or question the beliefs the patient has about their pain.

Has any one explained to you why they think your pain has lasted so long?

Patients generally have no idea of the neurophysiological changes that occur with chronic pain (see Chs 2-5). Re-formulating this information in an easy to understand and useful way is vital to help patients appreciate why, despite past injury, pain and increased sensitivity can persist. Understandably, once patients have this information they often start to feel in more control of what is happening.

Has anyone explained what a whiplash injury actually is?

Does the patient believe that his/her neck is very unstable and held together by 'ripped pieces of muscle and injured and crumbling joints'? Do they understand the structures involved in the injury and the mechanisms of repair, and why they have some of the sensations they have? Explaining many of these issues to the patient in a way they can understand is a high level skill and requires the therapist to have a thorough and up-to-date understanding of injury mechanisms (in this case whiplash) in the context of recent pain mechanism models.

What does the term ... mean to you?

Questions like this help to glean information about how patients interpret medical terminology. Patients often hear or see complex medical words and try to understand what they mean themselves. Unfortunately, they often misconstrue the seriousness of the words, which may add to their fear, and avoidance of physical activities. For example, the term arthritis means a serious, progressive and disabling disease to most people, including some health workers. Interpretations can vary from simple wear and tear, to crumbling of bones, worn out cartilage and bone rubbing bone, for example. In contrast, to physiotherapists it may imply a relatively benign state with stiff underused joints that with appropriate movement tends to improve. Being able to impart this sort of helpful information to patients during the course of intervention can have a tremendous influence on patients' eagerness to move.

Does that make sense to you?

This question is not supposed to sound patronising but is useful because it helps identify the level of control that patients may feel over their pain. It is understandable that if the pain does not make any sense, a sufferer can feel confused, misunderstood and disillusioned. Checking out what you say to patients is vital in giving patients the opportunity to go over things again.

Patients' activity levels (previous and current)

Identifying what patients are currently able to manage in their daily routines, gives valuable information concerning their level of activity. You are not so much investigating the aggravating and easing factors relating to their pain, as shifting your focus to a more functional and far less pain focused one.

These two questions may be helpful:

What sort of things are you able to do at home/work?
What do you do during the day?

Here, the focus is on achievements rather than on activities and tasks people avoid or cannot manage. Even at this early stage, the patient may well be starting to feel a higher sense of achievement than they would normally. It seems almost universal that we tend to be dominated by a focus on the things that we do not achieve, or do not complete 'well enough'. For patients with chronic pain this negative, unhelpful tendency is often greatly heightened. Physiotherapy, even on initial contact, can start to assist patients to develop a far more positive and helpful way of viewing themselves.

Gaining a picture about daily routines will also give you an idea about what is important for patients. You may find that they spend most of the day lying down, or wearing a collar at work, or that they never stop to take a rest. Knowledge here can help the patient and physiotherapist identify meaningful goals, which can then form the framework of intervention.

125

Work history

Do patients currently work, were they made redundant because of their pain, or did they seek early retirement? Enquire for specific answers to the above questions. Do patients believe that work is an unrealistic goal, or are they very keen to return to work? It is important that the role of work is normalised, and that work is seen as a part of normal life. Patients though are understandably unsure as to whether it is possible or not. Physiotherapists can help patients identify goals and plans and reinforce the idea that work can be a realistic goal.

Use of aids

During the assessment you will identify whether patients use any aids, such as collars, corsets or sticks, and establish when they are used. Most patients are aware that, in the long term, aids are detrimental, but that in the short term they can help them achieve better activity levels. The suggestion that aids are not necessary can be challenging. Throughout follow-up sessions you can explore with patients the advantages of reducing the use of aids. A reduction plan needs to do done in a paced and systematic way. In the long term, aids will increase dependence and disability and decrease patients' confidence in moving that part of the body or going out of doors.

An example of how to help patients reduce the use of a collar is described in the *pacing and planning* section below.

Patients goals and reasons for seeking help

Asking the patient, 'What would you like me to help you with?' and, 'If you were to become fitter what would like to be able to do or return to doing?' can help you and the patient set goals against which progress can be measured. By enquiring about sports and exercise goals, you are implying that these activities are quite achievable, so patients' expectations and confidence may increase.

This also gives you an insight into what patients expect from you and how realistic they are. For example, if a patient responds by saying, 'I want to be pain free', you will need to explore this further. Some patients will say this, but actually think it is not possible and can be relieved if you say that a cure is not possible. At other times, patients may give you a stream of goals and it is necessary to encourage them to prioritise. Goal setting and how to review them will be explained further in the management section.

Assessment of patients' movement

Ideally this is a hands-off assessment. The essence of a self-management approach is for the health practitioner to ascertain what the patient can do on his or her own.

A useful preparatory statement could be:

I would like to have a look at your movement—which parts are looser or stiffer— but I do not want you to have a big increase in pain. I will ask you to move in several directions and I would like you just to do what feels comfortable.

You are interested in observing and assessing the quality of movement: what moves in a relaxed and loose way, and patients' unconscious tension habits during movement as well as at rest. If you witness any efforts at relaxed and more natural movements, you can reinforce them (see below). Patients find it very encouraging if they are told that despite their movement being stiff and tight, some of it is being performed in a relaxed manner.

The way a patient moves will give you information about fear of moving. It is common for patients to be seen to perform normal free movements one moment, yet when focused on specific movements during physical examination to execute them with considerable tension and express much distress (see also Ch. 14). For many clinicians this amounts to proof of malingering. However, an enlightened consideration of patients' fear of moving parts that are focused on, and the simple physiological effect focusing has on opening the 'pain gate' to consciousness, should lead to a much needed reappraisal.

Important components of management

Below are key coping strategies that physiotherapists can teach patients and incorporate during sessions with patients.

Goal setting

The effectiveness of physiotherapy input with chronic pain patients is often measured by enquiring about patients' pain, for example:

How is your pain?
Is your pain better, the same or worse?

This approach poses an immediate problem if the aim of intervention is related to functional improvement and not pain intensity. Its use will only serve to confuse. If patients are aware that your focus is on function and the achievement of goals, they will immediately provide you with easily assessed measures of progress. For example, they may report being able to walk much more easily and for 2 or 3 minutes longer than previously. They may have managed to go out socially and meet friends they had abandoned due to their disability. Hence:

'Often people give up hobbies and interests, and social activities as well as work and chores. It is important that these quality of life activities are included in both short and long-term goals on which to be worked' (Harding, 1997).

Supporting and encouraging patients to set realistic and achievable short-term goals, for activities or problem areas they would like to return to, is vital.

Goals may be orientated towards work, pleasure, and social or physical activities. What is important is that they are determined by the patient and not by the physiotherapist. Once goals are identified, the factors that are hindering them need to be determined. Working these out together, and breaking down the goals into functional 'building blocks' provides a starting point for change. Pacing and planning can then increase these building blocks.

Reviewing goals regularly allows you both to reinforce changes. But as Harding (1997) points out, patients need to be flexible in the way they set them, learning to alter their expectations and adjust them to compensate for any changing circumstances.

The overactivity and underactivity cycle

Patients often cycle from days of overdoing activity to days of doing very little. This frustrating pattern of overactivity followed by underactivity links to days of less pain and days of more pain. The danger times are the days of less pain, since patients tend do more when things hurt less or they feel more confident. The problem is that overactivity and struggling on usually results in pain exacerbation, followed by further rest with its consequences of stiffness and weakness, and the ongoing perpetuation of the unhelpful cycle. Pacing and planning are strategies that can prevent this cycle from continuing, as described below.

Pacing and planning

Once building blocks for activities have been identified, measurements need to be taken from where they can be built. It is suggested that 2 or 3 measures are taken on consecutive days. Patients then take an average of the times for each building block or activity and start at 80% of the average. This is their baseline.

From this point the patient can decide on the pacing increments for each building block. For example:

	Baseline 1	Baseline 2	Average/80%	Pacing (weekly)	Start
Sitting	10 min	12 min	11 min / 8 min	+ 30 sec	8 min
Walking	20 min	10 min	15 min / 12 min	+1 min	12 min
Collar off time	1 min	2 min	1.5 min / 1 min	+ 10 sec	1 min

When anyone starts a new movement or action there is likely to be some training pain. Patients who have chronic pain need to very gradually get used to new or previously avoided activities, while at the same time slowly building up their confidence. This helps keep training pain to a manageable level and prevents unhelpful return to activity avoidance (see Ch. 13).

Pacing is a systematic approach of building on the amount that can be easily managed according to a quota system. Pacing is a means to an end. It is a strategy that will allow patients to increase their fitness and exposure to activities, in a gradual way (see graded exposure discussion, Ch. 13). It changes behaviour from pain dependent to time dependent. The patient will then be less likely to overdo as time is a far more helpful guide than pain. Harding (1997) describes the principles of pacing as:

- Make a plan. Prioritise what has to be done on a daily basis.
- Start activities with realistically low baselines, then build up tolerance to the activities gradually and systematically.
- Take regular rests between activities.
- Change position regularly while performing activities.
- Do small amounts often, rather than doing everything at once.
- Avoid long unbroken periods of either activity or rest.

Below is an example of how a patient can pace the reduction of a collar:

Week 1: Take collar off for 1 minute every hour (the time length can be decided by the patient, ensuring they feel confident they can achieve it even on days of increased pain). Add gentle stretches when collar is off, but encourage the patient to move little and often whilst the collar is on.

Week 2: Increase the time that the collar is off by a fixed increment e.g. 1 extra minute. Add further stretches to the routine, ensuring that they are done gently and slowly. Patients may report slight increases in their pain. Again, ensure that the exercises are done slowly and in a relaxed way. This is far more reassuring to the patient than telling them to stop doing them which can imply danger or damage.

Week 3: Continue to encourage the patient to decide on the time increase for removing the collar and building the stretches more frequently.

Exercise

As with activities, pacing is also applied to the introduction of routine exercises. The physiotherapist needs to help patients identify a baseline (starting point from where exercises can begin). This is the amount of stretch/movement or exercise that is easily manageable, can be done comfortably, and does not cause a flare-up in patients' pain (pain levels remaining higher than normal for a period of more than 2 hours later). As above, this process can be established over several days, thereby allowing for any natural fluctuation in patients' day to day pain behaviour. The baseline is determined by taking the average number (or time) of repetitions achieved over the trial days and reducing this by 20%. Once the baseline has been determined, a gradual increase can be introduced. For example, adding in 3 more repetitions of an arm exercise over a week.

Unfortunately many chronic pain patients all to quickly abandon exercises because of pain exacerbation and the associated fear of further damage. However, once they learn to start more gradually and take on the notion that pain or bodily sensations are not an important cue to stop, they more effectively increase their exercise tolerance and strength. It may be far better to help them reinterpret this as a reasonable response of very unfit and sensitive tissues to new activity, and to then encourage continued carefully graded practice.

Fordyce (1976) introduced the use of a quota system wherein pain patients decide specific exercise quotas to achieve prior to commencing. He found that pain levels notably do not determine patients' final targets and his use of a quota system in increasing patients fitness has been supported by others, e.g. Doleys et al (1982) and Lindstrom et al (1992). This model is commonly used within CBT pain management programmes, and is a useful and easily applied approach for individual patient-therapist settings. Reinforcement techniques, as mentioned earlier, can be used in conjunction to maximise the positive effects patients feel during exercise sessions and improve confidence.

The inclusion of specific exercises can vary but clearly should address relevant loss of function as well as being linked to activity goals. The following quote provides an appropriate message for the physiotherapist dealing with pain:

> Exercises should be linked to the restoration of function, especially if taught by a physiotherapist whom the patient is likely to perceive, based on previous experience, as providing interventions aimed at alleviating pain. When using the cognitive behavioural approach, the physiotherapist is acting more as a trainer, teaching the patient what she/he can do for him/herself, rather than providing the hands on treatments such as manipulation or massage that the patient may have previously received. (Nicholas 1996)

It is important that the exercise programme includes components that address movements and activities that have been persistently avoided. A programme of gradual exposure and mastery of these movements and activities is essential and reinforces the message that painful movements do not equate with damage when practised regularly and at an appropriate level (see also Ch. 13). At the same time patients are actively engaged in functional recovery, restoration of tissue health and confidence building. Patients with chronic neck pain for example, commonly avoid neck extension. A patient may decide on an initial baseline rate of looking up very gently for only 1 second every hour. If this is confidently achieved, however, it will help this patient to feel content to follow his/her quota system and to repeat it slightly further into range with an increase to 2 seconds the following week. The patient also learns that looking up does not have devastating effects, but actually plays a part in providing easier movements generally.

Flare-up plans

As with many ongoing conditions, chronic pain fluctuates and patients experience flare-ups and set backs (pain remaining high for more than 2 days). Plans to cope with these eventualities are extremely useful. They help patients to remain in control of their pain and take appropriate steps to minimise its increase. Helpful strategies for patients during flare-ups include:

- Precise pacing, checking that times are not exceeded.

- Systematic use of stretch, especially for muscles that are tighter. The patient may want to apply ice or heat to specific areas and then stretch. It is vital that patients do not stop exercising at these times.

- Problem solve with the patient possible causes and identify changes as necessary. Not all flare-ups have easily identifiable causes though.
- Regular rest and relaxation breaks are vital.
- Prioritise plans for the day, but do not move everything to the next day.
- Help patients acknowledge what they can manage and encourage them to reinforce themselves.

During set backs, where the pain is present for a lot longer, slightly different strategies are used: a systematic cut back of all tolerances and exercises, followed by a gradual increase over the following 3, 5 or 7 days. It is up to the patient to decide.

Reinforcement is fundamental to flare-up management. When a patient experiences a flare up it is important not to suggest trying something new or to stop the exercise plan as this sows seeds of concern that they may be doing the wrong thing at home. Telling a patient that they are doing the right things but that it may be worthwhile checking how they are doing the exercises can be particularly useful.

Information and patient education

Much of the information content has already been discussed throughout this book but it is important to be aware that patients' fears are unlikely to reduce with information alone. Patients will only come to believe the accuracy of what you say by trying things out in practice. It is only then that they learn that exercise, pain and damage are not directly or proportionately connected. Gratifyingly for patients, once they have overcome their fears and become fitter and more in control, the converse relationship is often found.

Equally, it is only fair to expect patients to be ready to make changes when they are well informed and in a position to make their own choices. This type of information clearly needs to be given prior to and alongside exercise programmes. It is always important to check what the patient has heard and understood, as well as allowing the patient time to ask a lot of questions. It is very surprising how what we as physiotherapists perceive as basic information, is for patients new and difficult information. Giving patients time to explore new information with us can be a major reason why patients are able to become confident with exercise and increased activity levels despite chronic pain.

Sports and hobbies

Sports and hobbies are far more enjoyable ways for patients to increase their fitness or maintain it. They are social, and are perceived much more now as a healthy component of any person's lifestyle. Goals setting will help patients identify what they are interested in, and physiotherapists' reinforcement of ideas can maximise patients' eagerness. Most sports should be encouraged, when paced and built up to gradually. There is no reason why patients with chronic pain should avoid them.

Rainville et al (1992) studied the association of strenuous physical activities with self-reported increases in pain in chronic low back pain sufferers. They found that after a rehabilitation programme all physical measures improved significantly, but there were no changes in reported pain measures. Significantly they concluded that patients with chronic pain could increase their physical performance within the same pain experiences.

Issues of maintenance

Harding (1997) provides us with this valuable quote, that should be remembered throughout the interaction with chronic pain patients. 'Helping patients by giving physical support, being the sole source of information and always coming up with solutions for problems results in patients being disempowered and unlikely to maintain improvement once they have left treatment.'

Central to any intervention aimed at helping patients manage their pain more successfully is that they are able to continue to maintain the changes and improvements without therapist assistance. Ideally physiotherapists do not want patients to ring up whenever they experience a flare-up or to ask for many further appointments. The ultimate goal is to give them the confidence in their skills to be able to manage their pain effectively and independently. This includes accepting and managing inevitable pain flare-ups.

By having previously encouraged patients to set their own baselines and quota increases, by having encouraged independence, personal goal setting, form filling and facilitating the patient to recognise their own achievements, therapists should find that patients are more likely to gain a higher sense of control and as a result be more likely to continue with a home programme. It is worth pointing out that any improvements patients make need to be perceived as being due to their own skills and inputs and attributed to their own coping efforts rather than to something done to or for them by a professional (see Hanson & Gerber 1990).

Talking through your plan of treatment and telling them well in advance when their last appointment will be helps patients prepare and plan questions for you. Sticking to your agreed plan is important and, unless you feel the patient definitely needs more time with you, it is best not to extend treatment sessions. Arranging a follow-up appointment in 6 months and encouraging the patient to ring you if problems arise can be very helpful. The reality is that patients rarely seem to do this if they know help is available.

Bear in mind that research has provided three possible reasons to explain why patients with chronic pain find it difficult to continue or make progress with treatment (Sluijs et al 1993).

1 The barriers that patients perceive and encounter.
2 A lack of positive feedback on their performance (see reinforcement section earlier).
3 The degree of helplessness they feel.

Hence, being aware of these and trying to minimise them through the strategies outlined can only add to changes a patient can make. If at discharge patients are asked what they feel they have gained, they often say that although the pain has not gone away they feel that are much more in control of it and that this is a very nice feeling. Patients who believe they have some control over their pain tend to report less pain and distress and exhibit lower levels of disability (Feuerstein & Beattie 1995).

Conclusion

The task of the physiotherapist in teaching a self-management approach to the chronic pain patient is undoubtedly a challenging one. There is often considerable discrepancy between patients' beliefs about their condition and hopes of treatment, and the information being provided by the physiotherapist. Most importantly, the approach instils a sense of control, which promotes the long-term maintenance of the gains made in treatment.

Physiotherapists are in a good position to help patients by using the cognitive-behavioural principles outlined in this chapter. They can provide patients with realistic hopes of improving function and mobility, and therefore quality of life, despite the presence of persistent pain. Patients can be helped to increase their self-esteem by informing them that it is quite possible to increase their fitness and function despite the pain and that pain will not stop them from getting fitter. Once patients can accept this they are likely to regain considerably better movement quality and far more enjoyable levels of activity. At the same time the therapist should be prepared to acknowledge that this goal is not an easy one and that it requires much effort to reach.

There are many reasons why physiotherapists find it difficult to help patients in chronic pain achieve their goals and it is likely that both the physiotherapist and the patients often feel frustrated, anxious and helpless during sessions. Fundamentally, this will occur much more when both parties have an unrealistic expectation of achieving pain relief and cure. Physiotherapists therefore, have a vital role in facilitating the adoption of a more helpful model and guiding patients towards more meaningful and satisfying lives.

REFERENCES

Battie M C, Cherkin D C, Dunn R 1995 Managing low back pain: Attitudes and treatment preferences of physical therapists. Physical Therapy 74:219–226

Cairns D, Pascino J A 1977 Comparison of verbal reinforcement and feedback in the operant treatment of disability due to chronic low back pain. Behavior Therapy 8: 621–630

Doleys D, Crocker M, Patten D 1982 Response of patients with chronic pain to exercise quotas. Physical Therapy 62:1111–1114

Feuerstein M, Beattie P 1995 Biobehavioural Factors Affecting Pain and Disability in Low Back Pain: Mechanisms and Assessment. Physical Therapy 75(4):267–280

Flor H, Fydrich T, Turk D C 1992 Efficacy of multidisciplinary pain treatment centers: a meta-analytic review. Pain 49:221–230

Fordyce W E 1976 Behavioural methods for chronic pain and illness. M O C V Mosby, St Louis

Fordyce W E, Roberts A, Sternbach R 1985 Behavioural management of chronic pain: A response to critics. Pain 22:113

Fordyce W E, Brockway J A, Bergman J A, Spengler D 1986 Acute back pain: a control-group comparison of behavioral vs traditional management methods. Journal of Behavioral Medicine 9(2):127–140

Gil K M, Ross S L, Keefe F J 1988 Behavioural treatment of chronic pain: Four pain management protocols. In: France R D, Krishnan K D D (eds) Chronic pain. American Psychiatric Press, Washington 376–413

Harding V H 1997 Application of the cognitive-behavioural approach. In: Rehabilitation of movement: Theoretical basis of clinical practice. Saunders, London 540–583

Hanson R W, Gerber K E 1990 Coping with chronic pain; A guide to patient self-management. Guildford Press, New York

Keefe F J 1982 Behavioural and cognitive-behavioural approaches to chronic pain: recent advances and future directions. Journal of Consulting and Clinical Psychology 60(4):528–536

Lindstrom I, Ohlund C, Eek C, Wallin L, Peterson L E, Fordyce W E, Nachemson A L 1992 The effect of graded activity on patients with subacute back pain: a randomised prospective clinical study with an operant behavioural approach. Physical Therapy 72:279–293

Linton S 1986 Behavioural remediation of chronic pain: A status report. Pain 24:125

Linton S 1996 Early interventions for the secondary prevention of chronic musculoskeletal pain. In: Cambell J N (ed) Pain 1996: an updated review: Refresher course syllabus. IASP Press, Seattle 305–311

Magni G, Moreschi C, Rigatli-Luchini S, Merskey H 1994 Prospective study on the relationship between depressive symptoms and chronic musculoskeletal pain. Pain 56:289–297

Melzack R, Wall PD 1996 The challenge of pain. Penguin, London

Nicholas M 1996 Theory and practice of cognitive-behavioural programs. In: Campbell, J N (ed) Pain 1996: an updated review: Refresher course syllabus. IASP Press, Seattle 297–303

Philips H C 1988 The psychological management of chronic pain: a treatment manual. Springer, New York

Rainville M D, Ahem D K, Phalen L, Childs L A, Sutherland R 1992 the association of pain with physical activities in chronic low back pain. Spine: 17(9):1060–1064

Sim J 1990 The concept of health. Physiotherapy 76(7):423–428

Simmonds M 1997 Pain and disability: A challenge for patients and practitioners. Physiotherapy Theory and practice 13:1–2

Sluijs E Kok G, Van der Zee J 1993 Correlates of exercise compliance in physical therapy. Physical Therapy 73:771–782

Turk DC, Meichenbaum D, Genest M 1983 Pain and behavioural medicine: A cognitive behavioural perspective. Guildford Press, New York

Turner J A, Clincy S, McQuade K J, Cardenas D D 1990 Effectiveness of behavioural therapy for chronic pain: a component analysis. Jour Consult Clin Psychol 58:573–579

Vlaeyen J W S, Kole-Snijders A M J, Boeren, R G B, van Eek H 1995 Fear of movement/(re)injury in chronic low back pain and its relation to behavioural performance. Pain 62:363–372

Waddell G 1987 A new clinical model for the treatment of low-back pain. Spine 12(7):632–643

Wells C 1997 Pain management: Pain clinic management of pain, intensity and distress from chronic whiplash. International Whiplash Conference. Ashton Court Manor, Bristol

Williams C 1996 Behavioural and Cognitive Section. UKCP News. UKCP 2nd Professional Conference: 3

Wolff M, Michel T H, Krebs D E 1991 Chronic pain: assessment of orthopaedic physical therapists' knowledge and attitudes. Physical Therapy 71:207–214

9

Patient assessment—case history

SUZANNE SHORLAND

The case history that follows illustrates the assessment and management strategies detailed in Chapter 8. It is a transcribed assessment based on an initial interview with a chronic pain patient four years after she sustained a whiplash injury. All personal details have been changed. The patient was seen individually, as an outpatient. The assessment occurred in a pain clinic where pain management principles are used. It is important to be aware that the direction an assessment takes is dictated in part by what the patient brings to the assessment and the questions that are raised. It is by no means definitive and should be adjusted to suit individual therapists and patients.

The referral received by the physiotherapist in 1997 was as follows:

This young patient (28 years old) sustained a whiplash injury in 1993. She has ongoing widespread pain, decreased fitness and is concerned about her future. No previous medical interventions have proved helpful; they included trigger point injections, acupuncture and medication. The patient has had a lot of previous physiotherapy.

Assessment. Session 1   1 hour

Physio: Good afternoon, Dr X has asked that we meet and today I would like to take the opportunity to get to know you and give you the opportunity to get to know me as well. I would like to chat about your experiences of exercise, what you think is causing your pain and then between us identify a future management plan. Dr X may have mentioned that the approach I use is likely to be different from that of previous physiotherapists you have met. I will not be doing any 'hands on' treatments, such as mobilisations or stretches on you. What I will aim towards is helping you incorporate some other strategies into your daily routine, whatever the environment. My experience is in helping people who have had pain a long time and are perhaps finding it difficult to keep fit, to know where to start exercising, to know what to do and when, or to increase their general level of activity. I will plan to expand on the ways this can happen during our meeting today. Have you had any physiotherapy before?

Patient: Yes, for about 2 years: 6 months initially after my accident, then a year later I had physiotherapy for another 8 months, and then in 1996 for about 8 months again; to be honest I am not sure why it stopped.

Physio: What sort of things did they do?

Patient: I reckon I've had the lot. First they tried traction—that made me worse—then ultrasound with some stretches. I remember that was quite helpful but the relief did not last for very long. I've had hydrotherapy, that was nice, but I got so tired afterwards I decided to stop.

Physio: You mentioned that you were unsure why the physiotherapy stopped, did the physiotherapist explain to you why?

Patient: Yes, she said that there was nothing she felt physiotherapy could help me with anymore.

Physio: Are you currently doing any stretches or other forms of exercise?

Patient: Well, I only do one or two occasionally. I've been told to do stretches every hour but I find them too painful, so I do my own thing really.

Physio: That's fine, what exactly do you do?

Patient: I turn my head to the left and right, I look downwards and if I feel OK I do some back arches and try to touch my toes. I'm not sure what else to do as they make me so sore. It's so frustrating though, I used to do so much exercise before the accident.

Physio: How often do you think you manage to do the exercises?

Patient: Oh, every morning I do the neck ones. If I remember I'll do some at work when I'm sitting.

Physio: That sounds like a helpful routine. Do you do much walking or other physical activities?

Patient: I occasionally walk to work instead of getting the tube, it depends on how I feel. If the pain is really bad I either stay indoors or avoid doing too much. My partner will take me places in the car. I actually think that not having been able to keep up with all the sports I used to do has not helped, but how do I do them when it hurts so much?

Physio: That is what we can explore and discuss today. What other medical treatments have you had?

Patient: The doctor here tried acupuncture. To be honest I was not sure what it was supposed to do, but it helped—though only at first. The day after, my neck was just as sore and stiff. I do think that my sleep pattern has improved since the doctor changed my medication. He has encouraged me to take weaker painkillers as the side effects were huge. I hope to gradually wean myself off them. The doctor seems really pleased with that. I also had some trigger point injections. They were agony, made me feel quite sick and I had a few headaches. The doctor stopped them because I was in more pain. Oh, I have also tried TNS; the machine seems to take the edge off so I can do a bit more. But then when I take it off, the next day seems really bad.

Physio: Have you noticed anything that leads to the bad days you mention?

Patient: My partner tells me I rush round the house and do everything when I feel in less pain. The next day then seems to be a bad day. But I really don't know—they seem so out of the blue.

Physio: It is a difficult concept, we'll come back to it later. Do you know if any of the doctors are planning any more medical treatments for you?

Patient: No there is nothing else they can do. I've just been told that you will help.

Physio: I'd like to ask you a little more about your pain. Can you tell me about the accident you had?

Patient: I had a whiplash injury in 1993. I was a passenger in a car. We were stationary at a set of traffic lights, I was talking to my partner who was the driver and a car hit us from behind. I remember hitting the headrest and the seat belt digging into me. I felt a headache come on over the next few hours and I think my neck became sore and stiff at about the same time. My partner felt OK, although I think he was a bit shocked.

Physio: What happened at casualty?

Patient: They told me I had sustained a whiplash injury, they X-rayed me, and told me I was OK. They gave me painkillers, a collar, and told me to go home and rest.

Physio: Were you given any advice on how much to use the collar?

Patient: I think I was told to take it off occasionally and gradually reduce its use, but my neck hurt so much I think I used it too much.

Physio: What makes you think that?

Patient: Well, I wonder if that's why I'm so stiff now, but it gives me such good support.

Physio: Do you still use it now?

Patient: Yes, for long journeys and when the pain is severe.

Physio: Do you travel in cars a lot?

Patient: Only when I have to, I still get pretty nervous. I was told that was normal though and that I should not avoid travelling in a car at all.

Physio: That's very helpful advice. If we go back to the accident again, can you briefly remember what happened between then and when you were referred here, to the pain clinic?

Patient: My pain continued to increase. My GP sent me back to casualty, they told me to get a referral to an orthopaedic specialist. My GP did this and the orthopaedic specialist gave me a MRI scan—but they told me it was clear. I also saw a neurosurgeon but I didn't want surgery and he was unsure if surgery would help my pain. I was then sent to see a physiotherapist in my local hospital. About 10 months ago I was referred here, to see the pain specialist. He said I have a chronic pain problem. I think that's why he asked me to see you, but I don't know why as there is probably nothing you can do for me.

Physio: It sounds as if you have seen a lot of different doctors and physiotherapists. Has anyone told you what a whiplash injury is or given you any explanations for why your pain has lasted?

Patient: No not really, they seem to say different things. I think whiplashes must be quite rare as they don't seem to know much. I know a whiplash injury is when your head goes forward and back very quickly, apparently it does not always come on from car accidents.

Physio: Can you remember any specific things people have told you?

Patient: In casualty I was told to rest, the physiotherapists told me to move, as I had a weak neck. After the X-ray I heard them mention wear and tear, something about degeneration. My GP has told me to get on with things but if I've got wear and tear surely I should keep still.

Physio: What do think?

Patient: I reckon my nerves are all caught up with my bones, the whiplash has shaken things up too much. Sometimes my head feels very unstable, I wonder if the muscles are working properly or maybe the doctors missed a slipped disc. To be honest I think some of the doctors think I am making it all up. They keep telling me the X-ray was fine and there is nothing to worry about and that my scan was clear. One doctor said it's been 4 years now and I should be back at work full time and playing sports again. The doctor here has explained a bit about chronic pain, how the brain is involved and why the brain registers chronic pain differently.

Physio: I would see it as important that throughout our sessions together we explore this more. Especially, how you can use some of the more up to date information about what you can do about your pain now, and how to increase your fitness despite the pain.

Patient: That would be helpful. Do you think I will ever be pain free?

Physio: What are your thoughts about that?

Patient: I'd love to be pain free, but don't think its possible now. The doctors and physiotherapists have tried everything and nothing helped. I think I've had the pain too long now, do you?

Physio: What I would say is that you are probably right in that you have had your pain such a long time now that a complete pain cure is unrealistic. But what I would say is that we can help you increase your fitness, strength, flexibility and endurance. That would then allow you to continue with or start new activities in your day-to-day routine. From the research and also my experience of working with people with chronic pain, it is possible to increase what you do despite the pain.

The different approach I mentioned earlier is based on helping you to become more in control of your pain. The focus of this approach is not on the pain itself. That is not because we don't think it exists or isn't real. We definitely believe you had a significant injury and have a real pain problem. The focus instead is on what you can do functionally and how together we can build on the things you would like to be able to do and hence improve your quality of life.

After any injury such as your whiplash, the body goes through a healing process, where everything mends itself. But in order for the body to heal in the most optimal way it needs to be moved, stretched and exercised little and often.

Patient: But I rested and wore a collar for ages.

Physio: Yes, but you also tried to do some exercises. The difficulty you have experienced is that when you tried to exercise the pain increased so you stopped.

Patient: That is exactly what happened.

Physio: What happens when the healing process occurs is that after about two days after the injury, the fibres start to mend together whilst there is still swelling. The swelling is vital to help promote healing but it is only required for a short period of time. If the area is kept still the swelling will stay there and its normal glue like properties tend to aggravate the healing process by sticking many of the tissues together—even the undamaged ones. The consequences are that the scar tissue, the result of the healing process, tightens around the whole area involved. The longer that area is kept still the tighter the scar tissue becomes and hence movement becomes stiffer and tighter.

Patient: So is that why my movement is getting worse?

Physio: Probably, because as you attempt to kept fit and active you are over-using the tight structures which actually have been under-used, so they go from one extreme to the other. But it is never too late to start stretching scar tissue, it loves to be stretched gently and daily. That is why we will include exercise in a management programme for you. You start at your level and then you can progress to more strengthening and aerobic exercises. What you will find though is that if you stop stretching, the scar tissue tightens up and movement becomes stiff again. There are also lots of other things involved in the healing process and the way the body responds to inactivity but we can cover that later in further sessions.

But so far, does that make sense to you?

Patient: It's different from what other people say; all I can do is give it a go.

Physio: That's the best approach, and take things at your pace. Can you tell me about the things you do during the day?

Patient: Well, I work 3 days a week in a primary school. It's getting harder though, as I have to sit with the children on their small chairs. My neck pain seems to have increased over the last year.

Physio: What exactly does your daily routine comprise?

Patient: I get up at 7.00, start work at 9.00 and finish at 3.00. I only work Mondays, Wednesdays and Fridays. I try to get to work earlier so I can prepare for the day, but basically once I'm at work I don't stop 'til 3.00.

Physio: Do you have any breaks during the day?

Patient: Yes, we get 45 minutes for lunch, which I usually use to prepare the afternoons lessons. We also get coffee breaks, which I never take.

Physio: Why is that?

Patient: Oh, I'm just so busy and I don't think I'm that organised to be able to spare the time.

Physio: What do you think would happen if you did take the coffee breaks regularly?

Patient: I don't know, no-one else seems to take theirs and just because I have a neck problem, doesn't mean I can't do the job.

Physio: Maybe this is something to come back to later. Do you do many social things in the evenings or at weekends?

Patient: Occasionally, but I tend to be so tired in the evenings. I save big things for Saturdays when I don't have to get up too early. My partner is getting a bit frustrated with me as we don't do much together, especially sports. But he's very good really, he does most of the cleaning and shopping, as I find it hard to carry and use my arms a lot. My partner says I should save my energy for work.

Physio: Do you find that helps?

Patient: Well it did initially, but I don't want to carry on like this. I seem no better or worse whether I do some things or not. I find it so peculiar as some days things are easier than others, although I'm doing exactly the same as the day before.

Physio: It's understandable that it seems peculiar and you mentioned earlier the unpredictability of your pain. Unfortunately it is the very process of fluctuating the amount of activity you do from day to day that is affecting your fitness and adding to your pain levels. Muscles like to be used little and often in a systematic way. If, for example you do a big shop every two weeks, as that seems easier than having to go often, you then demand of your body to do things it has not done for two weeks. If you think of athletes' training schedules—they will train daily for optimum fitness. The shopping example I just gave is like asking your body to run a marathon without any training.
Does that make sense?

Patient: Yes, but how do I build my fitness without increasing the pain levels. I don't want more pain.

Physio: No, but you do not want a lot of the training pain from overdoing things when your body is not used to it. We need to find a systematic approach you can take to exercise, thereby increasing your activity level and general fitness. The key is to start with a little amount of anything, that you can comfortably manage and then build on it daily or weekly. What you then do is exercise or stretch every day. You don't do more on the days you feel less pain and equally you don't do less on the days you are in more pain. On those days you may be even more gentle and take more time, but you are trying to avoid the swings in activity from good days and bad days, like the shopping example.

Patient: So will I be able to get back to badminton?

Physio: Yes, I think it is a great goal, if you slowly build on the building blocks that it involves and increase in a systematic and paced way. Are there other physical things you would like to return to or improve if you were to become fitter?

Patient: I'd like to feel stronger, get my stamina back. I used to love swimming, I've stopped now as my neck gets so stiff.

Physio: That's great that you'd like to swim again. Anything else?

Patient: Play golf, go to the gym with my partner, I'd love to return to horse riding. Sports were a major part of my life before the accident. Do you really think I can get back to them?

Physio: Bearing in mind what we have chatted about so far, what do you think?

Patient: Well no one else has said I could do sports. My GP told me never to horse ride again.

Physio: What do you think now?

Patient: We'll have to see but if I can build on my strength and stamina, and as you say build on things slowly.

Physio: The important think is to progress slowly as you said, because then your body, your muscles, and all the other soft tissues have time to build up within your limits and you will not be pushing your fitness levels. When you have pain flare-ups after you have done any exercise what do you think has happened to you body?

Patient: I'm not sure, I guess I've pulled a disc out or ripped a muscle. The pain can be so intense that I must have done something wrong.

Physio: Do you believe that the pain means you have done damage to your body?

Patient: I think so, yes. That's why I'm not sure about doing any exercise.

Physio: It's an understandable feeling because when you have previously exercised your pain has increased. What we definitely know though is that the pain increases you have are not because you are damaging yourself. What you are doing is overusing structures such as muscles, nerve sheaths—the surroundings of nerves, ligaments and tendons. These structures do not like being overused and consequently, you can feel a range of sensations after or during activities.

Patient: Is that why my right arm sometimes feels so peculiar and heavy?

Physio: Yes that could be because of a number of things. The blood flow around your muscles and nerves may be reduced because they are not being used fully; your muscles are weak and when overused give you training pain. What can happen is that you become very aware of all the sensations you feel in your body because you are so aware of your pain. The difficulty is that the sensations you feel are normal and are not warning signs of ongoing damage. This does not mean that the activities that cause them should be avoided; if anything it is the opposite. To reduce these sensations the more you practice the movements or activities the less they may occur and they will become less frightening to you as nothing awful happens when they occur.

Does that make sense?

Patient: Yes it seems so logical, why has no one told me this before?

Physio: Things are changing, we once thought that people should rest if things hurt, now the evidence is much stronger that exercise, when done slowly, gently and systematically, can help people increase and maintain their fitness despite pain. But it is also important to know that most clinicians are not taught much about chronic pain. Physiotherapists and doctors can become as frustrated as people who have the pain, especially when they are unsure of what to do. The approach is changing and it is not too late for you to start making changes.

Are there any other goals you have, that are not sports?

Patient: Well work is a problem really, I'd like to keep my job and build up to full-time. I'd also like to go on holiday abroad. I've avoided it because of the journey involved. Then there's all the household chores my partner does, I would like to be able to share them out with him more.

Physio: That is a great range, what I will ask you to do from session to session is to write them down and prioritise them, you can use them to see progress that you make. I have mentioned that the approach we use here is different, I will not be asking you about your pain itself, but about the things you can manage, for example, the exercises I will suggest, work issues that you decide to tackle and so on. You are in control of the goals you want to achieve, they are not mine, but we can work together to help you learn the strategies that will make achieving them possible.

Patient: That sounds great.

Physio: Can you tell me where exactly you have your pain? Do you have any neck pain?

Patient: It's here in the middle and then down to the right side.

Physio: Do you have pain on the left side of your neck?

Patient: Only on bad days when the pain is high. I also get pain down my right arm.

Physio: Where exactly?

Patient: Here, on the outside of the upper part and then in my elbow and occasionally in my forearm.

Physio: Do you have any pain in your left arm?

Patient: No.

Physio: Do you get headaches?

Patient: Yes, terrible; it feels like my head is being crushed.

Physio: Where do you get them?

Patient: Here, over the right side of my head and towards my eye. It's weird though, the top of my head feels really sensitive

Physio: I can explain about that later on. Do you have any pain from the neck down your back?

Patient: Not really.

Physio: So do you get some pain?

Patient: Occasionally I get sore between my shoulder blades and I'm aware that my lower back is getting stiffer, but I'm trying to ignore it.

Physio: Do you have any pain down your legs into your feet?

Patient: No, never.

Physio: Do you have any pins and needles or numbness?

Patient: I used to have lots of pins and needles, but they are less now. I get them in my right hand. Sometimes I have that odd heavy feeling in my right arm but I don't have any numbness.

Physio: Do you get dizzy?

Patient: Oh, yes a lot, especially if I do a lot. Why is that?

Physio: Possibly it is to do with the stiffness in your neck; we commonly see that people who have a stiff neck get dizzy. I can show you some exercises that will help. The key again is do them slowly and start with a realistic amount

Patient: OK.

Physio: Are you taking any pain medication?

Patient: I'm only having the occasional painkiller when the pain is really high. I have stopped the others I was taking last year.

Physio: Well done, that's quite an achievement. How do you feel about it?

Patient: I feel quite proud of myself, but I actually feel better in my self too; I'm not so sleepy and I think I'm able to concentrate more than before.

Physio: It's really great that you recognise the importance of having made those changes.

Finally, today I would like to see how much movement you have. I want to know what you are comfortable doing, I do not want you to have a flare-up from seeing me so its important that you don't push these. Firstly, if you look up towards the ceiling, and then down to your chest. How does it feel?

Patient: Tight here on the right side.

Physio: Why do you think that is?

Patient: Well I guess its because all my muscles and ligaments are tight and stiff because I have not moved much in these directions. Is it the scar tissue pulling?

Physio: That's correct. Next, if you turn to your left and then right.

Patient: Oh, I'm much tighter on the right but it pulls on the left a bit too?

Physio: Why do you think that is?

Patient: I don't know. I only occasionally get pain there.

Physio: Pain and stiffness though do not necessarily follow hand in hand. You could be very stiff and have little pain and visa versa. The body is very interconnected, if one part is not moving easily, other parts will be affected. The movement to your right is tight and that will affect the muscles and other structures on the left, this is why some people describe their pain as spreading.

Next, if you tilt your head to the right, keeping your face towards me. That's right, only move to your comfortable limit. And if you tilt to the left.

Patient: I never realised I was so tight.

Physio: Now I would like to see how much you can move your arms. If you lift your arms forward and up, how far do you feel comfortable moving them?

Patient: That pulls now.

Physio: It can be surprising how much the body misses movement. The tightness there indicates that your middle back, your thoracic spine is also stiff— which may be why you are getting some tightness there if you over-sit.

Patient: That makes sense.

Physio: I think it will be important to see how the rest of your body moves. I'll ask you next to do some back movements. If you slide your hands down the front of your legs how far does it feel comfortable to go?

Patient: Here, by my knees, then it starts to pull.

Physio: If you place your hands in the lower part of your back how for can you arch backwards?

Patient: This is tight, it makes me feel a bit dizzy.

Physio: Do you do it often?

Patient: No, I think I avoid it.

Physio: I wonder if there is a link there, between something you don't feel comfortable doing, and something that is very stiff and tight.

Patient: I've never thought of it that way.

Physio: It is worth thinking about. If you now slide your right hand down the outside of your right leg and then your left hand down your left leg. Are you able to crouch down, have a go?

Generally you are tight and stiff, I think we can help improve that as well as your muscle strength. But overall it sounds as if you have coped very well to get this far. I think I can help you to extend upon some of the things you are doing but also I can provide you with some new strategies that can help you increase your fitness, and the understanding of your pain—so that you may do more of the things that are important to you and hence improve the quality of your life.

All of what we have talked about I have written down, so you can go over it in your own time and then we can discuss it further. But have you any questions from what we have discussed today?

Patient: What exercises do you think I should do then?

Physio: What I suggest you do is try the following stretches. Remembering that you only take them to your comfortable limit, do not push them or try to push through the pain. That will tend to increase muscle tension and hence increase pain in that area. Hold each stretch for a count of 5 and then relax. Breathing as you perform each stretch will maximise relaxation. If we do the stretches together you can see what I mean.

Stand with your feet comfortably apart, and slowly take your arms out to the side, this will stretch your upper body, into your neck and back. Count to 5 and let it go. That was lovely and relaxed.

The next is the same but with your palms facing upwards to the ceiling. Just take it to you comfortable limit. Count to 5 and take your arms back down. That seems tight, how do you think I can tell?

Patient: I'm pulling faces and I don't think I'm relaxing enough.

Physio: Yes, the signs of trying too hard or pushing are screwing up your face, tensing your muscles such as your shoulders, and grunting or holding your breath.

The next stretches are again with your feet apart. Reach both arms up towards the ceiling, only as far as feels comfortable. Count to 5 and let go. That is good not to force your arms up higher.

Bend sideways, sliding one arm down the outside of your leg. Repeat the other way.

Repeat and raise the opposite arm up as you bend to one side. Repeat the other way.

With one hand holding onto the side of the chair, lean to the opposite side, tilt the head the same way and gently guide the head down (do not pull). Repeat to the other side.

Repeat but this time turn your head to the side instead of tilting it and then gently guide it. Repeat to the other side.

Do they feel manageable?

Patient: Yes, I need to remember to do them gently, it's so easy to get carried away and push them.

Physio: It is good that you are aware of the tendency to push. You could write 'gently' down on a piece of paper so you can see it when you do your stretches. It will help you remember. Try them daily, experimenting a bit to see what fits your routine. You can do them as many times as you like but remember that your body is not used to stretching at the moment, so spread them out. A lot of people decide to try it once a day at first. You may find that they will help you at work and that you can incorporate them into all your other activities.

The other thing to have a look at is the amount you are able to pace during the day, that is breaking things up into manageable amounts so you do not over do or under do. Try to spread things out evenly over the days. What I suggest you do is note your current habits and then we can discuss them next time we meet. Does that all sound manageable?

Patient: I'll give it a go. I have no choice really as the way that I am currently doing things is not helping. When shall we meet up again?

Physio: I think we should meet up a couple of times in order to discuss in more detail all the things we have mentioned today. Such as posture and ergonomics, use of your breaks at work, formulating a specific plan for you to reduce the use of your collar, joining a gym, going horse riding and any other things you would like to discuss. I propose we meet for 6 sessions and we can decide together how to spread them out. When would like to see me next?

Patient: Well it will take me a while to read the information you have given me and I would like to have a go at the stretches. How about 2 weeks?

Physio: That's fine. If you have any queries between now and then write them down, then we can discuss them when we meet.

Below is a brief outline of the important issues to be covered in future sessions.

- Regular review of achievements and goals.
- Discussion of stretch exercises done, difficulties encountered and problem solving them with patient.
- Paced plan for collar reduction during journeys and during flare-ups.
- Patient to identify and use flare-up and set-back plans.
- Introduction of strengthening exercises, e.g. arm circles, weights lifting with an increasingly filled water bottle, and impact exercises to build confidence in jolting e.g. stand-ups, jogging and jumping.
- Patient to develop plans for joining the gym, restarting horse riding, tennis, golf and swimming.
- Regular re-setting and evaluation of goals.
- Further discussion concerning the effects of inactivity on the body.
- Discussion on posture and ergonomics.
  Problem issues at work, especially use of breaks, stretch and walks during lunch breaks.
- Re-introduction of activities in the evenings in a paced way.

Handouts are given to patients to back-up the information given during sessions. They are detailed and are given as appropriate, dependent on the patients' needs. They can include:

- The overactivity-underactivity cycle.
- How to exercise with chronic pain.
- The healing process.
- What the body needs— information about bones, ligaments, muscles, joints and nerve tissue.
- Stretch exercises.
- Posture and ergonomics.
- Possible sensations associated with pain.
- Sports and hobbies.
- Sexual issues and chronic pain.
- Upper limb pain.
- Pregnancy and chronic pain.
- Travel stretches and tips.
- Timetable sheets—to help patients plan their days and weeks.

10

Understanding people with chronic pain following whiplash: a psychological perspective

KATHARINE F TREVES

Introduction

Originally defined as neck injury following a rear end motor vehicle accident (Crowe 1928), whiplash is now more broadly defined as any acceleration/deceleration injury to the neck sustained in a vehicular or similar accident (Gay & Abbott 1953). Increasingly a worrisome health problem in the Western world, neck pain (following whiplash injury) is seen by the Quebec Task Force as 'to the automobile what low back pain is to the workplace' (Spitzer et al 1995). Most people recover from injury but it is estimated that 10–25 per cent develop chronic symptoms, mainly neck pain (Barnsley et al 1994). Although there are sensible calls to conceptualise their experience as similar to that of any other individual with chronic pain (Merskey 1993, Wallis et al 1996), misconceptions and puzzlement about the clinical presentation associated with whiplash injury seem to persist, perhaps because of the frequency of complicating factors such as litigation. This chapter aims to untangle some of the psychological factors which may be contributing to the chronicity of disability and distress in people with chronic neck pain following whiplash injury. A case example is used throughout to enhance links between clinical presentation and theory, and pointers for the physiotherapist working with this population are offered.

Case example

Mr R., a 51-year-old engineer who prior to his whiplash injury five years ago had enjoyed an active work, social and leisure life, limped into the room for his assessment with a bent-over posture, using a stick, and wearing a neck collar. He was unable to sit still, seeming to find it most uncomfortable to remain in one position. Occasionally he stood up explaining that this relieved his pain.

Mr R. explained that he now spent most of his day sitting watching television. He was able to go shopping with his wife as long as he could sit down whilst they were out, but described being unable to drive, and no longer able to play snooker, dance or carry out household chores as before. For example, he reported that it had recently taken him six frustrating hours to change a car radio and he had been in bed for a week after with a significant increase in his analgesics.

Emotionally, Mr R. was depressed and had been seeing a psychiatrist for three years. He described his marriage as under considerable strain and reported that his sexual activity was significantly curtailed. His sleep was disturbed and he described his memory and concentration as 'terrible'. In addition, he described continued feelings of bitterness about the accident initiating his pain (he was hit from behind whilst waiting to join traffic on a roundabout) and subsequent legal proceedings, and considerable anger towards the driver of the vehicle which hit him.

Mr R. explained that he still found it hard to talk about what happened in the accident but that he had been 'thrown about like a rag doll'. He understood that he had 'wear and tear' in his discs but stated that this had been pointed out to him from a medical examination prior to his accident and not given him any trouble. He stated that it didn't seem reasonable to have so much pain if this was all that was wrong exclaiming, 'They only scanned my neck—I could have a tumour as far as I know'. He described his arm and back as feeling 'twisted' and his limbs as going 'dead and paralysed' when he slept, causing him to wake frequently to move.

He and his wife were tearful during the interview and, having felt that previous health professionals had not believed the amount of pain he was in, and were 'hiding behind closed doors', were despairing of further medical advice. They described being angry at the amount and range of treatments he had received (analgesics, antidepressants, TENS, mobilisation and ultrasound), of which none had been successful, yet were desperate for help.

So how do we understand what has happened to Mr R.? He was an active and busy working man with no previous psychiatric history or marital problems—yet following a whiplash injury he is now physically very limited, his scores on standard questionnaires suggest high levels of emotional distress, and some of his behaviour seems hard to understand. So is it 'all psychological'? Surely a soft tissue injury couldn't cause this much disruption to someone's life. Is there a serious underlying organic cause, hitherto undetected? Or maybe he is 'putting it on'—but for what reason, since he has just received his compensation settlement?

In fact these are the very type of questions that have probably been in many clinicians' minds on meeting a Mr R.; and, as with many chronic pain sufferers, have been subtly (or not so subtly) conveyed to him, thus adding to his overall sense of being misunderstood and resulting in feelings of isolation, confusion and anger. It is clear that 'something is wrong' and current understanding of whiplash certainly recognises the extent of injury to cervical muscles, ligaments, discs, capsules, spinal cord, roots and nerves that can be produced by the hyperextension of the neck in a motor vehicle collision (Amundson 1994). Given that it is now five years since the original accident, however, it is unlikely to be 'simply' soft tissue damage in the neck producing the range of difficulties Mr R. is experiencing. Indeed, current understanding of pain emphasises that it is an emotional as well as sensory experience (Merksey & Bogduk 1994) and reflects upon the evidence that cognitive, motivational, judgmental and psychologic processes can all have a significant effect upon the transmission of nociceptive impulses (Bonica 1979, see also Chs 2-5). An explanation is therefore far more likely to be found by looking at the whole picture—the complex interaction between nociception, pain perception, emotional suffering and behaviour (Loeser 1980).

As with any individual faced with a change in health, Mr R. will have attempted to make sense of what has happened to him, and endeavoured to cope in the best way he could. Some of the strategies he will have utilised will have served him well. Others, over the long term, may well have inadvertently compounded his difficulties.

Fear–avoidance

The cognitive-behavioural approach to pain (CBT) acknowledges that the likelihood and frequency of behavioural responses is influenced by the presentation and withdrawal of positive reinforcement, as well as by the initiation or avoidance of negative reinforcement (Bradley 1996). (So putting it simply, we are more likely to do something again if on a previous occasion it was followed by a rewarding outcome—either something good happening, *positive reinforcement* or something unpleasant ceasing, *negative reinforcement*.) However, where the CBT model has expanded upon the purely operant paradigm (Fordyce et al 1973) is in recognising the crucial role played by an individual's beliefs, thoughts and expectations in affecting their behaviour and emotional response (Turk & Rudy 1993).

Perhaps a good starting point in understanding Mr R.'s difficulties is an examination of his understanding of his pain—his thoughts and beliefs. Clearly he is perplexed by his condition, not reassured that it has been fully investigated, and fearful of what the pain might really mean—a tumour. He has also attempted to make sense of other sensations such as numbness in his limbs, but in the absence of adequate explanation (or perhaps explanation he has not retained, or that did not make sense to him at the time) and probably the experience of stiffness when he has made attempts to move after lying for a while at night, he has reached a catastrophic interpretation (see Harding & Williams 1995 for examples common in physiotherapy settings, also Ch. 12)—paralysis.

These beliefs are bound to have had a profound effect on Mr R.'s behaviour. He has probably become avoidant of movement and activity (the processes involved here having been discussed in more detail in Ch. 11) and hence physically de-conditioned; thus when he does move he almost certainly experiences increased discomfort, and his avoidant behaviour is thus negatively reinforced by the relief from pain it produces. His collar and stick further prevent movement, yet sadly compound his difficulties by creating further loss of muscle strength and greater lack of confidence. His tolerances for certain positions (especially sitting) has reduced markedly and hence he is fidgety and keen to adopt his most comfortable position—in this case lying down.

In addition, Mr R.'s beliefs and fears may have led to his becoming hypervigilant to bodily sensations (Salkovskis 1996)—thus he is constantly on the lookout for signs of paralysis and 'on the move' throughout the night as a means of reassuring himself that the worst has not yet taken place. Unfortunately this results in a necessity for alertness and is incompatible with restful sleep.

Others may also be anxious. His wife and family are probably just as perplexed about his pain as he is and fearful of him doing more 'damage' to himself. They may therefore encourage him to do less (also in the knowledge of the increased pain when he does do more) and hence his inactivity is also positively reinforced by them.

Secondary emotional consequences

Mr R. has clearly had to curtail many activities since his whiplash injury. He has stopped his job, which he enjoyed and was a major contributor to his self esteem, but has also relinquished previously enjoyed social and leisure activities. Social pursuits such as dancing, darts and snooker can all have positive effects on peoples' emotional well-being (Argyle 1996). Mr R. has thus lost several activities which not only gave him pleasure but probably a sense of achievement too, thus placing him at risk for the experience of low mood (Lewinsohn et al 1980).

Mr R. is now limited to watching television throughout the day which he contrasts sharply with his previous lifestyle, holding beliefs such as 'I'm a burden to my family—I'm worthless—a failure'. These are only to be confirmed, along with his sense of helplessness, when he attempts to push himself to carry out previous tasks and finds that with his now low physical fitness, flexibility and strength, his pain is significantly flared up and he is incapacitated for several days (as with his experience with the car radio).

Thoughts and beliefs such as these can lead to the experience of depression (Beck et al 1979). Again, however, this only compounds problems further. Depressed mood is likely to impair someone's interest in activities and when they do achieve a task it may well be evaluated negatively—'I used to be able to do far more'; or the tendency towards cognitive bias may mean it is not recognised at all in the context of so many other 'failed' activities. Depression may well also affect sleep, concentration and libido, although clearly this would be in combination with the effects that chronic pain can have on functioning in these areas, too (Pilowsky et al 1985, Crombez et al 1997, Ambler et al 1996).

150

The important point to note here is that the depression is secondary to the experience of pain, and mediated by cognitions. The experience of low mood may well have a deleterious effect on the person's pain and indeed many patients describe how feeling low makes it harder to cope with their pain. This is not to say however that the low mood is causing the pain, or playing the primary role in its severity, exacerbation or maintenance. The *Textbook of Pain* (Wall & Melzack 1989) states: '...evidence for the argument that severe or persisting emotional distress can trigger new pain or reinstigate old pain does not extend beyond clinicians' reports' (p. 224). This is reiterated by Merskey (1993) in his review of the psychological consequences of whiplash: '...the principal reason for psychological illness in association with cervical sprain injuries is the consequence of the illness itself.'

Trauma

In spite of probably having to recount his history many times, five years on Mr R. still finds it distressing to describe the car accident in which he received his initial injury. He is still phobic of driving and describes marked anger and bitterness towards the driver who hit him. His concentration and memory are described as impaired and his sleep is disturbed.

Mr R.'s difficulties fit the diagnostic criteria for Post-Traumatic Stress Disorder (PTSD), see Box.1.

Box 1   DSM IV Criteria for PTSD

A   The person must have witnessed or experienced a serious threat to their life or physical well-being and their response been one of intense fear, horror or helplessness.
B   The person must re-experience the event in some way.
C   The person must persistently avoid stimuli associated with the trauma or experience a numbing of general responsiveness.
D   The person must experience persistent symptoms of increased arousal.
E   Symptoms must have lasted at least a month.

Diagnostic & Statistical Manual for Mental Disorders (APA 1994)

When we think of PTSD we tend to think of the tragic events which have attracted significant media coverage (e.g. The *Herald of Free Enterprise* disaster) but evidence suggests that a significant number of individuals also become severely traumatised following involvement in road traffic accidents (Taylor & Koch 1995). In a study of 74 patients with whiplash injuries who presented at a Casualty Department in Oxford, for example, it was found that 12 per cent were experiencing significant psychological problems at one year (Mayou 1993). Patients were interviewed by a psychiatrist and they completed standard questionnaires. Eighteen per cent of the sample were experiencing significant travel anxiety and 5 per cent met the diagnostic criteria for PTSD at one year post accident.

Whilst initial post-traumatic reactions reflect a normal response to trauma, cognitive models of PTSD suggest that individual differences in the appraisal of traumatic events and their sequalae may be particularly important in explaining the persistence of the disorder in some individuals (Dunmore et al 1997). Mr R.'s description of himself as 'thrown about like a rag doll' is vivid: it perhaps indicates the lack of control he felt he had over events. His view of the world is changed as a result of the accident—'bad things' happen to him and his family which he cannot control, and with which doctors and other people in his life seem unable or unwilling to help. Basic assumptions of the world as a just, benevolent, predictable and controllable place have been 'shattered' (Janoff-Bulman & Frieze 1983). Given the all to common health care experiences of people suffering from chronic whiplash pain following their injury, it does not seem surprising that many develop this perspective. It would be erroneous to conclude that the experience of trauma per *se is* predictive of poor recovery from whiplash injury (Radanov et al 1996), but it would seem that the additional suffering and potential change in beliefs is unlikely to help individuals in their attempts to cope.

Effects of litigation

Mr R.'s experience of trauma was unlikely to end with the accident. Indeed, the legal proceedings following an accident such as this are often a major stressor in their own right. Mr R. has been interviewed by many 'experts' since his accident, who differed in their views. Unhelpful and unsubstantiable ideas that his pain is being mediated by his distress, depression and PTSD may have been postulated (Main & Spanswick 1995). He is aware that 'wrong was done to him' yet the process of 'putting this right' is frequently lengthy and time consuming.

The traditional view of the effects of litigation suggests that the patient's complaints of pain and trappings of disability only persist until the point at which legal proceedings have ceased, when the patient then walks collar free from the court room. The pejorative term *compensation neurosis* has been used to describe this phenomenon. In fact a comprehensive review of the literature (Shapiro & Roth 1993) finds no evidence that settlement of claim leads to resolution of whiplash related symptomatology.

Shapiro and Roth (1993) do however acknowledge the substantial emotional strain of legal proceedings for the patient, and the subsequent impact this might have on pain and coping, stating that 'it would be naive to assume that litigation has no effect'. They suggest that the 'myth of compensation neurosis' likely persists in the absence of empirical evidence, for reasons such as clinicians' frustrations in treating difficult patients with chronic pain, and dualistic notions of thinking that pain is either 'physical or psychological'. A more complex, multifactorial understanding is sensibly promoted.

Implications: approach to management

So, what are the implications for physiotherapy management? Clearly there are a range of important factors to take into account when treating Mr R. Perhaps the 'single handed' physiotherapist has little to offer? Indeed there is convincing evidence that multidisciplinary pain management programmes serve patients suffering from chronic pain well (Flor et al 1992). However, there is clearly much that the physiotherapist not working in this kind of setting can bear in mind and apply:

Believe in the patient's pain

In some ways there should be no need to 'state the obvious' yet professionals from all disciplines (psychologists included) find patients suffering from chronic pain perplexing. As has been discussed, myths abound in this area and with all good intentions, attitudes may be subtly conveyed to the patient who, from experiences with friends and relatives, as well as with previously consulted clinicians, will be hypervigilant for any sign that their pain is not being believed or being seen to be 'in their mind'. In order to engage the patient successfully in any treatment plans it will be essential that they feel understood and that treatment goals are shared (see also Ch. 7).

Provide information

Gentle, open ended discussion and prompting with questions such as 'How do **you** understand the reasons for your pain?', 'What have you been told?', 'What have scans shown?' will give some insight into the patient's beliefs, fears and understanding of their symptoms. Alternative explanations, information and education can then be provided, following Ley and Llewelyn's (1995) general principles for enhancing patients' comprehension and retention of information. Salkovskis (1996) emphasises the futility of simple reassurance that 'the worst will not happen' for patients with significant fears about their health. The importance of helping the patient to discover another less threatening but wholly plausible interpretation of his or her experience is advocated instead. For example, that limbs feeling heavy and lifeless is a result of their having been in one position too long, rather than an indicator that there is a risk of paralysis.

Provide opportunities for new learning

It is widely accepted in CBT that information alone is unlikely to lead to behaviour change. The person needs to learn by experience that their fears are not realised and that they were able to perform the desired activity. In order to build confidence and enhance the likelihood that the behaviour will be performed again, first steps need to be specific and achievable. For the person fearful of moving his/her head, therefore, doing chin retractions will involve just a small approximation to the full movement to begin with, which can later be built upon in a systematic way. Likewise, the neck collar can be removed for five minutes when sitting with the head supported on a pillow (or whatever the patient feels is the easiest place to begin). The physiotherapist will play a vital role in encouraging the person as they start, but later tailing this off as the person become self-reinforcing of their own success at increasing mobility.

Encourage graded return to activity

As confidence and mobility return, the person will find they are able to gradually do more. Self efficacy (Bandura 1977) increases and mood is improved as the person not only returns to enjoyable activities, but also experiences a sense of accomplishment with each new step forwards. The physiotherapist can do much to encourage return to activity but also in helping patients to set realistic targets and to pace their activities appropriately. For a more detailed discussion of the crucial elements of goal planning and breaking the over/underactivity cycle see Chs 8 & 9 and Williams (1993).

Be alert to psychological trauma and referral options

A graded approach to return to driving, combined with training in relaxation and diaphragmatic breathing, would be wholly appropriate for the person with a mild/moderate phobia of driving. In the acute stage, a careful and detailed history taking may well be quite therapeutic for the person distressed about their car accident. PTSD or severe phobia however requires specialist diagnosis, assessment and intervention from a clinical psychologist or psychiatrist trained in cognitive-behavioural therapy. Possible signs to the physiotherapist at the initial assessment that someone is suffering from PTSD include marked distress on talking about the accident or inability to do so, in addition to the symptoms described previously, and would be an indicator for specialist referral.

Conclusion

Mr R. began a programme of graded return to activity in treatment. Learning to carry out exercises in a graded and systematic way helped increase his confidence with movement and this in addition to explanation about the physical sensations he was experiencing, helped him to change his beliefs about his pain. He gradually began to remove his collar and walk without a stick for precise amounts of time and used the same kind of timed approach for returning to household and leisure pursuits, making sure that his daily routine incorporated regular brief rests and changes in position. This had positive effects on his mood and interactions with his family, but Mr R. had to remind himself often of the need to be realistic about the rate of progress, to recognise that there would be set backs, and that each small step towards progress was a significant achievement. Three months later his scores on standard questionnaires indicated an improvement in his mood and confidence in his ability to manage his pain. His results on tests such as a timed walk and number of stairs completed in one minute showed significant improvement and his use of analgesics reduced.

Individuals suffering chronic pain following whiplash injury have frequently accrued a substantial number of negative experiences subsequent to their original injury. Recognising their beliefs about their condition, themselves and others, which have formed as a result of these experiences, is crucial for understanding their presentation. Much can be achieved in treatment by taking this as the starting point.

REFERENCES

Ambler N R, Williams A C de C, Cratchley G, Gunary R M, Hill P A 1996 Sexual difficulties in chronic pain sufferers. Abstracts of 8th World Congress on Pain IASP Press, Seattle

American Psychiatric Association 1994 Diagnostic and Statistical Manual for Mental Disorders. American Psychiatric Association, Washington, DC

Amundson G M 1994 The evaluation and treatment of cervical whiplash. Current Opinion in Orthopaedics 5(11):17–27

Argyle M 1996 The social psychology of leisure. Penguin Books, London

Bandura A 1977 Self efficacy: Towards a unifying theory of behaviour change. Psychological Review 84:191

Barnsley L, Lord S, Bogduk N 1994 Whiplash injuries. Pain 58:283–307

Beck A T, Rush A J, Shaw B F, Emery G 1979 Cognitive therapy of depression. Guilford Press, London

Bonica J J 1979 Letter. Pain 7:203

Bradley L A 1996 Cognitive behavioural therapy for chronic pain. In: Gatchel R J, Turk D C (eds) Psychological approaches to pain management. Guilford Press, London

Crombez G, Eccleston C, Bayaens F, Eelen P 1997 Habituation and the interference of pain with task performance. Pain 70:149–154

Crowe H 1928 Injuries to the cervical spine. Presentation to the annual meeting of the Western Orthopaedic Association, San Fransisco

Dunmore E, Clark D M, Ehlers A 1997 Cognitive factors in persistent versus recovered post-traumatic stress disorder after physical or sexual assault: A pilot study. Behavioral and Cognitive Psychotherapy 25:147–159

Flor H, Fydrich T, Turk D C 1992 Efficacy of multi-disciplinary pain treatment centres: a meta-analytic review. Pain 49:221–30

Fordyce W E, Fowler R S, Lehmann J F et al 1973 Operant conditioning in the treatment of chronic pain. Archives of Physical Medicine and Rehabilitation 53:399–408

Gay J R, Abbott K H 1953 Common whiplash injuries of the neck. JAMA 152:1698–1704

Harding V H, Williams A C de C 1995 Extending physiotherapy skills using a psychological approach: cognitive-behavioural management of chronic pain. Physiotherapy 81:681–688

Janoff-Bulman R, Frieze I H 1983 A theoretical perspective for understanding reactions to victimisation. Journal of Social Issues 37:105–122

Lewinsohn P M, Mischel W, Chapelin W, Barton R 1980 Social competence and depression: The role of illusory self perceptions. Journal of Abnormal Psychology 89:203–12

155

Ley P, Llewelyn S 1995 Improving patients' understanding, recall, satisfaction and compliance. In: Health psychology: processes & applications. II edn. edited by A Broome & S Llewelyn, Chapman & Hall,

Loeser J D 1980 Low back pPain. In: Bonica J J (ed) Pain. Raven Press, New York

Main C J, Spanswick C C 1995 'Functional overlay', and illness behaviour in chronic pain: Distress or malingering? Conceptual difficulties in medico-legal assessment of personal injury claims. Journal of Psychosomatic Research 39(6):737–753

Mayou R, Bryant B, Duthie R 1993 Psychiatric consequences of road traffic accidents. British Medical Journal 307:647–51

Merskey H 1993 Psychological consequences of whiplash. Spine, State of the Art Reviews 7(3):471–480

Merksey H, Bogduk N 1994 Classification of chronic pain. IASP Press, Seattle

Pilowsky I, Crettendon I, Townley M 1985 Sleep disturbance in pain clinic patients. Pain 23:27–33

Radanov B P, Begre S, Sturznegger M, Augustiny K F 1996 Course of psychological variables in whiplash injury—a two year follow-up with age, gender and education pair matched patients Pain 64:429–434

Salkovskis P M 1996 The cognitive approach to anxiety: threat beliefs, safety seeking behaviour, and the special case of health anxiety and obsessions. In: Salkovskis P M (ed) Frontiers of cognitive therapy. Guildford Press, London

Shapiro A P, Roth R S 1993 The effect of litigation on recovery from whiplash. Spine: State of the Art Reviews 7(3):531–556

Spitzer W O, Skovron M L, Salmi L R 1995 Scientific monograph of the Quebec task force on whiplash associated disorders: redefining whiplash and its management. Spine 20(Suppl):10s–73s

Taylor S, Koch W J 1995 Anxiety disorders due to motor vehicle accidents: Nature and treatment. Clinical Psychology Review 15(8):721–738

Turk D C, Rudy T E, Boucek D C 1993 Psychological factors in chronic pain. In: Warfield C A (ed) Pain management techniques. Martinus Nijhoff, Boston

Wall P D, Melzack R 1989 Textbook of pain, 2nd edn. Churchill-Livingstone, Edinburgh

Wallis B J, Lord S M, Barnsley L, Bogduk N 1996 Pain and psychologic symptoms of Australians following whiplash. Spine 21(7): 804–810

Williams A C de C 1993 In-patient management of chronic pain. In: Hodes M, Moorey S (eds) Psychological treatment of disease and illness. Gaskell, London

2

Fear-avoidance beliefs and behaviour

11

Fear-avoidance theories

PATRICK HILL

A good introduction is to start with a conclusion. An important message is best summed up in the following quote:

> Simple single construct models of low back pain have limited usefulness as theoretical foundations for clinical intervention (Rose et al 1995).

This chapter aims to explore this conclusion through discussion of fear-avoidance and other theoretical models in relation to chronic back pain.

Fear-avoidance is based on the work of Philips (1974) who proposes that pain comprises physiological, subjective, and behavioural dimensions. Although these aspects of pain inter-relate with one another, they may also 'de-synchronise' under certain conditions. A good example of this is a common situation found in chronic pain where the physiological basis of pain stays static or resolves but the emotional or subjective component increases. This basic idea allows the concept of psychological or affective components being dominant in a multi rather than single construct model of pain.

The fear-avoidance model

The fear-avoidance model has been shown to be a good predictor of chronic low back disability particularly if used in conjunction with other variables such as the physical and psychosocial. Klenerman et al (1995) and Waddell et al (1993) have demonstrated the predictive value of the fear-avoidance concept in patients with chronic low back pain.

The model (Fig. 11.1) proposes a continuum upon which people with acute back pain may exist and then proceed to either *coping wellness* or *chronic illness*.

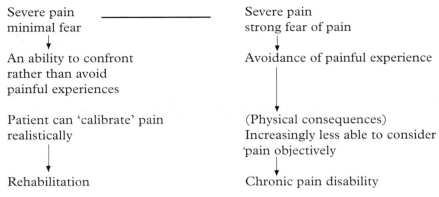

Fig. 11.1 The fear-avoidance model

Development of fear-avoidance in the individual

Researchers using the model have proposed that a number of factors including the following contribute to the development of fear-avoidance in the individual:

- Life events—as proposed by Holmes and Rahe (1967)
- Personality factors—such as tendency to 'somatise'
- Previous pain experience—recurrent episodes of severe pain
- Normal coping strategies—passive or active.

But overall the research shows that the best predictions as to who will become chronically disabled come not from single factors but from using a combination of physical and psychosocial variables.

Health psychology models

Other models from the health psychology literature also fall into the same difficulties.

The health belief model

The Health Belief Model (HBM) (Rosenstock 1974) is a model widely used by social psychologists studying health care. The HBM attempts to identify those factors which influence individuals to act in a way that prevents disease, including the use of health services.

The HBM rests on the assumption that whether a person will act depends on:

a) the value placed on a certain goal (e.g. the desire to avoid illness)
b) the belief that a specific action will achieve that goal.

For example, going to the dentist for a checkup will reduce the chance of dental problems.

Rosenstock, in 1974, pointed out that social pressures influenced the way people behave, so that considering the way people think, in isolation from the context in which those thoughts occur, is clearly assuming a false idea.

The theories of reasoned action and planned behaviour

The theory of reasoned action (Fishbein & Azjen 1975) is more elaborate than the HBM and offers greater predictive value, as does Azjen's 1988 theory of planned behaviour; but still falls foul of the same problem: considering beliefs and intentions in social isolation.

This all points to the need for not necessarily more complex, but perhaps more comprehensive models. Johnston 1996, in an important paper discussing models of disability, argues for a combination of existing models, such as the WHO model of disability (WHO 1980), with the theory of planned behaviour. Johnston adds two additional variables:

*   internal representations of the behaviour
*   external eliciting cues.

Towards a multidimensional model

If we take the fear–voidance concepts as useful ones, which seem to account for at least part of the variance, it is perhaps useful here to take some of the concepts apart and add in one or two others. For example, one question to ask is, where might the fear come from?

From clinical experience, fear in people with chronic pain often seems to originate from the commonly held 'acute pain' belief that:

$$Pain = Damage$$

It is understandable that if the person with back pain believes that any increase in their pain relates to some (further) damage occuring, then it is likely that they will avoid doing the activities which may cause any increase in their pain, such as exercise. History may give an indication as to where these strongly held beliefs may originate.

An historical perspective

There has been an enormous increase in low back pain related disability, relatively recently. The historical perspective on the current situation is an important factor to consider. The 1994 OPCS survey showed very clearly that the recorded incidence of low back pain has changed very little, since records began, but the *disability* reported due to low back pain is reaching epidemic proportions.

Two key ideas from the 19th century laid the foundation for our modern approach to back pain: *that it came from the spine* and *was due to injury*.

Previously, backache was thought to be a rheumatic condition that was, by and large, 'one of life's problems'. However, the change in thinking led to the idea that medical treatment of back pain was possible and until very recently, has been dominated by the orthopaedic principle of therapeutic rest.

Chronic disability due to back pain only began to appear in the late 19th century, escalating after World War II . Some observers feel that this relatively recent phenomenon has been aided by the improved social support which makes rest possible.

So perhaps history can help partly to explain:

Fear of Pain (= damage) ►Avoidance = rest

People demonstrating disability in relation to chronic pain seem to suffer with two other problems:

a) failure to switch their concepts from 'acute' to 'chronic'
b) pre- morbid lack of coping skills in areas such as
  • Stress management
  • Communication
  • Problem solving
  • Goal setting and pacing.

Lay concepts: acute vs. chronic models of pain

The switch from regarding their pain as an acute, treatable, finite problem, to a chronic condition, requiring long term management, is a difficult change in concepts for most people. The idea of having to cope with back pain as a chronic or long term problem is a concept that most people do not adopt readily.

Self regulation theory

Leventhal and Nerenz (1983) have proposed that coping with chronic illness can be examined within the framework of Self Regulation Theory, which basically states that people view their illness in the context of their efforts to cope with the perceived problems and their emotional reactions to them. The individual's coping efforts are directed at the person's own objective assessment of their problems, not that of other people.

Previous research showed that people order their thoughts or beliefs in a consistent way, to provide an internal representation or cognitive model of their illness, which serves as a basis for action. The analysis of thousands of descriptions of ordinary people's experience of illness led to the discovery of 5 themes along which people tend to organise their thoughts into 'schema' or themes about an illness:

1 **Identity:** which comprises a label and any associated symptoms.
2 **Timeline:** finite, cyclical or indefinite.

3 **Consequences:** the major effects having the illness will impose.
4 **Cause:** single or multiple.
5 **Cure:** whether a cure is available and how it might be achieved.

These schema are thought to combine to form *lay models* of illness which may be

- **Acute:** with a single cause, predictable consequences including well defined treatment and a finite timeline
- **Chronic:** with multiple aetiology, unpredictable consequences and an open ended timeline.

In most aspects of health and illness people adopt an 'acute model' as it is the most accessible and the most widely publicised in the media. It also 'fits' with the modern view of back pain as a phenomenon amenable to treatment, taking the historical perspective into account. The acute model of pain incorporates the most widely understood lay concepts of pain, as a warning sign indicating damage or injury.

In practice, in accordance with an acute model and its concepts of 'cure', in the earlier stages of chronic back pain few people do nothing. Coping often involves seeing a number of orthodox and complementary practitioners including orthopaedic specialists, osteopaths, physiotherapists, or acupuncturists, naturally seeking information to make sense of what is happening and/or someone who will provide them with a cure.

For someone developing a chronic problem, failure to achieve a cure coupled with a belief that their persistent pain is a product of continuing damage or deterioration, reinforced by concepts such as 'a crumbling spine', it is understandable if they develop a fear which leads to avoidance of aggravating factors.

'Life skills' deficiency

A number of studies have shown that people with chronic back pain tend to score higher on scales which measure hypochondriasis, 'hysteria' and depression, (Sternbach 1974). Clinical experience indicates that people often find difficulty coping with chronic pain because of a lack of what might be termed 'life skills'. These may be represented by a tendency for physical and mental health problems and somatising emotional problems they do not have the skills to deal with. Lack of an ability to manage stress, problem solve, set goals or communicate well with others, let alone deal with strong emotion, means that a person without these resources may very quickly enter one of a number of vicious circles when encountering long term pain.

For example: the person may well try to exercise as they've probably been told, but if they are unable to set themselves appropriate goals, then they are likely to overdo it and the pain will get worse, which leads to more stress, inactivity and an increase in the physical problems (reduced mobility, muscle tone etc).

This sequence can also reinforce the acute model concept of *pain = damage* and increases the fear of movement and avoidance of 'things I know will make it worse'.

Understanding the person's beliefs is one of the keys to understanding their attempts to cope or health related behaviour, at a given moment. This can help to explore where fear-avoidance may come from.

In order to understand the person's beliefs we must take other factors into account such as culture, history and social aspects.

Maintenance of fear-avoidance: the A-B-C model

To introduce the social context element, another model which is worth consideration is a simple operant behaviour model of pain, which might help to look at the factors which maintain the vicious circles set up under the fear-avoidance idea in the long term—and give some practical ideas as to what we can do about this.

The operant behaviour or A-B-C model

Simply put, an operant model states that any behaviour is reciprocally linked directly to its contingencies. Consequently if the contingencies are altered, then the behaviour is also altered. For example:

A = Antecedent, stimulus or cue for action
A person with chronic back pain goes to see their GP, having had a row with their partner the night before, who is fed up with the unremitting pain problem, which means that they have to do all the housework, garden etc and seemingly 'nothing is being done' to cure the pain. The person is told by their GP, 'There's nothing more we can do except give you these pain killers. What you must do is take some exercise.'

B = Behaviour
Person takes painkillers and tries to exercise—doesn't pace themselves or set realistic goals, the pain killers help to deaden the pain, so they do far too much.

C = Consequence
The person ends up in bed for two days. Not only does the pain get worse but their partner gets even more stroppy.

So seeking medical help, and often trying to self help, can be a very *punishing* experience for the person with chronic pain. Using an operant model, the idea is that by altering *both* As and Cs into a positive and rewarding equation, you are more likely to achieve the desired B in the long term. For example:
A *Physio:* 'You need to exercise, but you need to set achievable goals and this is how to do it. You would expect it to hurt a little more initially but this will get easier if you stick to the plan we make together' (see Chs 7,8,9,13 & 14).
B Exercise is undertaken in a more sustainable fashion.
C *Physio:* 'Well done!' Person has a sense of achievement, and eventually feels benefits thus undoing fear-avoidance loop.

Figure 11.2 puts a new model together taking all these aspects into account.

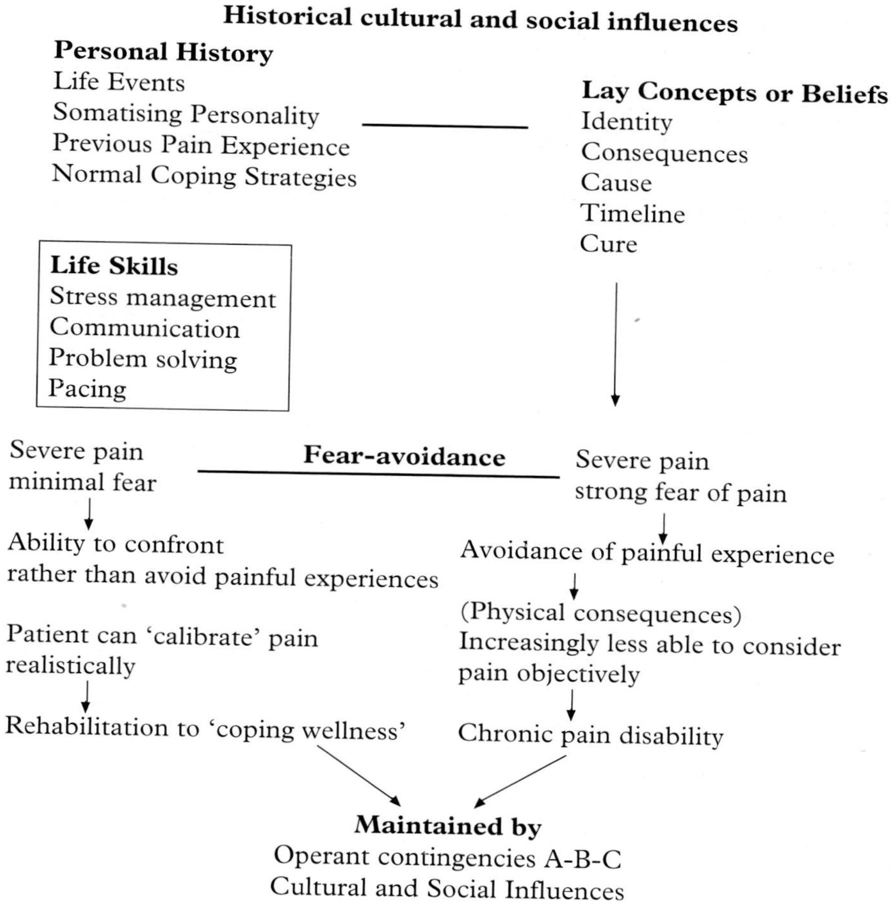

Historical cultural and social influences

Personal History
Life Events
Somatising Personality ———————
Previous Pain Experience
Normal Coping Strategies

Lay Concepts or Beliefs
Identity
Consequences
Cause
Timeline
Cure

Life Skills
Stress management
Communication
Problem solving
Pacing

Severe pain   **Fear-avoidance**   Severe pain
minimal fear   ————————————   strong fear of pain

Ability to confront   Avoidance of painful experience
rather than avoid painful experiences

Patient can 'calibrate' pain   (Physical consequences)
realistically   Increasingly less able to consider
                                       pain objectively

Rehabilitation to 'coping wellness'   Chronic pain disability

Maintained by
Operant contingencies A-B-C
Cultural and Social Influences

Fig. 11.2 A multidimensional model of chronic back pain

Conclusion: the practical consequences

Our original conclusion was: 'Simple single construct models of low back pain have limited usefulness as theoretical foundations for clinical intervention' (Rose et al 1995). In discussing fear-avoidance concepts and other models, we arrived at the idea of a multidimensional model. In practice therefore in considering assessment and intervention in chronic pain, this means that addressing the needs of people with chronic pain requires adopting a biopsychosocial model with a strong emphasis on the need for multi rather than uni-disciplinary assessment.

BACKGROUND READING

Radley A 1994 Making sense of illness. Sage, London
Hanson R, Gerber K 1990 Coping with chronic pain: A guide to patient self-management. Guilford, New York

REFERENCES

Azjen 1988 Attitudes personality and behaviour. Open University Press, Milton Keynes

Fishbein M, Azjen I 1975 Belief, attitude, intention and behaviour. Addison-Wesley, Reading

Holmes T H, Rahe R H 1967 The social readjustment rating scale. Journal of Psychosomatic Research 11:213-218

Johnston M 1996 Models of disability. The Psychologist 9(5):205–210

Klenerman L, Slade P, Stanley M, Pennie B, Reilly J, Atchison L,Troup J, Rose M 1995 The prediction of chronicity in patients with an acute attack of low back pain in a general practice setting. Spine 20(4):478–484

Leventhal H, Nerenz D 1983 Self regulation theory in chronic illness. In: Burish T, Bradley L A (eds) Coping with chronic disease: Research and applications. Academic Press, London

OPCS 1994 Low back pain. Survey. HMSO, London

Philips C 1974 A psychological analysis of tension headache . In: Rachman S (ed) Contributions of medical psychology. Pergamon Press, Oxford

Rose M, Reilly J, Slade P, Dewey M, 1995 A comparative analysis of psychological and physical models of low back pain experience. Physiotherapy 81(12):710–716

Rosenstock I 1974 The health belief model and preventive health behaviour. Health Education Monographs 2:354–386

Sternbach R 1974 Pain patients: traits and treatment. Academic Press, New York

Waddell G, Newton M, Henderson I, Somerville D, Main C 1993 A fear avoidance beliefs questionnaire (FABQ) and the role of fear avoidance beliefs in chronic low back pain and disability. Pain 52:157–168

World Health Organisation 1980 International Classification of Impairments Disabilities and Handicaps. WHO, Geneva

12

Iatrogenic disability and back pain rehabilitation

MICHAEL J ROSE

Introduction

The financial costs of low back pain to health care and the Exchequer are well documented as are the costs to employers of those who suffer (Rosen 1994). Such has been the increase in numbers of individuals deemed unfit for work because of back pain that the symptom has been popularly labelled as a modern epidemic (Waddell 1987).

This pressure has resulted in a significant research focus on back pain. The consensus view now suggests that back pain should be managed within a framework which recognises the equal importance of biological, behavioural, cognitive, affective and socio-economic variables. This model has been described as 'biopsychosocial' (Waddell, 1987).

Academic efforts have now influenced providers of health care to the extent that the Department of Health Clinical Standards Advisory Group (Rosen 1994) suggests that *'management and advice given to all low back pain patients must take full account of the psychosocial and occupational assessment'* and back pain and disability are better understood and managed as a clinical syndrome which includes important physical, psychological and social interactions.

Fear-avoidance and iatrogenesis

A significant component of the biopsychosocial model concerns the notion of fear-avoidance which is described in Chapter 11. Briefly, it is suggested that fear of pain leads to avoidance behaviour which, in the context of mechanical back pain, can result in increased disability, physical deterioration and psychological distress (Troup & Videman 1989, Lethem et al 1983, Klenerman et al 1995). The cognitive determinants of fear and subsequent avoidance behaviour have been the focus of much attention (Nicholas et al 1992, Waddell et al 1993) and the role of health professionals in generating fear in patients has been forcefully articulated by Waddell (1993) who views much chronic back pain as being 'iatrogenic'.

This view is supported by statements made by many chronic low back pain patients referred to a rehabilitation unit (Taylor & Rose 1997 p.152). The majority of patients believed themselves to have diseased or vulnerable backs:

The spine is just built up with a series of cushions and these go flat. They dry out, become loose, slack and wobble out. Muscles move and get damaged during physical exertion .(female, age 31)

It's like the whole of my back is made of ground glass. (female, age 42)

And their behavioural responses tend towards avoidance:

It's going to get degeneratively worse. I know my limitations now, which perhaps I didn't before. I know that if I take the curtains down I'm going to be in agony so I don't do it. (female, age 42)

I just know I'm going to get worse. I mean, I can't do exercises to keep my weight down. (female, age 31)

Waddell's notion of iatrogenesis is also supported in terms of information provided by professionals:

I saw the physiotherapist here and she was brilliant. She drew diagrams and told me the bottom of my spine was deformed. (female, age 41)

I did a lot of sport and I just put it down to wear and tear but I went to the doctor and he told me that I had a curvature of the spine. (male, age 33)

I had a scan and they said the disc had collapsed. (male, age 42)

and also in terms of advice given:

And when I went for the X-ray they said it was spondylitis and I would be better looking for another job. (female, age 42)

For the first 4 or 5 years I was seeing osteopaths and they were strapping me up and saying you mustn't bend. (male, age 40)

One patient appeared to have developed considerable insight into the problems associated with the back pain management and the health care process.

What I think has done me the world of good, in all honesty, having had a month in hospital, seeing doctors, specialists and physiotherapists, from February I haven't seen a soul and I feel so much better (female, age 31).

Back pain rehabilitation

The move towards a biopsychosocial model of back pain and the recognition that health professionals' words (see Chs 7 & 14) may be at least as important as their actions, have led to the growth and philosophy of back pain management programmes. Initially, they drew upon strict behavioural principles (Fordyce 1976). The evolution of cognitive-behavioural interventions represents an extension of the behavioural model and a recognition that pain is a complex and dynamic experience. The basic rationale of back pain management programmes can be defined as the alteration of behavioural, cognitive and affective variables which interfere with adaptive functioning.

The content of most programmes is similar and generally patients are treated as part of a group (Peters et al 1992, Richardson et al 1994). However, the intensity of treatment on such programmes ranges from a few hours' out-patient attendance to several weeks' in-patient admission (Nicholas et al 1992, Flor et al 1992). Rose et al (1997) conducted two studies designed to:

1 compare the effects of applying closely similar cognitive-behavioural pain management approaches to individuals and groups of patients; and
2 identify, within the parameters of 15 and 60 hours, the optimum duration of treatment.

Their results demonstrated that in terms of patient centred outcomes such as psychological distress, disability, cognitions, affect and 'distress' there was an overall improvement for up to six months after completion of a programme. However, there were no significant effects of group or individual treatment or length of programme.

Wirral Hospital Trust Back Pain Rehabilitation Unit

This work led to the development of a service-based programme at Wirral Hospital Trust. The programme was designed to operate within a service environment rather than be driven by controlled research and was a response to waiting list pressures. Wirral Hospital is a general acute provider unit serving a population of 350 000. Analysis of the orthopaedic out-patient waiting list demonstrated that 30% could be accounted for by mechanical low back pain.

The service takes the form of a discrete unit staffed by psychological and physical therapists. Patients are referred directly by general practitioners or hospital consultants and assessed by physiotherapists. Patients complete a questionnaire which measures disability, pain and psychological distress. In addition to providing baseline data and informing the assessor in terms of appropriate management, the questionnaire functions as an 'agenda' for a semi-structured interview which is designed to explore in detail the relationship between psychosocial and organic variables in patients' presentation. The assessment process also includes a physical examination, the aim of which is to measure 'inappropriate pain behaviour' and identify dysfunction which requires medical or physiotherapeutic intervention.

The unit operates two programmes, both of which are staffed by a physiotherapist and psychology assistant. The first is designed for individuals who have become disabled and distressed by their pain. Patients attend for five consecutive days in groups of eight as out-patients. The content of this programme includes education about the function of the spine, the physical, psychological and social dynamics of back pain experience, pain theory (with an emphasis on the difference between 'hurt' and 'harm') and the general benefits of exercise. In addition, patients are expected to exercise for an hour a day and are encouraged to pace themselves according to their individual level of fitness. Follow-up sessions are offered at three and six months. The second programme is designed for individuals who are less disabled and not distressed by back pain. Its focus is preventive rather than therapeutic. Patients attend for one day (six hours) in groups of eight. This programme includes spinal anatomy, pain mechanisms and the benefits of exercise. Patients re-attend at six months for follow-up and de-briefing. The central theme of both programmes concerns the notion that mechanical back pain is not a symptom of severe damage and that exercise and normal activity are likely to result in increased or maintained levels of function. The aim of both programmes is to reduce 'fear of pain'. Reduction of pain is not an aim of the intervention.

An audit was undertaken of the first 500 patients referred from primary care or by hospital consultants to the unit (Taylor & Rose 1997, p.152). The large majority of patients were managed within the unit without recourse to referral to consultant surgeons or physicians. Significant reductions in medication use, disability and distress were maintained by patients for at least six months after completion of a treatment programme and orthopaedic surgeons within the hospital were relieved of a significant proportion of patients with mechanical back pain from their waiting list.

Conclusions

Chronic low back pain is complex and multifactorial and the majority of acute back pain patients recover. However, the minority of acute patients who go on to become chronic sufferers account for a disproportionate drain upon available resources. Measures designed to reduce chronic back disability may result in a significant reduction in the distress experienced by the sufferer and the overall cost of the problem to society.

It is evident that, although therapeutic intervention designed to reduce the organic component of pain experience may have a role in the overall management of low back pain, the way in which patients are 'managed', the information that is provided by health professionals and the circumstances of health care can profoundly influence the outcome of such intervention. Indeed, interventions which focus primarily upon the delivery of appropriate information and which recognise the importance of the 'communication' process between patient and professional may be shown to be more relevant in terms of back pain management than treatments based upon the traditional view of pain experience. It would appear that group therapy and short, focused programmes (15 hours or maybe less) address and fulfil issues of economy and therapeutic potential.

The Wirral Hospital programme is physiotherapy-led with consultants and psychologists being involved minimally. The use of these short yet effective interventions has kept the costs low, which should put such units within the financial reach of many district hospitals enabling most people to be treated as outpatients by their local hospital. The unit was a response to practical issues within a health service setting and based upon theoretical constructs which have already been tested and described widely in the literature. The Wirral experience may represent what might be expected if a similar organisation were to introduce a unit of the kind described.

Contemporary thinking and the experience of the author suggest that a significant proportion of back pain disability and distress could be prevented by the application of psychosocial principles at the acute stage of the symptom's natural history. The Wirral unit is therefore collaborating with a local community trust in order to test this hypothesis (Beattie et al 1996).

REFERENCES

Beattie G M, Rose M J, Stanley I M 1996 Establishing and evaluating a co-ordinated service for patients with back pain in primary care. Funded by North West Regional Health Authority

Flor H, Frydrich T, Turk D C 1992 Efficacy of multi-disciplinary pain treatment centres; a meta analytic review. Pain 49:221–230

Fordyce W E 1976 Behavioural methods for chronic pain and illness. Mosby, St. Louis

Klenerman L, Slade P D, Stanley I M, Pennie B, Reilly J P, Atchison L E, Troup J D G, Rose M J 1995 The prediction of chronicity in patients with an acute attack of low back pain in a general practice setting. Spine 20(4):478–484

Lethem J, Slade P D, Troup J D G, Bentley G 1983 The fear avoidance model of exaggerated pain perception-1. Behaviour Research and Therapy 21(4):401–408

Nicholas M K, Wilson P H Goyen J 1992 Comparison of cognitive behavioural group treatment and an alternative non-psychological treatment for chronic low back pain. Pain 48:339–347

Peters J, Large R G, Elkind G 1992 Follow-up results from a randomised controlled trial evaluating in- and out-patient pain management programmes. Pain 50:41–50

Richardson I H, Richardson P H, Williams A C de C, Featherstone J, Harding V R 1994 The effects of a cognitive-behavioural pain management programme on the quality of work and employment status of severely impaired chronic pain patients. Disability and Rehabilitation 1:26–34

Rose M J, Reilly J P, Pennie B, Bowen-Jones K, Stanley I M, Slade P D 1997 Chronic low back pain rehabilitation prgrammes—a study of the optimum duration of treatment and a comparison of group and individual. Spine 22(19):2246-2251

Rosen M 1994 Back pain: Report of a clinical standards advisory group committee on back Pain. HMSO, London

Taylor D, Rose M 1997 Psychophysiological and psychological techniques for the treatment of low back pain. In: Adams N (ed) The psychophysiology of low back pain. Churchill Livingstone, New York

Troup J D G, Videman T 1989 Inactivity and the aetiopathogenesis of musculoskeltal disorders. Clinical Biomechanics 4:173–178

Waddell G 1987 A new clinical model for the treatment of low back pain. Spine 12:632–643

Waddell G, Newton M, Henderson I, Sommerville D, Main CJ 1993 A fear–avoidance beliefs questionnaire (FABQ) and the role of fear–avoidance in chronic low back pain. Pain 52:157–168

13

Cognitive-behavioural approach to fear and avoidance

VICKI HARDING

In Chapter 11 Patrick Hill described current and historical models and theories about fear and avoidance, emphasising clearly that multidimensional biopsychosocial models are needed rather than unidimensional models. Treatment approaches for fear and avoidance therefore also need to be multidimensional. Attention is therefore given to the behavioural and cognitive changes that are necessary as well as to physical re-conditioning, and all are placed within patients' various social contexts.

The behavioural models and approach to treatment of fear and avoidance

Watson and Rayner in 1920 described classical conditioning anxiety in 'Little Albert', an 11-month-old infant, by pairing the appearance of a white rat with a loud noise. This conditioned anxiety generalized to similar stimuli such as the experimenter's white hair and cotton wool. Jones in 1924 adopted Watson's recommendations for treatment and found two treatment methods that were consistently effective:

1 Associating the feared object with an alternative pleasant response such as eating.
2 Exposing the child to the feared stimulus in the presence of other children who were not fearful (social conditioning, modelling).

Classical and operant conditioning were proposed by Mowrer (1947, 1960) to then explain fear and avoidance behaviour with a 2-factor model:

1   Fear of a specific stimulus is acquired through classical conditioning—as in the example of 'Little Albert'.
2   As fear is aversive, the animal learns to reduce it by avoiding the conditioned stimulus. The reduction in anxiety then becomes negatively reinforcing.

Solomon and Wynn (1954) observed that stimuli previously linked (classically conditioned) with very strongly aversive stimuli were extremely resistant to extinction. In this case, avoidance of a harmless stimulus could continue long after the earlier conditioning had stopped e.g. fear of keyboards continuing long after healing of tenosynovitis; fear of weight-bearing continuing long after healing of a knee injury. (In these cases there is also the double bind, since avoidance leads to stiffness or reduced fitness/ability to do a task, and also to disuse pain/hypersensitivity. Thus, to the patient, it appears that the fear of the harmless stimulus—typing a few words or weight-bearing evenly—is wholly justified, since the activity is still painful, as well as frightening.)

Behavioural treatment for phobias developed particularly from the work of Wolpe (1958, 1961) on systematic desensitization. Unhelpful learned behaviour is unlearned and more helpful adaptive reactions are learned instead. This is achieved by 'graded exposure'. By approaching rather than avoiding, patients have the opportunity to learn that these situations are not in fact dangerous. The child who never goes near the dog (or white rat!) that frightened them again may remain fearful, while the one who approaches it is likely to regain confidence. Treatment, therefore, requires that patients repeatedly make contact with the things they fear, and remain in contact with them until the fear subsides. Exposure is defined as facing something that has been avoided because it provokes anxiety. *For optimal effectiveness exposure should be graduated, repeated, and prolonged* (e.g. Marks 1981, Emmelkamp 1982, Matthews et al 1981).

Patients first identify all the things that are avoided, ordering them according to difficulty in a 'graded hierarchy', for example:

Weight-bearing through left leg

- Resting a little weight of the foot on the floor—when sitting
- Resting a little weight of the foot on the floor—when standing
- Walking with crutches, putting a little weight through the foot
- Walking as above, more weight
- Going up stairs using handrail, mainly using good leg
- Walking without a crutch for a short distance
- Walking further, less limp
- Going up stairs using handrail and both legs
- Jogging on the spot
- Walking, no limp at all
- Going up stairs 2 at a time
- Jogging up stairs

Once the level of the feared activity that is just manageable has been decided, a plan to help frequent and regular exposure is needed. Reinforcement provided by the patient (self-reinforcement) and by others (staff or friends) is invaluable, but the 'Primack' principle can also come in handy here too. This is to make a hierarchy of activities engaged in with greatest likelihood. For example:

Activity hierarchy

- Sit down with a chocolate biscuit and a cup of coffee
- Watch a TV programme
- Sit down with a good book
- Ring a friend to arrange when to meet
- Practice relaxation
- Read handout from pain management programme
- Do your stretch routine
- Use a timer to help pace gardening
- Go window/clothes shopping when the sun is shining
- Do your exercise programme
- Go swimming with the children
- Ring your mother to tell her you can't visit
- Work on weightbearing evenly while walking without crutch
- Use a timer to help pace ironing

The idea is then to choose activities from the end of the list that are least likely to be done, and some that are more likely to be done, making sure that the least likely to be done are done first. This process, as well as ensuring that uncomfortable/disliked tasks are completed, also provides its own natural reinforcement.

Cognitive model of anxiety/panic

In this model (Clark 1986, 1988) patients misinterpret a range of body sensations such as breathlessness, aches, pains, pins and needles, palpitations and dizziness, in a catastrophic way. They may perceive them as signs of imminent physical or mental danger or disaster.

Two processes contribute to the maintenance of anxiety/panic disorder:

1 Because patients are frightened of certain sensations, they become hypervigilant and repeatedly scan/check their body. This allows them to notice sensations which many other people would not be aware of. Once noticed, they are taken as further evidence of a serious physical or mental disorder.

2 Certain forms of avoidance tend to maintain patients' negative interpretations by preventing them collecting contrary evidence (Salkovskis 1988).

Example

A patient with back pain and referred coccydynia avoided sitting completely. He was concerned about the strength of the spine having been told that a disc was crumbling and whenever he experienced symptoms from his lower back he immediately became anxious that this was further evidence of damage and deterioration. He therefore believed that by avoiding taking weight directly through the spine this would reduce the chances of the spine crumbling further. However the effect of the avoidance was to prevent the patient learning that when he sat this would NOT lead to collapse of the spine.

Personal evidence

Panic attacks can be preceded by heightened anxiety or by bodily sensations due to other emotional states (excitement, anger) or harmless things such as getting up quickly (dizzy, palpitations), exercise (breathlessness, palpitations), or drinking coffee (palpitations) which appear to come out of the blue. Patients often take the absence of any obvious triggers for these attacks as evidence that they are due to serious physical disorder. Psychologists find that identifying the antecedents of a spontaneous attack can be a helpful way of challenging patients' catastrophic interpretations. They might use the following exercise to do this:

Identify antecedents of 'spontaneous attacks'

1   Description of main problems: e.g.
    * Feeling tired much of the time
    * Being tense at work and at home
    * Having difficulty coping with pressures at work and meeting people.

2   For each obtain a description of a recent occasion:
    * What was it?
    * Where were you?
    * Who were you with?
    * What were you doing?
    * What did you notice happening to your body, what sensations did you experience?
    * What went through your mind?
    * What did you do?
    * How did the other person react?
    * What did the other person say/do?

Once the antecedents have been identified, patients will have both cognitive and behavioural material to work with:

* Use relaxation in the presence of previous cues for anxious feelings or physical tension

- Graded exposure to the situation
- Challenge unhelpful cognitions, including utilising new helpful information
- Awareness of reinforcers for certain behaviours so that contingencies can be changed; Use/obtain the reinforcer for behaviour incompatible with the behaviour to be changed
- Problem solve other practical alternatives, including use of communication skills.

Minor symptoms = major pathology

Some patients attribute the onset of their pain to a relatively innocuous routine activity such as bending lifting or twisting. They may appraise the experience as, 'My back just gave out', or 'I felt it snap', or 'Something seemed to pop out of place'. Their experience seems to be that fairly minor physical trauma produces quite frightening 'pathology'. This can then lead to the kinds of beliefs which generate strong avoidance behaviours. This is compounded when the chiropractor tells them they have 'put the disc back in', the doctor tells them they have 'wear and tear' and to rest (it will obviously wear out if you don't), or the physiotherapist tells them NEVER to bend over or do situps.

Beliefs

A traditional medical myth is that the back is a delicate structure, to be protected carefully from strain or damage. In their efforts to explain the cause of recurrent back pain, doctors and physiotherapists often point to various structural defects. Terms like *degeneration* and *spondylosis* are used despite the lack of evidence relating them to pain or disability. Patients report being told they have crumbling spines/discs/bones, slipped discs, pinched nerves, trapped nerves, that they will end up in a wheelchair..., with relatives confirming that these statements were made. The horrors and mystique that has built up around arachnoiditis, RSI, irritable bowel, or ME are not entirely the patients' fault.

Integrating the cognitive and behavioural approaches

It is easy for fear-avoidance to be seen mainly as a behavioural problem, however it is important to pay attention to the underlying cognitions. The avoidance of, or relief from, distressing emotion including fear, is frequently an immediate effect of a problem behaviour, and is often the most potent maintaining factor. Helping patients explore the thoughts behind these unpleasant emotions, then challenging them with alternative thoughts and collecting plausible evidence to the contrary, is often immensely helpful in bringing about rapid behaviour change as well as relief from the emotion.

Box 1 Examples of avoidance behaviours

Avoidance of

- Being touched on painful area by clothes or others
- Weight through bottom, or right or left of bottom
- Weight through right or left leg
- Bending low back
- Pain—trying to 'run away from it' by using distraction
- Lying down
- Lying on right or left side
- Kneeling/squatting
- Stairs

Avoidance of activities

- Keyboards
- Eating
- Jarring activities
- Social activities
- Driving
- Writing
- Lifting/carrying
- Going out of the house
- Crowds
- Travelling/public transport

Cognitive avoidance

Patients can also avoid:

- Thinking of anxiety provoking situations, past or present
- Rest or relaxation—thoughts crowd in.

Using sleeping pills, anxiolytics, tranquilisers etc. can be a means of mental avoidance as they dull the patients' cognitive state, and stop them thinking about distressing events or situations.

Recognising avoidance

When considering helping patients overcome fear and/or avoidance, it is a salutary exercise to look at one's own avoidances and fears, in order to realise that patients' responses are often quite *normal*. The following activity has been presented as a workshop exercise. For the first few examples contributions from participants in the workshop are included and shown in italics, you should add your own responses in the space provided or on a separate sheet.

178

Things you avoid

Going to the dentist
Spiders
Confrontation
Injury
Eating salad
Paying bills
Speeding

Things you have to force yourself to do because you would rather avoid them:

House work
Writing
Changing nappies
Going to Sainsburys
Sex
Getting up early to go to work

When is avoidance appropriate?

When distress would otherwise be too high
Benefits outweigh costs
There are alternatives
Safety/survival

What are the benefits of avoidance?

Physical
Stay alive
Conservation of energy
Less pain
Comfort
Emotional
Reduce distress and anxiety
Feel in control
More relaxing
Comfort
Social
Cheaper
Someone else will do it

One can go on to explore avoidance, looking at instances where it is not helpful for coping with problems.

What are the dangers of physical avoidance?

Physical

....

Emotional

....

Social

....

What are the dangers of cognitive avoidance?

Physical

....

Emotional

....

Social

....

What may patients who avoid activities believe are the benefits?

....

How can patients use reinforcement to help overcome avoidance?

....

Cue strength hierarchy

Cues that patients may pick up that confirm their fears can be very, very subtle. Cues that the therapist needs to supply (in the form of information and disconfirming evidence) may have to be supported strongly by much believable and varied repetition, and reinforced strongly and very convincingly. Going over their options with patients is helpful. When the therapist feels the message has been heard despite overwhelming fear, then patients need to be weaned off information and left to make a decision/make a change.

Understanding does not of itself lead to behaviour change

It is important that the therapist does not fall into the trap of delaying progress in behaviour change by substituting information and theoretical understanding for gathering the practical evidence patients need—in other words giving it a go. The therapist needs to be aware of the risks of reinforcing avoidance by continuing to provide information well beyond where behaviour change might be expected to have begun given the circumstances. Patients may have been taught to avoid activities by using quite complex arguments against change. As well as genuine misunderstandings, many of these arguments will have actually been provided and legitimised by physiotherapists and doctors in the past. Remaining in the position of 'Aunt Sally' or focusing on complaints about previous management or professionals however, can divert attention from the avoided activity.

Patient self attribution

In order to feel a sense of achievement—*I did it*—patients need to have reasons for attributing success to themselves and not to the therapist. It is therefore important that the therapist minimises reasons for patients to attribute their success to the therapist.

Very occasionally the fear of an activity, combined with very little or no skill in performing the new behaviour, means the therapist needs to give more direction and even physical help. Provided this is done in such a way that patients are still able to attribute improvement to themselves, there is no harm in this at all. One will be using the principle of graded exposure as for phobias, from mild exposure with the therapist helping, to exposure with the therapist present, to finally strong exposure without the therapist present.

Example

Weaning a patient off crutches or from support from another person while walking can occasionally seem to stop progressing. The patient may get off one or both crutches, but still be walking hanging onto walls. She may even be willing to try a few steps into a room away from the walls, but can seem to be unable to co-ordinate 1) swinging the arms, which gives her balance, with 2) relaxing and 3) an even right left gait, despite your modelling. Provided you know what is a meaningful reinforcer for her, it is quite OK to start by taking her hand.

Begin with swinging the arms holding hands, then walking on the spot swinging the arms, then set off at an easy rhythmical pace into the room swinging the arms with her. Provide constant reinforcement in addition to the reinforcement of your help, then move up the hierarchy of difficulty. Walk as before with your hand on her back, still modelling a rhythmical relaxed pace with your other arm swinging, then walk with her without touching her but staying close, then gradually move further away, until she walks across on her own. All the time provide meaningful reinforcement. At the end make sure she is pleased with HER achievement, and drum up praise and acknowledgement of the achievement and huge improvement from other staff, patients or, preferably, friends and relatives

Rapid exposure like this to the feared activity is very, very effective. Because it provides the patient with a lot of evidence of success it is likely to maintain well, though of course it needs frequent practice in the early stages to 'set' the new behaviour.

Role of friends and relatives

It must be remembered that patients' friends and relatives will have also learnt a vicarious fear avoidance, and are likely to have unhelpful cognitions and make statements that can undermine improvement. They will have had to 'pick up the pieces' in the past, dealing with intense distress or panic attacks, falls, actual injury and worry about damage. They may be modelling what they have seen doctors and therapists do. They may also have been present when doctors or physiotherapists said 'NEVER go up stairs without your crutch', 'If you do that the fusion will break/you'll end up in a wheelchair/the pain will get worse/I won't treat you any more' etc. They will also need help with behaviour change, though it is not usually possible for you to provide all of it in person on a programme. They can however have access to patients' handouts, and patients can learn to reassure and reinforce their friends and relatives and make allies of the ones who are most helpful and find it easier to change. Patients may have to learn to challenge their relative/friend's worries and be assertive in doing what they feel is best for them.

Patient self reinforcement

Certain patients may have had little skill in the past at gathering evidence of achievement and much skill at looking for evidence of failure—'Yes, but ...'. They may need help at first, with the therapist modelling for them how to challenge their unhelpful 'Yes, buts' and how to recognise seemingly small achievements as actually large in their context. If the therapist finds that this is not reinforcing cognitive and behaviour change, then it is necessary to help patients look in more detail at their cognitions about the situation.

Functional analysis

It is not always easy to find out what functions as a reinforcer for a particular patient, nor sometimes to immediately make the links between a patient's behaviour and the cues and reinforcers in the environment. It is helpful in these situations to establish what is happening by doing a functional analysis. A simple way to approach functional analysis is via the acronym ABC: Antecedent (cue), Behaviour, Consequence (reinforcer).

Antecendents to behaviours can be found in the setting of the behaviour or as triggers. The setting may be a place, perhaps with unpleasant associations from the past, or it may be the setting of existing beliefs based on previous information. This may for instance have been given to them by doctors: 'I've fused your spine together, but don't bend over, do sit-ups or anything silly, or you might have to come back and have another operation', or might even be from such sources as the Internet: 'If you have arachnoiditis you may end up in a wheelchair'. Personal experience is also a source of evidence and contributes to the setting of the patient's beliefs: the knee gives way and they have fallen down the stairs three times. Triggers can be external—provided by other people or the sight or sound of something with past consequences—or may be internal, such as various thought patterns, or feelings such as anxiety.

Feelings usually have an external trigger, but this may not be at all apparent to the patient. In this case the person may feel quite at the mercy of their feelings which seem to come out of the blue. Helping them recognise and understand the cues and reinforcers that operate in their case, is the first step to learning to gain control over them and changing behaviour.

The following examples are of simple functional analyses of avoidance behaviours in patients, but also look at the behaviours of therapists, relatives and friends, which may be helpful or unhelpful to the patient. Features that can come up in pain management and illustrate likely cues and reinforcers are in italics.

Avoidance learning

* Patient behaviour

Antecedent (cue)		Behaviour	Consequences
Setting *Physio Dept./stairs* Beliefs *Pain means don't do it, it'll wear out* Previous information: *Dr. said don't do.* *Degeneration on Xray* Personal evidence: *Exercise made me worse* *I ended up in hospital* *I fell down the stairs*	**Trigger** External *request: 'come on'* *exercise on sheet* Internal thoughts *'She'll make me.'* *'I can't, my leg!'* Feelings *- anxious* *- not in control*	AVOIDANCE	*Reduces fear* *Reduces pain* *Reinforced by others* *eg. family, therapist* *beliefs confirmed* *and strengthened:* *'I'll be OK if I don't* *do it'*

* Patient behaviour (continued)

Antecedent (cue)		Behaviour	Consequences
Setting *Experience/information* *physio challenges old* *information.* *Provide new information* Other patients' evidence: *'They tried & managed'* Personal evidence: *'I had no spasm when I* *did much less'*	**Trigger** External *How request made* *'It's up to you'* Internal thoughts: *'I only need to go* *up by a little'* Feelings: *- in control*	GRADED EXPOSURE	*Reduces fear* *Feel more in control* *Beliefs affected* *'It seems to work'* *'Maybe pain does* *not mean damage,* *maybe pain does* *not mean spasm'*

* Therapist behaviour

Antecedent (cue)		Behaviour	Consequences
Setting/External Trigger Patient statement: *'Last time …'* *'Every time I …'* *'If you make me….'* Patient emotion: *- anger* *- fear/panic* Patient behaviour: *- scream in pain* *- catastrophising*	**Trigger** Internal therapist thoughts: *'S/he clearly can't'* *'It's cruel'* *'Litigation?'* Therapist feelings: *- apprehensive* *- not in control* *- out of her/his* *depth*	THERAPIST COLLUDES IN PATIENT AVOIDANCE THERAPIST AVOIDS PATIENT OR SITUATION	*Lowers therapist fear* *Therapist feels* *back in control* *Beliefs affected* *Therapist reinfor-* *ced by patient* *(anger and fear* *reduced, grateful)*

* Therapist behaviour (continued)

Antecedent (cue)		Behaviour	Consequences
Setting/External triggers *as above*	**Trigger** Therapist thoughts: *'There's nothing* *really wrong'* *'It's put on'* *'What a fuss'* *'Hypochondriac'* Therapist feelings: *- exasperation* *- annoyance*	Therapist: MAKE DEMANDS BLAMES PATIENT GET ANGRY MAKE THREATS DISCHARGE PATIENT	Patient: *> fear/panic* *behaviour increases* *Beliefs confirmed* *and strengthened* *Doesn't return* Therapist: *Beliefs confirmed* *and strengthened:* *'The patient* *doesn't want to* *get better.'*

* Relative/friend behaviour

Antecedent (cue)		Behaviour	Consequences
Setting	**Trigger**	ENCOURAGES	*Reduces their fear*
Scene of previous aversive	Patient anxiety	PATIENT	*and patient's pain*
experience	Thoughts:	AVOIDANCE	*Beliefs confirmed*
Beliefs	*'Last time .....'*	JEOPARDISES	*and strengthened*
Consequences not worth it	Feelings:	ALL ATTEMPTS	*Reinforced*
Previous information:	*– anxious*	BY PATIENT	*(patientand*
GP: 'Bones are crumbling'	*– not in control*	TO OVERCOME	*therapist/doctor)*
Personal evidence:	*– not needed*	FEARS AND	*Feel needed*
Took weeks to recover		AVOIDANCE	

* Relative/friend behaviour (continued)

Antecedent (cue)		Behaviour	Consequences
Setting	**Trigger**	REINFORCES	*Reduces fear*
Challenged unhelpful	External	PATIENT	*Feels more in*
information	*Patient confidence*	FOR	*control*
Read programme handouts	Internal thoughts:	ACHIEVEMENTS	*'Improvement is*
New evidence from patient	*'That's a first,*		*possible this way'*
or other patients	*and no fall!'*	STOPS	*Reinforced by*
	Feelings:	REINFORCING	*patient and feels*
	– in control	AVOIDANCE	*needed in other*
	– hopeful		ways

The following two case studies demonstrate how patients with a high degree of fear and avoidance may be approached. The first gives examples of cognitive-behavioural principles in action with a patient. An ABC and question and answer format is used so that you can see how the patient may be helped. The second asks similar questions and you may like to think how they could be answered and what you might do in the given situation.

Case study 1

Claire is a 25-year-old ex-nurse attending a pain management programme with back pain and sciatica following an accident at work. She had a laminectomy which made no difference to her pain. She has moved back to live with her parents, and although she has stopped work she still goes out with her friends and does voluntary work as a hospital visitor once a week. She walks with two crutches and is unable to weight-bear at all on her left leg.

Comments she has made on the programme have included:

*'I'm not going to walk without my crutches, I **can't** put weight through my left leg, the pain is just too bad. It's stupid to do something that makes the pain worse when you don't have to. My surgeon said I shouldn't put weight on my leg. I know my pain, I've lived with it for 4 years, you can't tell me, you don't have pain, you don't know what my pain's like, I know what's best for it.'*

What have the likely cues for avoidance been in the past?

Setting

Environment: Hospital ward

Beliefs: Pain means damage, one shouldn't have to suffer—doctors/pills can do something; if I avoid the pain it will go away or at least get less, if I make it worse it may stay worse, my back is so bad it needed an operation—I've got to look after it or it might collapse/crumble/need another operation.

Previous information: Surgeon told her not to put weight on the leg; physiotherapist seemed annoyed with her for weight-bearing when she tried, and said she might fall.

Personal evidence: Pain when she weight-bears, unbearable pain when she weight-bears a lot, as a nurse saw hospital patients in similar situations.

Triggers

Presence of physiotherapist
Presence of other patients/family/friends
Exercise sheet
Increased pain
Thoughts: 'I can't', 'They don't understand'
Feelings: anxiety, anger

Resulting behaviour

Avoidance
Refusal
Muscle tension
Clanking of the crutches etc.

Previous reinforcers

Immediate avoidance of increased pain
Crutches provide visual cue for help (seats in trains, buses etc)
Invalidity/mobility allowances
Sense of worth—'brave disabled'
Anxiety/panic avoided

What might the patient be thinking—catastrophising?

'Aaaaaaaaaaaah, walking without my crutches!!'

'The physiotherapist obviously doesn't understand otherwise she wouldn't tell me to do it.

When I put more weight on my leg the pain is terrible; it's obvious it's something serious and that I mustn't do it.'

'I tried it before with a physio. She was really pushy and tried to tell me it would be alright—I should do it whether it hurt or not. God, I ended up with the most terrific pain, I couldn't move, the back seized up as well as the leg, my father had to come and get me. And, I don't want to end up in hospital again!'

What could happen if you told her to just get on with it?

* A general increase in pain and disability behaviours, especially noisy ones
* Continue with outright refusal
* Angry response—'You just don't understand, I've met your sort before, I'd like to see you try it'
* She will provide you with evidence that she can't do it, or that the cost is too high
* There is a high risk that she will lose any remaining trust in you and leave the programme.

How might you approach this, rather than telling her what to do?

* Acknowledge fears, difficulties and pain, and the dilemma that conflicting information brings. (This often does not alter behaviour immediately, but is essential for continuing to work with her.)
* Be very careful not to do anything that might be construed as coercion, with judicious use of 'Only do what you can manage, it's up to you how much you do', and keep your distance from her so she doesn't feel crowded/watched/imposed upon etc.
* Problem solve with her (link to goals)

Remembering to observe ABC, what might you reinforce?

With body language and your interest:
* Listening to you.
* Relaxing tense neck, shoulder or back muscles.
* Referring to her information folder.
* Bracing shoulders less and taking less weight through the crutches.
* Appearing calmer and less angry.
* Not 'Yes-butting'.

With praise:
* All other helpful exercise behaviours.
* Problem solving and thinking things through.

- Considering a baseline on weight-bearing through the left leg, e.g. resting it gently on the floor to start with, or gently patting it on the floor—perhaps in sitting initially.
- Any actual weight-bearing—but with great care that she feels believed not patronised, and cannot construe your response as 'I told you so' or 'I caught you out'.

What strategies could you use if your attempts at reinforcement are met with a lot of 'Yes, but...'s?

- Reduce your eye contact as soon as the 'Yes, but' comes up or look neutral rather than interested (as you were when reinforcing her) and don't get into any discussion that can be construed as 'Yes you can/no I can't... etc'.
- Stop praising her for the moment—your praise may be a cue for the 'Yes, buts'—leave it until a discussion after she has finished her exercises when she will have more evidence that can be counted as success rather than failure.
- Reflect back to her what she is doing ('Yes butting')—'It sounds as if you are being quite hard on yourself', then help her look at more realistic views.
- Help her think about how it makes her feel to say these things (low, fed-up, etc).
- Get her to generate a list of advantages and disadvantages of progressing in weight-bearing. Go through it with her to help generate options and link to goals (NB goals she mentioned at her screening interview to come on the programme can be useful, if she finds it hard to think of weight-bearing goals).
- Go over with her her images of what it feels like and what she may feel is happening inside her back/leg when she takes weight on it, then help her challenge these images and generate more helpful ones.

What is likely to happen when she actually does start weight-bearing?

- Pain behaviour will increase (pain, fear and you are cues).
- She may catastrophise.

How should you respond?

- Praise her +++ for weight-bearing as well as for not weight-bearing very long (she chose a sensible low baseline).
- Recognise that the task was harder to achieve due to her pain and apprehension, and therefore a bigger success. (You will not have paid attention to the pain behaviour, you are using your reference to pain as part of your reinforcement of her achievement, thus modelling/strengthening her self-evidence that weight-bearing is not totally impossible).
- Recognise HER achievement—'Are you pleased?...Good, you *should* be, because that was a real achievement. I'm impressed that you gave it a try!'

Case study 2

Michael is a 40-year-old train driver who now works as an announcer. He reports that he fell down a hole in 1985 and 'got a displaced pelvis for two years', then a scout dropped a pole on his leg in 1990. Later in 1990 someone ran into him with a loaded luggage trolley at the airport and his knee was bent backwards. He has been told by Mr X. (orthopaedic surgeon) that the impact was similar to an estate car hitting him at 10 mph. In 1992 he fell down some steps and hurt his back. He has used crutches since then.

He has knee pain that radiates down the shin like a red hot knife warning him to stop walking. He describes his hip coming out, and that the leg locks and suddenly collapses with no warning. The knee is very sensitive to touch and can disturb his sleep. He walks with 2 crutches—recommended by a physio, who told him 'NHS crutches give you wrist problems'—and a leg brace. He generally keeps the brace locked at the knee.

He has seen a sports injuries physiotherapist who gave him exercises. He was given loads of advice, including not to exercise when the pain increases. The physiotherapitst has said that the natural locking of the knee muscles has gone and if he doesn't wear the brace then his knee will collapse backwards and the ligaments will tear. Mr X. has said his knee will never be the same again—he has had 3 serious accidents on the leg. He also said some of it is 'in the mind'. The physio said something is very wrong— the muscles are not developing as they should. He has had 6 scans where they found a syndrome affecting the nerves, tissues and bones. The physio said that is what he'd guessed, only 1 person in 6-7000 got it—he is quite unique.

Michael lives with his parents who are both 74, and goes shopping with his mother. Both parents are very supportive, and drive him to the station in the mornings. He avoids anything with steps or climbing. He still works as a scout leader but can't lead long hikes any more and has been told by the District Commissioner, 'You're not much use to scouting'. He can't ski any more, but enjoys DIY (he recently re-decorated his own room), and working on hobbies. His parents response when his knee goes is to say, 'Is the knee playing up?, OK, let's wait'. Michael is not sure if they can always tell the pain has flared up, but if he holds it or is short-tempered, they probably guess. He is unsure about the future 'I think I've got to accept it now. I assume if I get older and there's no answer then it will get worse'.

I hope you can see from these examples that the cognitive-behavioural approach makes it quite possible to understand patients' circumstances and behaviours without blaming them e.g. for being weak, malingering or stupid, or feeling frustrated, annoyed and helpless yourself. It also provides the means for helping patients to understand their situation, and to learn to make meaningful changes in their lives.

What have the likely cues for avoidance been in the past?

Setting   Triggers
Environment

....

Beliefs

....

Previous information   Thoughts:

....

Personal evidence   Feelings:

....

What have been previous reinforcers for avoiding stairs and steps?

....

When it is time for Michael to tackle stairs, what might he be thinking?

....

How might he reply if you tell him to get on with it—'Come on you can do it'?

....

How might you approach beginning a graded exposure programme to stair climbing?

....

What strategies might you help Michael to use to challenge his fears?

....

What might happen when Michael first tries to go up a step?

....

How will you respond?

....

BACKGROUND READING

Clark D M 1989 Anxiety states: Panic and generalized anxiety. In: Cognitive behaviour therapy for psychiatric problems: A practical guide. Hawton K, Salkovskis P M, Kirk J, Clark D M (eds) Oxford Medical Publications, Oxford

Fordyce W E, Shelton J L, Dundore D E 1982 The modification of avoidance learning pain behavior. Journal of Behavioural Medicine 5(4):405–414

Philips H C 1987 Avoidance behaviour and its role in sustaining chronic pain. Behavioural. Research and Therapy. 25(4):273–279

REFERENCES

Clark D.M 1986 A cognitive approach to panic. Behavioural Research and Therapy 24:461-470

Clark D M 1988 A cognitive model of panic attackes. In: Rachman S, Maser J D (eds) Panic: psychological perspectives. Lawrence Erlbaum, Hillsdale NJ pp 71-90

Emmelkamp P M G 1982 Phobic and obsessive-compulsive disorders: theory, research and practice. Plenum, New York

Jones M C 1924 The elimination of children's fears. Journal of Experimental Psychology 7:382-390

Marks I M 1981 Cure and care of neurosis. Wiley, New York

Matthews A M, Gelder M G, Johnston D W 1981 Agoraphobia: nature and treatment. Guilford Press, New York

Mowrer O H 1947 On the dual nature of learning—a reinterpretation of 'conditioning' and 'problem solving'. Harvard Educational Review 17:102-148

Mowrer O H 1960 Learning theory and behavior. Wiley, New York

Salkovskis P M 1988 Phenomenology, assessment and the cognitive model of panic. In: Rachman S, Maser J D (eds) Panic: psychological perspectives. Lawrence Erlbaum, Hillsdale NJ pp 111-136

Solomon R L, Wynn L C 1954 Traumatic avoidance learning: the principles of anxiety conservation and partial irreversability. Psychological Review 61: 353-385

Wolpe J 1958 Psychotherapy by reciprocal inhibition. Stanford University Press, Stanford California

Wolpe J 1961 The systematic desensitization treatment for neurosis. Journal of Nervous and Mental Diseases 132: 189-203

14

Are we being patientist?

VICKI HARDING

Doctors, nurses and health professionals allied to medicine are mainly trained in a traditional unidimensional approach to patients and their problems. Physiotherapists' training does emphasise a rehabilitation approach, yet this traditionally had roots in unidimensionalism where the doctor/therapist was the expert dispensing wisdom and advice. Importantly, even when as physiotherapists we begin to use a more multidimensional and biopsychosocial approach to our patients, it is still very hard to throw off the ways we learnt so well. We need to be aware of factors in the traditional approach to chronic pain that encourage a single construct model of pain or that take autonomy away from the patient. Some of the traditional terminology we might use can not only lead us back to thinking unidimensionally, but can also, in or out of context, encourage prejudiced or patientist thinking. It is the use of terms or labels in relation to patients with chronic pain that is the focus of this chapter.

Labelling pain behaviour

The psychiatric approach to chronic pain arose from a more medical approach to illness (Gamsa 1994). Black (1975) called it the *chronic pain syndrome* relating it to patients with 'no clear organic pathology, only symptoms'. He was thus implying that if pain is not physical then it must be mental. This had developed from the psychosomatic school of psychiatry where physical symptoms are said to be produced by psychological factors; e.g., asthma is separation anxiety. This has never been proved, and the movement in chronic pain is now more towards physical illness maintained or made more problematical by psychological factors. Psychiatrists still tend though, to see things in terms of pain due to psychological mechanisms and try to find explanations that are purely psychological. Black still mentions 'no physical findings', though admits that this depends on modern technology and where you look.

I think this is a warning to us to be careful in the way we think and speak about patients with chronic pain. We may be utterly convinced that all pain has a physical component as well as psychological and social components, and be only too well aware of the limitations of medical diagnosis. If, however, we use phrases like 'no physical findings', 'symptoms out of proportion to the injury' or 'inappropriate signs', it will not be too long before patients hear us say this, read it in a letter, or hear it repeated second hand from a colleague. They can then quite rightly feel angry at our betrayal, feel misunderstood, and realise that we have our colours pinned to a different mast than we are espousing. Importantly, it will affect our approach to patients even if this appears quite minor initially. It is an indication that there is a mismatch between our actions and our understanding of the biopsychosocial approach. It indicates that fault or blame are creeping into our view rather than degrees of responsibility based on a wider view of a patient's difficulties.

Patients' past experiences

Patients have had to contend with many disbelieving and blaming health professionals in the past. These clinicians may have stated as well as implied that pain is in the patient's mind, they may have displayed irritation when the patient was not able to 'comply' with instructions exactly, and may have used a 'pull yourself together' tone of voice at times. When a patient has had experience of this, it inevitably leads to heightened sensitivity and defensiveness for these attitudes. If patients think you are being judgemental they will hear that message rather than the message you want them to hear. We need to be extremely careful that we do not use words, phrases or a tone of voice that could in any way indicate a digression from the wider biopsychosocial model. If not, this makes it much harder to work with the patient and tends to break what therapeutic alliance has existed until then.

Terms that may provoke misunderstandings

The term *somatisers* appears in the psychological as well as psychiatric literature, and is also being used in the biopsychosocial approach to chronic pain and illness. However, the label of somatiser is generally derogatory, and implies an individual who 'complains' a lot, makes a fuss, seems weak willed and easily frightened, and dwells on illness and fear; *somatiser* blames patients for 'needlessly focusing on ordinary symptoms' rather than 'pulling themselves together' and getting on with life. Equally, since people are aware of the futility of *telling* someone to stop focusing on symptoms, it is easy to see how a therapist might feel helpless or even irritable in the face of these images. The patient may then be seen as the link to or cause of these feelings. However, if we look at the wider picture and gain a better understanding of the mechanisms involved, this now presents a picture whereby the patient is seen to be behaving quite logically or normally considering their beliefs about their illness and their past and present circumstances. Also, importantly, it suggests the means to changing the way the patient manages their situation—both in terms of their behaviour and cognitions—and points to what may be changeable in the environment so that the patient gains control over their situation.

Other words we use also need to be used with care, and it may well be preferable to use and become familiar with less emotionally-loaded terms.

Conditioning can be associated with training rats in a laboratory or seem like tricking people or manipulating them.

Learning is a more helpful and jargon-free term. Operant learning can be used in place of operant conditioning, and its use indicates that the user is familiar with the practical application of operant techniques in a value-free patient-orientated way.

Behaviour is usually associated with bad behaviour, and in chronic pain, with unwanted behaviours. Any behaviour, however, has a context in which it is appropriate.

Habit is a much less loaded word—everybody has them, good and bad, we all know they are difficult to break, and patients possibly accept more readily that their therapist's expectations for change are not set unrealistically high, so they are less likely to feel under pressure.

Avoidance and, to a degree, **fear** need to be used with care. Avoidance can sound like something the patient is blamed for—'brave' people don't do it— just like fear is only for wimps. There may be no direct alternative so we need to be aware that other professionals need to know what we mean, and preferably not use the term in front of patients—they rarely after all *completely* avoid anything at all times; **tend to avoid** may be more accurate. Fear is a word that really needs to come from the patient. If you are helping them recognise the feelings associated with certain situations or cognitions, **apprehension** may be kinder. Wait until the patient uses the word *fear* before you adopt it in relation to them.

Positive thinking and **negative thinking** are sometimes used by patients, particularly those who may have heard of the book *The Power of Positive Thinking*. Occasionally these terms have crept into the physiotherapy literature. We perhaps need to remind ourselves that these terms are very simplistic, and imply that all one has to do is 'think positive'. This does not recognise the difficulties patients can have with complex cognitive issues, and the potential futility of just 'thinking positive'. Positive thinking can quite easily feel hollow and empty and unable to meaningfully challenge those thoughts that are responsible for anger, distress or low mood. Some things can be inherently without a positive dimension, so patients could get very frustrated or distressed by trying to pursue positive thoughts about their husband dying or about having chronic pain for the rest of their lives. If *negative thinking* is considered bad, then avoiding it may prevent patients from addressing what is difficult or painful for them, much of it based on all too evident reality. More useful terms to use are *helpful* and *unhelpful* cognitions or thoughts. These terms are not loaded, and will tend to lead patients towards useful coping self statements and problem solving rather than just mantras.

Active and *passive* can also be quite loaded or judgemental, particularly when applied to 'active and passive coping strategies', terms that are creeping into the literature but are possibly not helpful. Rest can be termed a 'passive' coping strategy, yet is a vital part of pacing provided it is not too long and reinforces activity. Like cognitions, coping strategies perhaps need to be deemed *helpful* or *effective* versus *unhelpful*. This allows one person's unhelpful coping strategy to be another's helpful coping strategy, based on their pathology and circumstances and not on something good or bad.

Shoulds and *musts* 'must' not creep into our language. Emphases need to be watched—. remember 'Musturbation'! Since we wish patients to gain control 'patients *may*...' rather than 'patients should...'. We need to recognise that patients are different and do not readily fall into uniform groups. We also need to watch that any of our preconceived ideas don't influence our view of patients. People can be happy in certain types of relationships that research indicates may increase the likelihood of dependence or disability. It is not up to us to rock the boat or make assumptions, merely to help patients try things out, look at the evidence and their options, and make their own informed choices.

Pain complaints and *complaining* are words that tend to sound judgemental: what we don't want to hear. It seems to the patient like: 'Stop complaining, just put up with it', i.e. be more stoic. The behavioural approach aims to help patients cope better under difficult circumstances. It does not aim to make people more stoic—this is in fact often counterproductive since patients can easily come unstuck if they try to ignore the pain and battle on. It often leads to increased physical tension which causes movement and function deterioration and can result in a cognitive backwards step: 'I knew I couldn't manage it, I'll never get any better', 'It's all in my mind', or 'It's mind over matter'.

Why pain behaviour might appear to be 'inconsistent'

Inconsistent pain behaviour is a phrase that is sometimes used, and which can imply that the patient's symptoms are not genuine and are therefore blameworthy. It is thus worth looking at what is happening and how it can be interpreted:

- Pain behaviour varies in response to the same stimulus—many stimuli are present, that stimulus might be only one remaining the same.
- Behaviour varies in different settings—this indicates the complexity of chronic pain and the many and varied cues and reinforcers operating, usually at unconscious levels.

- Behaviour inconsistent with statement about behaviour—'I can't...' when patient is able to partly do something. There are degrees of 'can' as well as 'can't'. We may be looking at the degrees of can when the patient only rates 'can' when it is perfect. Addressing or arguing with them about 'can't' may be unhelpful until they can recognise the benefit of looking at the degrees of 'can'.

Patients' pain behaviour can be reinforced by others, however it is worth looking at hypotheses for other reasons for 'variation in pain behaviour':

- ★ Good day/bad day/time of day—these will all influence parameters such as pain, stiffness and tiredness that affect movement and behaviour directly.
- ★ Have we correctly identified stimulus/meaning?
- ★ Faking—people with no pain can fake a limp, but it is hard to maintain for long, as concentration turns to other activities. A patient with a long established limp will maintain that limp long past their (or anyone else's) concentration span, indicating that non-conscious mechanisms are involved. The notion that someone is consciously controlling or 'faking' a limp across all contexts and across time is far fetched.
- ★ Distress/emotions—during times of increased anxiety or lower mood, patients' ability to cope is reduced. This may influence behaviour relating to pain.
- Gradual extinction of behaviour—while behaviours are undergoing extinction there will be increases and decreases in frequency and strength of those behaviours in response to the intermittency or extinction of reinforcement.
- Secondary gain—this implies deliberate manipulation to get something from another. This may of course be the case, but usually occurs when patients do not appear to have other, more worthwhile, options. Perhaps rather than looking at secondary gain it is helpful to see if this could be re-framed as secondary loss, i.e. the patient is behaving in this way as a result of having lost important skills or opportunities. Then the patient can be helped to see if perhaps there are other options that would be more valuable. If there are not, perhaps their response could be judged to be reasonable and fair given their present circumstances—not an impression given by use of the term secondary gain.

Some of these hypotheses are likely to be operating with an individual, some not, and some should be rejected even if they are held by others.

Hypothesis testing

It is useful exercise to test the hunches we have about our patients' behaviours. There are several ways to do this:

- Observe—more careful and lengthier observation of cues, behaviours and reinforcers may help us confirm or disconfirm our hypotheses.

a   Monitor details of the situation—it is sometimes necessary to actually measure frequency and timing in order to uncover which cues and reinforcers are most powerful.

- Ask—asking the patient is empowering, though choosing the right question is important. It is vital to avoid the implication that you are trying to catch them out, since patients will likely have been sensitised to this by professionals or relatives in the past.
- Provide feedback—discuss your observations with the patient, provided again you avoid the implication that you have been trying to catch them out. Use of words like *habit* are very useful here, as is evidence that others are responding this way too, so that the patient is not made to feel unusual or stupid.
- Experiment with contingencies—it is very difficult to be consistent with providing cues and reinforcers which may be why behaviour appears to be inconsistent. Experimenting can help clarify the situation.
- Video and private detective—if it is your aim to catch the patient out and try to prove dishonesty, this method may seem appropriate. However it is expensive, unethical, and more importantly not valid, since it is only a snapshot of a short period of time and does not record any of the other contingencies operating, e.g. as above, pacing and pain level.
- Research findings can be turned to for elucidation—however, these are based on group data and group trends, and not on the individual. Group data should merely guide some of the content or emphases of group pain management. Its relevance to the individual needs to be established separately every time.

Finally, it is worth considering whether *any* behaviour is consistent, and why we should expect patients' pain behaviour to be consistent when our own behaviour is variable. Just as Salkovskis (1996) states '...there is no place in the [cognitive] theory or the therapy for the idea of the therapist defined 'wrong thinking', which is inappropriately judgemental', so it should be also for habits or behaviours.

REFERENCES

Black R G 1975 The chronic pain syndrome. Surgical Clinics of North America 55:999

Gamsa A 1994 The role of psychological factors in chronic pain. I. A half century of study. Pain 57:5–15

Salkovskis P M 1996 The cognitive approach to anxiety: threat beliefs, safety-seeking behavior, and the special case of health anxiety and obsession. In: Salkovskis P M (ed) Frontiers of cognitive therapy. Guilford Press, New York

15

Structure-oriented beliefs and disability due to back pain

Reproduced with kind permission from Australian Journal of Physiotherapy 1998, 44:13-20

MAX ZUSMAN

Introduction

During the course of this century there has been an exponential increase in the numbers of individuals in Western societies who are disabled by the symptom (low) back pain (Waddell 1987). As far as can be determined there has been no corresponding change in the fundamental nature of back pain, or sciatica, itself (Troup 1996, Waddell 1995). Historically, the incidence and prevalence of back pain appear to have been relatively stable (Fordyce 1995). In other words it has been difficult to attribute this modern epidemic to some inexplicable dramatic increase in the generally recognised 'specific' diagnoses (Waddell 1992).

Nor have proposals attributing back pain to everyday lifestyle factors been particularly convincing. For instance, in the USA, a number of these lifestyle factors were modified by, among other things, the extensive and expensive introduction of seemingly promising applied ergonomic knowledge and an array of mechanical labour-saving devices (Mooney 1987). However, during the same period, disability due to back pain increased 14 times the population growth (Cats-Baril & Frymoyer 1991). This costly addition to the ranks of the chronically disabled was in excess of that for all other health disorders (Frymoyer & Cats-Baril 1991). During the time that disability awards for all conditions rose an average of 347 per cent, those for back pain soared 2,680 per cent. Similar figures are reported for other Western societies, including Great Britain and Sweden (Cats-Baril & Frymoyer 1991).

The change considered to be associated with this uniquely 20th century phenomenon are beliefs as to the basis for back pain and, therefore, the way(s) in which it should be managed (Allan & Waddell 1989). Namely that pain is evidence of some injury or otherwise induced structural/biomechanical fault with the spine (Waddell 1992). As such, the treatment of choice would be rest, perhaps some intervention which actually or purportedly altered structure, or both (Loeser & Sullivan 1995, Long 1995, Nachemson 1992, Wardwell 1993). However, rather than being effective, the disabling consequences of this approach have left a legacy of profound personal, social and economic loss (Fordyce 1995, Loeser 1996, Nachemson 1996, Volinn 1996, Waddell 1987). Hence, it has been suspected that many of the manifestations of back pain, in particular chronic 'intolerance to activity', are a result of factors other than simply underlying pathoanatomy (Fordyce 1995, Loeser 1996).

There is now mounting pressure to halt, and hopefully reverse this '...twentieth-century health care disaster' (Waddell 1995, p.595). Considerable effort is being expended on endeavouring to uncover those diagnostically 'non-specific' factors which could contribute, albeit unintentionally, to growing numbers of individuals becoming crippled by the essentially benign and mostly self-limiting symptom, back pain (Fordyce 1995). Research to date suggests that these non-specific factors fall into three mutually influential categories; namely: 'iatrogenic' (medical professionals of all types), the 'system' (compensation-legal) and 'biobehavioural' (claimant/patient).

Non-specific components of back pain

Iatrogenesis

Iatrogenic factors relate mainly to the impairment-disability label and deconditioning consequences of (prolonged) pain-contingent therapeutic rest together with the need for correction of apparently faulty structure/movement of the spine (Loeser & Sullivan 1995, Vernon 1996, Volinn 1996, Waddell 1995). Therapeutic rest and both invasive, and non-invasive correction of structure are largely the result of anatomical and imaging-driven opinions as to an injury/tissue damage and structural/biomechanical basis for back pain (Hadler 1995, Vernon 1996, Waddell 1995). However, this structurally-based view has been challenged for the overwhelming majority (approximately 80 per cent) of cases, which are now labelled 'non-specific' back pain (Fordyce 1995, Hall & Hadler 1995, Loeser 1996). Non-specific back pain has been described as 'Back pain complaints occuring without identifiable specific anatomical or neurophysiological causative factors.' (Fordyce 1995, p.3).

Decades of conditioning have bred a convinced and expectant lay public who, abetted by medical professionals of all types (Frymoyer & Cats-Baril 1991), tends to believe that pain is evidence of some potentially correctable structural/biomechanical impairment of the spine (Borkan et al 1995, Cherkin & MacCornack 1989, Cherkin et al 1988, Salmon et al 1996, Zusman 1984). The corollary belief being that, in the presence of such presumed or occasionally actual impairment, normal function is impossible or at best dangerous (Jensen et al 1996, LaCroix et al 1990, Vlaeyen et al 1995, Waddell et al 1993). This sort of reasoning appears to underly the findings of several studies including Riley et al (1988). These authors demonstrated that patients' incomplete performance of routine examination, and disability assignment, ranges of trunk and leg movements correlated with the belief that pain implied some structural/damage problem with the spine. This correlation was found to be independent of the actual contribution of reported pain (Riley et al 1988).

The system

Conceived and instituted with theoretically humane and responsible motives, the modern-day compensation-disability system is considered to be a major contributor to the current back pain problem (Hadler 1995, Long 1995, Seres 1995). There is the growing opinion that its original purpose of providing sustenance pending the resumption of gainful employment has been distorted with, particularly in the case of back pain, devastating consequences (Hadler 1995, Fordyce 1995, Loeser 1996).

For example, a recent study of 2000 low back pain patients found that involvement in litigation was the only variable statistically capable of predicting return to work (Long 1995). In contrast to non-litigants all of whom resumed working, not one of the 400 (20 per cent) litigants in the sample returned to work. This was despite their having achieved seemingly satisfactory improvement in work capacity, and comparable pain relief (Long 1995). Findings such as these prompted Seres (1995, p.131) to conclude that the back pain problem is '...not in the iatrogenesis of disability, but in the system that creates the problem.' Specifically, 'Pain and suffering cannot be dealt with rationally in a compensation system based upon the concept that [structural] impairment leads to disability' (Loeser & Sullivan 1995, p.120). This critical issue has been clarified by Hadler (1995, p.648) while decrying the use of impairment rating as a basis for disability determination: 'It is a fantasy that supports an industry whose efforts are iatrogenic! Anyone who has to prove he or she is disabled cannot get better. In fact, they can only get more disabled ...'.

It might be readily understood how individuals compelled to operate within such a system would have additional incentive to embrace iatrogenically reinforced beliefs as to some structural/biomechanical basis for their pain/impairment, and so temporary or permanent intolerance to activity (Fordyce 1995). It is also possible that beliefs of this type pervade the general public and are not simply confined to those individuals required to negotiate the 'iatrogenic gauntlet' demanded by the modern compensation-disability-legal systems (Borkan et al 1995, Cherkin & MacCornack 1989, Cherkin et al 1988, Hadler 1995 and 1996, Salmon et al 1996)

Biobehavioural

Many of the factors included in this category are discussed by Feuerstein and Beattie (1995) under the headings: psychological/cognitive-perceptual, behavioural-environmental and psychophysiological. Tables may also be found in Bigos et al (1991), Frymoyer (1992) and Gatchel et al (1995).

Investigation of biobehavioural factors, compiled from a large number of studies, arose out of acknowledgement of the inability to understand, or treat, back pain in terms of ontogenetic changes, or injury, to structure (Fordyce 1995, Hadler 1995, Loeser & Sullivan 1995). To date, diagnostic and therapeutic models based on notions of applied (patho)anatomy and biomechanics have been incapable of explaining either the onset or severity of most back pain (Fordyce 1995, Kraemer 1995, Nachemson 1996, Saal 1995). Perhaps more importantly such anatomic interpretations have failed to predict the duration of pain or its (lack of) response to a vast array of conservative and invasive interventions (Bigos & Davis 1996, Fordyce 1995, Hadler 1995, Nachemson 1996, Twomey 1992). In fact, the structure-oriented approach to the cause and management of back pain developed during the course of this century is itself considered to have contributed significantly to the situation that exists at the present time (Fordyce 1995, Hadler 1995, Loeser & Sullivan 1995).

A basis for biobehavioural factors

The modern epidemic of disability due to back pain is currently seen as largely a behavioural rather than a strictly medical problem (Barsky & Borus 1995, Fordyce 1995, Loeser 1996). As such, the focus has shifted away from pain-contingent wasteful and ineffective passively received interventions and the need for rehabilitation (Bigos & Davis 1996, Spitzer et al 1987, Teasell & Harth 1996). The currently recommended approach is for early active management (eg return to some form of work) along with attempted prevention (Indahl et al 1995). The major thrust with respect to the latter has been to isolate factors which are considered to be predictive of disability and, with this, determine those individuals most at risk. The most striking feature of the predictive studies so far has been the relative insignificance of biologic, and the dominance of psychosocial influences (eg Burton et al 1995, Gatchel et al 1995, Hazard et al 1996).

Identification of biobehavioural factors is clearly critical. However, it is acknowledged that in a number of instances their underlying basis and precise make-up are still insufficiently understood (Feuerstein & Beattie 1995). The contribution that biobehavioural factors make to the modern epidemic of disability due to back pain will probably necessitate more extensive investigation (Troup 1996). An example would be the factor known as 'perceived disability' (Feuerstein & Beattie 1995, Waddell and Turk 1992). Research has shown that patients' refusal to engage in everyday activities stemmed from the belief that they were physically incapable of doing so (Waddell & Turk 1992). However, this opinion was not supported by relevant structural changes to the spine (Waddell & Turk 1992). The correlation of perceived disability with (poor) performance, but not necessarily identifiable impairment or even levels of pain, has often been observed (Riley et al 1988, Waddell & Turk 1992, Waddell et al 1993).

It would be advantageous to understand what lay behind such erroneous dysfunctional beliefs (Troup 1996, Turk 1996). The known association of perceived disability with 'fear of (re)injury' (Feuerstein & Beattie 1995, Vlaeyen et al 1995) does suggest the invariable connection between pain and structure (Beattie 1996, Cherkin & MacCornack 1989, Kraemer 1995, Nachemson 1996, Vernon 1996). In other words, the belief that pain, especially when mechanically provoked (eg by movement, posture or pressure), is evidence of some problem with the physical intregrity of the spine (Borkan et al 1995, Cherkin et al 1988, Cherkin & MacCornack 1989, Jensen et al 1996, Rose et al 1993, Salmon et al 1996, Vernon 1996, Vlaeyen et al 1995, Zusman 1995). In fact, the presence of pain is not always essential; simply its anticipation is known to be sufficient to prohibit activity (Phillips 1987, Turk 1996, Waddell & Turk 1992).

Fear–avoidance

It is not difficult to appreciate how such structure-oriented beliefs could have detrimental consequences. It might be deemed inefficient (Borkan et al 1995), and also dangerous (Beattie 1996, Jensen et al 1996, McCracken et al 1992, Rose et al 1993, Vlaeyen et al 1995, Waddell et al 1993), to attempt functional activity while harbouring a hypothetical uncorrected structural fault with the spine (Borkan et al 1995, Cherkin & MacCornack 1989, Cherkin et al 1988, Coulehan 1985, McCallum et al 1996, Rose et al 1993, Salmon et al 1996). The perception or anticipation of mechanically provoked pain is not the only stimulus for engaging in these sorts of structure-oriented cognitions (Turk 1996). Aspects of the clinical encounter, including the prescription of therapeutic rest (Volinn 1996), and the use of imaging techniques diagnostically (Beattie 1996, Cherkin & MacCornack 1989, Cherkin et al 1988) have also been found to be highly influential (Borkan et al 1995, Loeser 1996, Loeser & Sullivan 1995). Moreover, fear–avoidance theory predicts that simply the anticipation of pain is sufficient for the maintenance of protective behaviours such as decreased ranges of joint movement and activity intolerance (Fordyce 1995, Phillips 1987, Turk 1996). Fear–avoidance of everyday work and leisure activities has been clearly linked with beliefs about the presence of faulty structure (Borkan et al 1995, LaCroix et al 1990, Riley et al 1988, Waddell et al 1993) and the likelihood of mechanically produced (re)injury of the spine (Jensen et al 1996, McCracken et al 1992, Vlaeyen et al 1995).

It is tempting to detect the influence of simplistic pain-structure cognitions, and costly disabling clinical impressions (Volinn 1996), on a number of identified biobehavioural factors, as well as on common behavioural responses, associated with back pain. For example, what might actually be involved in the factor 'fear of pain' (Feuerstein & Beattie 1995)? It could be simply an aversion to activity-provoked or anticipated pain per se, or perhaps a dread of the iatrogenically conditioned meaning and prognosis often attributed to such pain. The inclusion, and validation, by McCracken et al (1992), of items such as (pain means that) '...I am damaging myself' and '...I might become paralysed or totally disabled' (if I continue) with their instrument for measuring fear of pain, suggests recognition of the latter possibility. According to these authors, fear can function to drive avoidance behaviour which in turn can serve to reduce the distress associated with back pain (McCracken et al 1992), although not necessarily the pain itself (Phillips 1987, Waddell et al 1993). This view was endorsed by positive responses to questionnaire items such as: 'When I feel pain I try to stay as still as possible', 'When I sense pain I feel dizzy and faint' and 'My thoughts are agitated and keyed up as pain approaches' (McCracken et al 1992). A somewhat similar rationale seems to be applicable to the factor 'disease conviction'. Here, distress arising out of the belief that pain is evidence of a major physical problem can effectively increase pain perception by reducing pain tolerance (Feuerstein & Beattie 1995). With one widely used instrument for the evaluation of pain (Illness Behaviour Questionnaire), the combination of the factors disease conviction and 'somatic focussing' was found to be highly predictive of response to treatment for back pain, including surgery (Pilowsky 1995). Distress and pain perception may be further supplemented by the deconditioning sensory-motor consequences of severely reduced activity (Fordyce 1995, Waddell et al 1993).

Transferred to the workplace the scenario could be as follows (identified biobehavioural factors italicised): Constant complaints and reluctance to carry out obligatory functions and responsibility (*job dissatisfaction*) lead eventually to *loss of support* of supervisor, employer and even fellow workers. Denied or disinterested in *limited employment* and no longer willing to suffer the distress associated with being obliged to go on *damaging oneself*, an obvious and necessary recourse is to seek *compensation*. Contending with the powerful employer group (which is perceived to be basically to *blame* for the permanent 'damage') along with its ally the (orthodox) medical-legal-funding organisation, demands the services of a (known to be sympathetic) *lawyer* (factor reference: Frymoyer 1992). Demonstrable impairment-based disability is a virtual guarantee of successful claim outcome (Fordyce 1995, Hadler 1995, Loeser 1996). However, as has been pointed out, once legally overseen medically executed disability determination that is '...objectively grounded in pathoanatomy' is set in motion, full recovery is, if not impossible, then at best seriously compromised (Hadler 1995, p.642).

Structure-oriented beliefs, fear–avoidance and disability

There is now increasing recognition of the critical role patients' beliefs play in the cause, prognosis and management of back pain (Turk 1996). Indeed Waddell et al (1993, p.164) are adamant that: 'In their final expression it is the patient's beliefs rather than the underlying physical reality which govern behaviour.'.

The recent report by Jensen et al (1996) provided further confirmation of the common clinical observation that low levels of functioning correlated with beliefs that pain was evidence of structural damage to the spine, and therefore physical disability. Details surrounding such beliefs, as expressed in their own language were forthcoming from a sample of general practice patients studied by Salmon et al (1996). Patients thought that the origin of back pain was hidden and serious but nonetheless potentially detectable and correctable. The major causes were considered to be structural damage/strain, 'something out of place' and the internal buildup of pressure. The stereotype of age-related wearing out, 'hardening' and failure to work of musculoskeletal structures also emerged as a perceived basis for pain and the inability to function normally. Items believed to be of help diagnostically and therapeutically included X-rays/tests, consultation with a specialist and surgery. Similar beliefs were expressed by subjects in the study of Borkan et al (1995). Pain was said to be the result of their back 'going out'. It was believed that this predisposition was because there is '...some [structural] defect ...in my spine'. There was also the certain knowledge that surgery would reveal that everything '...is completely rotten in my vertebrae' (Borkan et al 1995, p.981).

These structure-oriented beliefs were found to have quite specific backgrounds and consequences, involving the cause of pain, attitude to activity/work, choice of treatment and opinion of providers (Borkan et al 1995, see also Cherkin & MacCornack 1989). Subjects were resigned to the inevitability of potentially disabling back pain because of convictions of genetic-hereditory predisposition together with the presence of congenital defects of structure. Most were able to nominate the presumed primary pain-producing physical insult, sometimes occurring as far back as childhood. This may have been compounded by some subsequent trauma (eg bump following a slip, jumping from a height, pregnancy, car accident) and by age and work related structural degeneration/'wearing out'. Together, these and other cognitions had a significant impact on lifestyle. The dominance of (anticipated) pain, 'ergonomic preoccupation' and, despite peer disapproval or self recrimination, the open evasion of certain tasks and responsibilities, were all evident. Expressions of fear of never being able to walk or run again and the 'nightmare' quality of the inescapable feeling of disability were not uncommon. Yet subjects' fondest desire (expectation) was to be 'better'. That is, to be pain free without recurrences or loss of function. Anything short of this resulted in a spiralling pattern of excessive resource utilisation involving pill substitutions, therapy changes and doctor shopping, with their attendent distress and illness behaviour (Borkan et al 1995).

Costly erroneous and dysfunctional structure-oriented beliefs emerged as the only variable to consistently predict return to work in the study by LaCroix et al (1990). Patients entering the study with the belief that back pain was the product of a 'disintegrating' spine for example, were far less likely to have resumed working when reassessed one year later. An obvious link would be that between fear of (further) structural damage and the prohibition of functional activity. In this regard, Klenerman et al (1995) observed that the best predictor of failure to recover after one year was a positive score for the authors' fear-avoidance screen obtained at one week and again at two months following pain onset. Vlaeyen et al (1995) provided support for the proposal that patients tend to believe that pain is evidence of some structural damage or fault with the spine, and that fear of (re)injury underlies their often profound reluctance to engage in everyday activities. The authors stressed the need to specifically probe and, when present address, such outcome-influencing beliefs, since patients may be otherwise indistinguishable in terms of existing organic pathology, pain intensity or 'nociception' (Vlaeyen et al 1995). Turk (1996) likewise advocated the early identification, and rectification, of patients idiosyncratic beliefs, and cautioned against viewing all patients with the same medical diagnosis as similar. Szpalski et al (1995) found with their culturally diverse sample that the most powerful influence on illness-related practices (eg bed rest, medication consumption) and resource utilisation (eg professional visit, X-ray) was the expectation that back pain would be a lifelong problem. These behaviours were not necessarily dependent on the actual frequency of pain. The probable structure-oriented basis for this opinion may be found in the authors' proposed model which begins with a beliefs/behaviour instigated radiologic (ie structural) diagnosis and ends with failed back surgery and chronic disability (Szpalski et al 1995 p.441).

Turk (1996) has discussed consequences of the common misinformed belief that it is dangerous to engage in activity while experiencing pain, and that pain perception is the signal for retreating into temporary or permanent disability. The impact of such beliefs on patients mood, as well as on behaviour, can have a significant indirect influence on the pain experience itself (Turk 1996). Moreover, according to the operant conditioning model, cognitively instigated perceptions and behaviours may be maintained by reinforcement long after any initial soft tissue damage has healed (Fordyce 1988). Disability increases as a result of the process known as stimulus generalisation whereby avoidance expands to include activities that are only suspected of being potentially painful. Knowing, and addressing from the outset, patients idiosyncratic beliefs were also considered to be critical for optimal treatment planning and an accurate understanding of examination and treatment findings (Turk 1996).

As well as contributing to convictions of disability, increased focus on and preoccupation with the body and pain, may predispose to disturbances of routine physiological processes, with potential misinterpretation of the sensory consequences (Ciccone & Grzesiak 1984). For instance, Flor et al (1995) showed that simply the topic of pain was sufficient to produce site specific changes in back muscle activity (measured electromyographically) with back pain patients. Main and Watson (1996) found a significant correlation between patients fear-avoidance beliefs and abnormalities of muscle action displayed on surface EMG. Restoration towards normal muscle patterns followed a specific pain management programme designed to address these beliefs. No relationship was found between ranges of lumbar movement or pain intensity;

the only observed association was with reductions in patients' fear of activity-related hurt and harm. Interestingly, it appears that even routine physiological responses are somehow distorted in patients with back pain. Following an experimental noxious stimulus to the upper limb (cold pressor test), normal subjects demonstrated the anticipated reflex increase in surface EMG activity in the upper trapezius. However, this shoulder muscle activity was not only absent in patients with back pain, it appeared instead in muscles of the relevant lumbar region (Main & Watson 1996).

Main and Watson (1996) concluded that largely because of the self-perpetuating disabling fear-avoidance behaviour to which they give rise, patients' harm-signalling beliefs about pain and work are a major risk factor for the development of chronicity. Recent studies of acute back pain clearly demonstrated that beliefs held at or soon after the time of initial pain onset exert a powerful influence on treatment outcome (Main & Watson 1996). According to these authors an essential element to prevent unnecessary chronicity is to include such entities as beliefs about the cause, meaning, prognosis and therefore appropriate management of back pain in the initial assessment (Main & Watson 1996). Similar sentiments were expressed by Waddell et al (1993, p.165): 'To prevent chronicity, such inappropriate fear-avoidance beliefs would need to be recognised from the acute stage, tackled directly and changed early before they become fixed. Indeed it is possible that the first step to successful rehabilitation may be to overcome mistaken fear-avoidance beliefs.'

The need for belief management

As Saal (1995) has pointed out, the structural paradigm for (low) back pain failed to meet the challenge; any validation this may have had has begun to fall apart. Large disc herniations with unequivocal evidence of nerve compression may be asymptomatic. Changes in reported pain occur independently of decompression following the structure altering interventions discectomy and chemonucleosis (Saal 1995). Nachemson (1996) has been critical of the hit or miss symptomatic results for structure/movement altering surgery (fusion) in patients having presumably the same physical indicators. There was an even weaker relationship between the subjective indicator, patients' reports of 'same pain' to mechanical provocation (discography), and post surgical functional outcome (Nachemson 1996). Similar uncertainty and criticism continue to surround other structure-based diagnostic labels such as 'facet syndrome', radiographic 'instability' and sacroiliac joint 'dysfunction' (Jackson 1992, Nachemson 1992 and 1996, Pope et al 1992, Sato & Kikuchi 1993).

It is well known that the entire spine undergoes readily visible structural changes from birth to death which are not paralleled by the morbidity curve (Kraemer 1995, Twomey 1992). Furthermore, the natural history for the vast majority of causes and episodes of back pain is benign; even for many of the so-called specific diagnoses the prognosis is generally good (Fordyce 1995,

Kraemer 1995, Nachemson 1992 and 1996). Increasingly, the recom–mendation has been to attempt to avoid invasive, truly structure-altering interventions wherever possible. This recommendation is based on both bitter experience and substantial sound research evidence (Fordyce 1995). On the other hand, also as a result of observation and (lack of) investigation, there is little enthusiasm for many of the currently available conservative treatments for back pain (Bigos & Davis 1996, Long 1995, Reitman & Esses 1995). A singular, and some might say unlikely, exception is (chiropractic) manipulation (Curtis 1988, Hadler et al 1987, Meade et al 1990, Nachemson 1992). It should be made clear, however, that the current endorsement of this manoeuvre is not dependent on knowing, or even the existence, of an acceptable specific therapeutic mechanism (Cherkin 1992, Coulehan 1985, Hadler 1996). Postacchini (1996, p.1385) is probably not alone in suspecting that for discogenic back and radicular pain '...conservative treatment corresponds to no treatment, the outcome reflecting the natural history'. Identical success rates (80 per cent) claimed for a wide range of diverse treatments, and providers, have led Deyo and Phillips (1996) to question whether in fact there had been any modification of the natural history. Similarly, Waddell (1987) came to the conclusion that with very few barely clinically significant exceptions, no treatment for back pain was that much better than a combination of natural history and placebo. Hadler has stated that for the bulk of back pain the cause is inderterminate, the natural history benign and that nearly all interventions do not alter the outcome (Hall & Hadler 1995).

Thus Kraemer (1995) is confident that, given time, even a 'specific' diagnosis such as discogenic back and sciatic pain will generally subside. It is certainly reasonable to attempt to keep most types of pain to a minimum with relatively inexpensive and justifiable treatment. Nevertheless, in the overwhelming majority of instances it can be confidently expected that pain curves will drop (Kraemer 1995). The involved parties (patient, provider, funder) need only to exercise sufficient and reasonable patience and endurance (Fordyce 1995, Kraemer 1995, Nachemson 1996). Unfortunately, at least in part because of the modern structure-oriented understanding as to the cause, meaning, prognosis and appropriate management of back pain, this is rarely the path taken (Waddell 1987 and 1995). Instead, management is surrendered to a preferred professional(s); various appropriate and inappropriate interventions are undertaken. Functional recovery depends largely on two factors: the extent to which these interventions, along with a host of psychosocial factors influence the perception of pain; and the handling of fears of structural relapse. Even with specific diagnoses, indication for the well intentioned prescription of a procession of (unsuccessful) interventions has often been patients belief-driven distress and illness behaviour (Waddell 1987, Fordyce 1995). However, it is with the so-called non-specific presentations—in other words the bulk of back pain—that erroneous structure-oriented beliefs have the greatest potential to be unnecessarily disabling.

One way in which this occurs has been described by Beattie (1996, p. 606) while commenting on the impossibilty, and the danger, of attempting to classify, or guide the treatment of back pain on the pathoanatomic findings of imaged structure (in this case with MRI): 'All but the most severe findings of disk degeneration or herniation visible on MRI are non-specific for LBP or radiculopathy. The finding of disk abnormality, however, may have a profound effect on a patient's belief regarding the severity of his or her clinical condition. This perception may lead the patient to believe that his or her spine is permanently damaged and that he or she will be permanently disabled.'. McCallum et al (1996) were sufficiently concerned with the potential clinical and rehabilitative impact of such dysfunctional structure-based cognitions to offer a highly successful 'radiology conference' as a component of their (back) pain management program. Following expert explanation as to the true meaning and significance of various radiological and anatomical findings, patients volunteered expressions of relief at discovering that most visible structural changes were not significant and that graduated activity was quite safe. There were also expressions of anger at having been unnecessarily concerned and functionally impeded by past conflicting misinformation (McCallum et al 1996). Clearly there is the urgent need to question how it is that lay populations of the Western world came to hold such erroneous, distressing and potentialy disabling structure-oriented beliefs in the first place. This inquiry is probably a necessary prerequisite to the introduction of a concerted campaign for their eradication. As mentioned earlier, the costly social and economic consequences of these beliefs are the fear-avoidance and compulsive resource consuming behaviours they tend to instigate when combined with the mechanically provoked perception, or even simply the anticipation, of pain.

The actual nature of the sensory input and mechanisms responsible for the ongoing perception of non-specific back pain(s) is a matter of some importance and disagreement, and the subject of a separate discussion in itself (see for example Waddell et al 1993, Zusman 1997a and 1997b). Any tendency, on the part of both patient and provider, to mislabel and misinterpret 'non-pathological' sensory input would add a further dimension to the potentially disabling consequences of dysfunctional structure-oriented beliefs regarding back pain (Barsky & Borus 1995, Ciccone & Grzesiak 1984, Main & Watson 1996, Pilowsky 1995, Turk 1996, Waddell et al 1993). Mistaken inferences are also fundamental to the proposal by Rose et al (1993) who concluded that chronic disability due to back pain was largely a result of misinformation as to the meaning of perceived pain. The familiar picture of distress, illness behaviour, excessive resource utilisation and lack of function was considered to be a direct consequence of the seemingly unreasonable (and unnecessary) expectation and demand by patients for complete pain relief. However, this need could be readily understood in terms of the misinformed belief that since pain was evidence of some serious underlying structural pathology, its lingering presence meant that recovery was incomplete. In other words, that some hypothetical physical impairment remained uncorrected. Therefore, until pain had totally disappeared, routine activity could not be safely contemplated (McCallum et al 1996, Rose et al 1993, Salmon et al 1996). Again it was noted how grateful patients were to be given an accurate understanding of perceived pain, and angry at having been unnessessarily stressed by the unfounded and frequently unrealistic belief in the need for its complete elimination. These authors also made reference to the ease with which common 'stiffness pain' might be misconstrued as serious and pathognomonic, and so become grounds for activity avoidance and the demand for passive treatment (Rose et al 1993, see also Fordyce 1988).

Conclusion

Troup (1996) is probably correct in asserting that successful control over back pain patients' dysfunctional and costly beliefs and behaviours will require a thorough investigation and understanding of their cause. The need by patients to have their pain 'legitimised' by the explicit or implicit message that it has some purported pathoanatomical origin is understandable. Among other things, this is necessary in order for them to successfully negotiate the modern compensation system with its structure-based method of impairment rating and disability determination (Fordyce 1995, Hadler 1995). This disabling demand is one of the major reasons why there has been a concerted call for the disbandment of the current system (Fordyce 1995, Hadler 1995, Loeser 1996). Furthermore, patients' self respect and sanity demand that pain could not possibly be 'all in the head' (Barsky & Borus 1995, Borkan et al 1995). However, from a providers perspective it might be noted that, far from being a success, the clinical management of back pain in Western societies, particularly during the latter half of this century, has been an unqualified failure. And, whether because of ignorance, blind adherance to the purported infallibility of clinical impressions or seemingly informed logic, the bestowing of inappropriate and incorrect diagnoses, and therefore related interventions, is now recognised as being largely responsible. As the evidence clearly demonstrates patients pay an undeservedly high price in return for structure-oriented diagnoses and treatment of their back pain.

Acknowledgements

I would like to thank Dr Patricia Sullivan, Lorna Rosenwax and Dr John Quintner for their comments and advice.

REFERENCES

Allan D B, Waddell G 1989 An historical perspective on low back pain and disability. Acta Orthopaedica Scandinavica 60:1–23
Barsky A J, Borus J F 1995 Somatization and medicalization in the era of managed care. Journal of the American Medical Association 274:1931–1934
Beattie P 1996 The relationship between symptoms and abnormal magnetic resonance images of lumbar intervertebral disks. Physical Therapy 76:601–608

Bigos S J, Davis G E 1996 Scientific application of sports medicine principles for acute low back problems. Journal of Orthopedic and Sports Physical Therapy 24:192–206

Bigos S J, Battie M C, Spengler D M, Fisher L D, Fordyce W E, Hansson T H, Nachemson A L, Wortley M D 1991 A prospective study of work perceptions and psychosocial factors affecting the report of back injury. Spine 16:1–6

Borkan J, Reis S, Hermoni D, Biderman A 1995 Talking about the pain: a patient-centered study of low back pain in primary care. Social Science and Medicine 40:977–988

Burton A K, Tillotson K M, Main C J, Hollis S 1995 Psychosocial predictors of outcome in acute and subchronic low back trouble. Spine 20:722–728

Cats-Baril W L, Frymoyer J W 1991 Identifying patients at risk of becoming disabled because of low-back pain. Spine 16:605–607

Cherkin D C 1992 Family physicians and chiropractors: what's best for the patient? The Journal of Family Practice 35:505–506

Cherkin D C, MacCornack F A 1989 Patient evaluations of low back pain care from family physicians and chiropractors. Western Journal of Medicine 150:351–355

Cherkin D C, MacCornack F A, Berg A O 1988 Managing low back pain—a comparison of the beliefs and behaviours of family physicians and chiropractors. Western Journal of Medicine 149:475–480

Ciccone D S, Grzesiak R C 1984 Cognitive dimensions of chronic pain. Social Science and Medicine 19:1339–1345

Coulehan J L 1985 Chiropractic and the clinical art. Social Science and Medicine 21:383–390

Curtis P 1988 Spinal manipulation: does it work? Occupational Medicine: State of the Art Reviews 3:31–44

Deyo R A, Phillips W R 1996 Low back pain a primary care challenge. Spine 21:2826–2832

Feuerstein M, Beattie P 1995 Biobehavioural factors affecting pain and disability in low back pain: mechanisms and assessment. Physical Therapy 75:267–80

Flor H, Turk D C, Birbaumer N 1995 Assessment of stress-related responses in chronic back pain patients. Journal of Consulting and Clinical Psychology 53:354–364

Fordyce W E 1988 Psychological factors in the failed back. International Disability Studies 10:2–31

Fordyce W E 1995 Back pain in the workplace. IASP Press, Seattle

Frymoyer J W 1992 Predicting disability from low back pain. Clinical Orthopaedics and Related Research 279:101–109

Frymoyer J W, Cats-Baril W 1991 An overview of the incidences and costs of low back pain. Orthopedic Clinics of North America 22:263–271

Gatchell R J, Polatin P B, Mayer T M 1995 The dominant role of psychosocial risk factors in the development of chronic low back pain disability. Spine 20:2702–2709

Hadler N M 1995 The disabling backache. Spine 20:640–649

Hadler N M 1996 Point of view. Spine 21:355

Hadler N M, Curtis P, Gillings D B, Stinnett S 1987 A benefit of spinal manipulation as adjunctive therapy for acute low back pain: a stratified controlled trial. Spine 12:703–706

Hall H, Hadler N M 1995 Low back school. Spine 20:1097–1098

Hazard R G, Haugh L D, Reed S, Preble J B, MacDonald L 1996 Early prediction of chronic disability after occupational low back injury. Spine 21:945–951

Indahl A, Velund L, Reikeraas O 1995 Good prognosis for low back pain left untampered. Spine 20:473–477

Jackson R P 1992 The facet syndrome. Clinical Orthopaedics and Related Research 279:110–121

Jensen M P, Romano J M, Turner J A, Good A B, Wald L H 1996 The survey of pain attitudes: further evidence for validity. Abstracts 8th World Congress on Pain Seattle: IASP Press p 73

Klenerman L, Slade P D, Stanley M, Pennie B, Reilly J P, Atchison L E, Troup J D G, Rose M J 1995 The prediction of chronicity in patients with an acute attack of low back pain in a general setting. Spine 20:478–488

Kraemer J 1995 Presidential address: natural course and history of intervertebral disk diseases. Spine 20:635–639

LaCroix J M, Powell J, Lloyd G J, Doxey N C S, Mitson G L, Aldam C F 1990 Low back pain factors of value in predicting outcome. Spine 15:495–499

Loeser J 1996 Back pain in the workplace II. Pain 65:7–8

Loeser J D, Sullivan K 1995 Disability in the chronic low back pain patient may be iatrogenic. Pain Forum 4:114–121

Long D M 1995 Effectiveness of therapies currently employed for persistent low back and leg pain. Pain Forum 4:122–125

McCallum K, Large R G, Petrie K 1996 'The radiology conference': helping patients demystify their pain. Abstracts 8th World Congress on Pain Seattle: IASP Press, p.66

McCracken L M, Zayfert C, Gross R T 1992 The pain anxiety symptoms scale: development and validation of a scale to measure fear of pain. Pain 50:67–73

Main C J, Watson P J 1996 Guarded movements: development of chronicity. Journal of Musculoskeletal Pain 4:163–170

Meade T W, Dyer S, Browne W, Townsend J, Frank A O 1990 Low back pain of mechanical origin: randomised comparison of chiropractic and hospital outpatient treatment. British Medical Journal 300:1431–1437

Mooney V 1987 Where is the pain coming from? Spine 12:754–759

Nachemson A L 1992 Newest knowledge of low back pain. Clinical Orthopaedics and Related Research 279:8–20

Nachemson A L 1996 Lumbar disc disease with discogenic pain. Spine 21:1835–1836

Phillips H C 1987 Avoidance behaviour and its role in sustaining chronic pain. Behaviour Research and Therapy 25:273–279

Pilowsky I 1995 Low back pain and illness behaviour. Spine 20:1522–1524

Pope M H, Frymoyer J W, Krag M H 1992 Diagnosing instability. Clinical Orthopaedics and Related Research 279:60–67

Postacchini F 1996 Results of surgery compared with conservative management for lumbar disc herniations. Spine 21:1383–1387

Reitman C A, Esses S I 1995 Modalities, manual therapy, and education: a review of conservative measures. Spine: State of the Art Reviews 9:661–672

Riley J F, Ahern D K, Follick M J 1988 Chronic pain and functional impairment: assessing beliefs about their relationship. Archives of Physical Medicine and Rehabilitation 69:579–582

Rose M J, Reilly J P, Pennie B, Slade P D 1993 Chronic low back pain: a consequence of misinformation? Employee Counselling Today 5:12–15

Saal J A 1995 The pathophysiology of painful lumbar disorder symposium. Spine 20:1803

Salmon P, Woloshynowych M, Valori R 1996 The measurement of beliefs about physical symptoms in English general practice patients. Social Science and Medicine 42:1561–1567

Sato H, Kikuchi S 1993 The natural history of radiographic instability of the lumbar spine. Spine 18:2075–2079

Seres J L 1995 Physicians do not cause disability due to low back pain but they inadvertently contribute to the problem. Pain Forum 4:129–131

Spitzer W O, LeBlanc F E, Dupuis M 1987 Scientific approach to the assessment and management of activity-related spinal disorders. Spine 12:S22–S30

Szpalski M, Nordin M, Skovron M L, Melot C, Cukier D 1995 Health care utilization for low back pain in Belgium. Spine 20:431–442

Teasell R W, Harth M 1996 Functional restoration returning patients with chronic low back pain to work—revolution or fad? Spine 21:844–847

Troup J D G 1996 Review essay. Social Science and Medicine 42:561–563

Turk D C 1996 Psychological aspects of chronic pain and disability. Journal of Musculoskeletal Pain 4:145–153

Twomey L T 1992 A rationale for the treatment of back pain and joint pain by manual therapy. Physical Therapy 72:885–892

Vernon H 1996 The role of joint dysfunction in spinal myofascial pain. Journal of Musculoskeletal Pain 3:99–104

Vlaeyen J W S, Kole-Snijders A M J, Boeren R G B, van Eek H 1995 Fear of movement/ (re)injury in chronic low back pain and its relation to behavioural performance. Pain 62:363–372

Volinn E 1996 Between the idea and reality: research on bed rest for uncomplicated acute low back pain and implications for clinical practice patterns. The Clinical Journal of Pain 12:166–170

Waddell G 1987 A new clinical model for the treatment of low-back pain. Spine 12:632–644

Waddell G 1992 Biopsychosocial analysis of low back pain. Baillieres Clinical Rheumatology 6:523–557

Waddell G 1995 Modern management of spinal disorders. Journal of Manipulative and Physiological Therapeutics 18:590–596

Waddell G, Newton M, Henderson I, Somerville D, Main C J 1993 A fear-avoidance beliefs questionnaire (FABQ) and the role of fear-avoidance beliefs in chronic low back pain and disability. Pain 52:157–168

Waddell G, Turk D C 1992 Clinical assessment of low back pain. In: Turk D C, Melzack R (eds) Handbook of pain assessment. Guilford Press, New York, pp. 15–36

Wardwell W I 1993 Chiropractic: history and evolution of a new profession. Mosby Year Book, St Louis

Zusman M 1984 Spinal pain patients' beliefs about pain and physiotherapy. Australian Journal of Physiotherapy 30:145–151

Zusman M 1995 The clinical variable of primary significance. In: Shacklock MO (ed) Moving in on pain. Butterworth-Heinemann, Sydney pp. 27–31

Zusman M 1997a Instigators of activity intolerance. Manual Therapy 2:75–86

Zusman M 1997b Nociception maintaining post-healing 'mechanical' back pain. In Proceedings of MPAA 10th Biennial Conference, Melbourne: Manipulative Physiotherapists Association of Australia pp. 224–229

Index

Introducing ...

NOI PRESS

NOI Press is a new publishing house owned by physiotherapists, publishing books by physiotherapists for physiotherapists. We understand the needs of the profession, and we aim to publish quality books at an affordable price.

We offer a 30 day money back guarantee if you are not completely satisfied with your purchase, so you can order our books with confidence.

Contact your nearest NOI office for a list of our new and forthcoming titles and for details of NOI courses. Addresses appear overleaf.

NOI PRESS
Falmouth and Adelaide

NOI Press UK
Kestrel
Swanpool
Falmouth
Cornwall TR11 5BD
UK
Ph: (+44) 01326 312156
Fax: (+44) 01326 211149
Email:louisgifford@compuserve.com

NOI Press Australia
31 Angus Street
Goodwood
South Australia 5034
Australia
Ph: (+61) 08 8271 8147
Fax: (+61) 08 8271 8147
Email:butlergore@compuserve.com

Neuro Orthopaedic Institute - USA
1507 S. Vona Ct.
Superior, CO   80027
U.S.A.
Ph: (+1) 303-494-9826
Fax: (+1) 303-494-9807
Email:noi@tesser.com

Neuro Orthopaedic Institute - Europe
Post Graduate Study Centre
Badstrasse 33
CH 8437 Zurzach
Switzerland
Ph: (+41) 056 2695290
Fax: (+41) 056 2695178

Neuro Orthopaedic Institute - Europe
Stobbenkamp 10 (onder voorbehoud)
7631 CP Ootmarsum
Nederland
Ph: (+31) 0541 294001
Fax: (+31) 0541 294002
Email:h.piekartz@wxs.nl